A Shuddering Dawn

A
Shuddering Dawn

Religious Studies and the Nuclear Age

Edited by

Ira Chernus and Edward Tabor Linenthal

With a Foreword by

Ninian Smart

91-428

State University of New York Press

Published by
State University of New York Press, Albany

© 1989   State University of New York

For information, address State University of New York
Press, State University Plaza, Albany, N.Y., 12246

Library of Congress Cataloging-in-Publication Data

A Shuddering Dawn.

     1. Nuclear warfare—Religious aspects.   I. Chernus,
Ira, 1946-   II. Linenthal, Edward Tabor,
1947-
BL65.A85S54   1989   291.1′7873   88-38013
ISBN 0-7914-0084-0
ISBN 0-7914-0085-9   (pbk.)

10 9 8 7 6 5 4 3 2 1

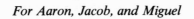

For Aaron, Jacob, and Miguel

Contents

Foreword

    Ninian Smart   ix

Acknowledgments   xi

Introduction

    Ira Chernus *and* Edward Tabor Linenthal   xiii

Part I. History of Religions

1. Nuclear Images in the Popular Press:
The Age of Apocalypse
Ira Chernus   3

2. War and Sacrifice in the Nuclear Age:
The Committee on the Present Danger
and the Renewal of Martial Enthusiasm
Edward Tabor Linenthal   20

3. Nuclear Images in the Popular Press:
From Apocalypse to Static Balance
Ira Chernus   33

Part II. Sociology of Religion

4. "I Am Death . . . Who Shatters Worlds":
The Emerging Nuclear Death Cult
James A. Aho   49

5. Performing the Nuclear Ceremony:
The Arms Race as a Ritual
Robert D. Benford *and* Lester R. Kurtz   69

Part III. Psychology of Religion

6.   Growing Up in the Nuclear Age:
     Psychological Challenges and
     Spiritual Possibilities
          John McDargh   91

7.   The Nuclear Horror and the Hounding of Nature:
     Listening to Images
          Daniel C. Noel   105

Part IV. Reflective Religious Thought

8.   Approaching Nuclearism as a Heresy
          G. Clarke Chapman   125

9.   God and Her Survival in a Nuclear Age
          Susan B. Thistlethwaite   140

10. Doing the Truth:
     Peacemaking as Hopeful Activity
          Walter J. Noyalis   152

Part V. Conclusion

11. The Religious Dimensions of the Nuclear Age
          Ira Chernus *and* Edward Tabor Linenthal   167

Notes   177

Contributors   209

Foreword

The modern study of religion has something important to say about the Bomb. Many readers will be familiar with the idea of the Christian or Jewish theologian who comments on matters of moment from an angle of commitment. Such prophetic voices are part of living religion. But the modern study of religion stands in a sense at a higher level, commenting on the nature of religious symbols, myth, rituals, experience, doctrines, and so on. It has learned to stand apart in order to understand, and so it is not speaking from within the midst of commitment. But by that somewhat detached stance it can throw light upon the significance of human practices and ideas, and this is the logic of the present book: to use the resources of religious studies to help us to understand some of the deeper meanings of the Bomb in contemporary life, especially in America.

As the editors themselves point out, their division of the field into four subdisciplines is somewhat artificial (though convenient). For whether we are thinking about some facet of human life from a sociological, psychological, historical and comparative, or reflective theological angle, we shall primarily be trying to understand the emotional and symbolic forces that direct our attitudes and select our concepts. The present age is, of course, unique in human history in that we now have the power to destroy all of civilization. This unnerving thought, coupled with the blinding power of nuclear fission, is enough to stir symbolic forces within us. The Bomb takes on a kind of religious power.

There are plentiful sources for expressing and repressing our terror. Western history has in part been shaped by the fear of the numinous, hoping and dreading in the face of the End, a sense of disquiet in face of the incomprehensible. Such themes are evident in a new and secular way as a result of the discovery of the art of nuclear Bomb making. It is not surprising that J. Robert Oppenheimer should have quoted from the *Bhagavadgita* when the first atomic explosion proved to be a "success." It was awesome enough then, but the potential for terror has been increasing ever since. The fateful conjunction of the Bomb with the development of computers, for guidance, and rockets has brought annihilation a few minutes away from us all. Yet though we know this, we go on living as though it were not so. Thus it is important for us to analyze the symbolic meaning of the Bomb in order better to understand the polar responses that we have to the new force.

The editors of this book have brought together essays that are bound to stir in us reflection. For human beings there is no neutral stance in the face of the Bomb; but there is a higher level from which it can be viewed. This book might be described as "applied religious studies." It brings the resources of the field to help us analyze and judge the phenomena associated with the violent edge of the nuclear age. The two sides of the quest for application are brought out in the two parts of this volume.

From the first five essays we gain some understanding of the way the study of religion can depict the realities of the nuclear situation and, in particular, the ways in which people, whether technically involved or not, tend to view the Bomb. The latter essays explore some practical alternatives—not proceeding from a faith-community's commitment as such, but rather looking at some of the insights that religion and religions can share—for example, the life and thought of Gandhi and their relevance to the peacemaking process.

We in religious studies are concerned with world view analysis—which looks to the structures of values controlling human life—and such analysis tends to emphasize the importance of ideational factors over economic and material causes. The relative importance of mental and material factors is something that we can discover only in the actual grain of history, and the distinction in any case cannot be neatly made. But insofar as we emphasize the spiritual dynamic in nuclear Bomb wielding we are surely right. What makes war between the superpowers possible and even at times perhaps likely is that they have their rockets targeted on one another. But why? The answer is largely ideological. They have cast each other as rivals. In short, the causes of destruction ultimately will turn out, if the horrific ever happens, to be mental; that is, located in the beliefs and values and fears of the elites (and to some extent peoples) of the two superpowers. We shall not resolve our problems by technological means but ultimately by mental means. This is why the modern study of religion, which so emphasizes the symbolic, mythic, and emotional factors in human behavior, is important for the ongoing nuclear debate. The editors and contributors to this volume are to be commended for providing us with much to ponder on. And pondering before action is wise. While we still have time, let us, then, ponder.

NINIAN SMART

Acknowledgments

We thank the following publishers for their generous permission to use copyrighted material:

NTL Institute, for permission to reprint "Performing the Nuclear Ceremony: the Arms Race as Ritual" by Robert D. Benford and Lester R. Kurtz, pp. 463-482. *The Journal of Applied Behavioral Science,* Vol. 23, No. 4, copyright 1987.

Journal of Feminist Studies in Religion, for permission to reprint "God and Her Survival in a Nuclear Age" by Susan Thistlethwaite, *JFSR* I, no. 1 (Spring 1988).

Soundings, for permission to reprint "The Nuclear Horror and the Hounding of Nature: Listening to Images," by Daniel C. Noel, *Soundings,* vol. LXX, no. 3-4, Fall/Winter 1987, pp. 289-308.

Union Seminary Quarterly Review, for permission to reprint "Approaching Nuclearism as a Heresy: Four Paradigms," by G. Clarke Chapman, Jr., from Volume 39, Number 4, 1985, pp. 255-268.

University of Illinois Press. Some of the thoughts expressed in Chapter 2 appear in another version in Edward T. Linenthal, "Restoring America: Political Revivalism in the Nuclear Age," in *Religion in the Life of the Nation: American Recoveries,* edited by Roland A. Sherrill, published by the University of Illinois Press.

IRA CHERNUS and EDWARD TABOR LINENTHAL

Introduction

The nuclear age was born in the desert of New Mexico on July 16, 1945, and grew to maturity a few weeks later with the destruction of Hiroshima and Nagasaki. News reports immediately communicated two immutable truths of this new age to Americans: they were the possessors of a new, almost unimaginable power, and when the "secret" of this power fell into the hands of the nation's enemies, as it inevitably would, Americans would be potential victims of this great power.

Manifestations of awesome power have always been of interest to students of religion. In *The Idea of the Holy,* a seminal work of modern religious studies, Rudolf Otto interpreted religion as human awe in the face of power that might be considered sacred or "wholly other." There has never been a technological construction like the Bomb, a human creation of unlimited power wholly other than any humanity has previously known. Such a power evokes what Otto and others would understand as primal religious feelings of numinous awe and dread. The Bomb, in short, has become an object of veneration. So it is appropriate that the field of religious studies should begin to explore its many meanings.

Prior to American culture's recent period of passionate debate about nuclear weapons, the great majority of students of religion wrote about the nuclear dilemma from the standpoint of religious ethics. They began with the question: "Why, and under what circumstances, *should* we possess and use nuclear weapons?" And they generally answered this question on the basis of particular theological, ethical, or faith commitments. The authors in this book begin with a different question. From diverse methodological perspectives within religious studies, they ask: "Why *do* we presently have nuclear weapons and a continuing nuclear arms race?" Some then go on to ask: "What kinds of changes would have to occur in order to stem and reverse the buildup of nuclear armaments?" And they answer these questions with academic and intellectual analyses that presuppose little or no formal religious commitment on the part of writer or reader.

The essays presented here are a representative sampling of the new approaches to the nuclear issue explored by academics in religious studies during the 1980s. All of the authors believe that the proximate and ultimate resolution of the nuclear dilemma begins by delving more deeply into the dilemma. When we go as deeply as we can, we arrive at the depth dimension of nuclear weapons, which is their religious dimension. Many of the essays reflect the popular and widespread intellectual fashions of the late 1970s and early 1980s that were used to criticize the nuclear status quo. In particular, many assume that the nuclear arms race is a form of disease, a dangerous and perhaps ultimately suicidal aberration of the human spirit. Many of the authors would certainly agree with psychologist Robert Jay Lifton, who characterizes veneration of the Bomb as the secular religion of "nuclearism." (See Chapter 8 of this book for an analysis of nuclearism.)

We hope that this collection of essays will point others toward the challenging task of detailing the rich inner history of the nuclear age and its religious dimensions. There is still much to be done. Each of the contributors to this book breaks new ground that suggests fertile areas for further research. Moreover, there have been significant statements by major church bodies since the publication of the American Catholic Bishops' Pastoral Letter, *The Challenge of Peace: God's Promise and Our Response,* that call for analysis. And a systematic study of evangelical Christian responses to the Bomb has yet to be written. Future studies must also examine antinuclearism, the activity and thought of antinuclear activists, as a cultural construct with important religious implications.

The first five chapters in this collection set forth in some detail the human response to the primal power of the Bomb. These responses have been expressed in a wide variety of symbolic forms, which emerge from ambivalence toward that which is considered sacred. The Bomb appears as both creator and destroyer. It engenders deep fears and deep allegiances. It has become arguably the most powerful and enduring religious symbol in the modern world.

In the first chapter, Ira Chernus examines the apocalyptic imagery that marked the first two decades of the nuclear age. Drawing on popular magazine accounts, he delineates the stark and seemingly contradictory messages the Bomb communicated—the message of absolute destruction and the message of ultimate salvation—and the interplay between the two. Edward Linenthal agrees with Chernus that political events are most accurately described as religious dramas. From this perspective, he discusses how and why the

Committee on the Present Danger (CPD) revived the Cold War vision and helped to shape public perceptions of nuclear weapons in the late 1970s and early 1980s. Linenthal argues that groups like the CPD are the modern secular equivalent of religious revivalists, preaching a message of doom and degeneration while calling for restoration and salvation. For the CPD, nuclear weapons function as the primary symbol of national strength and willingness to make the ultimate martial sacrifice in holy war against the forces of evil.

In the third chapter, Chernus describes the latest phase in the development of popular nuclear imagery. He believes that in the 1980s the Bomb's inner tension as symbol of destruction and salvation was put aside in favor of a new symbol: the Bomb as linchpin of a global rational balance. The real enemy, he argues, has become instability itself. Consequently, the popular hope is that arms control and arms buildups can be perfectly balanced so that a perfect equilibrium, maintained by technological experts, will be the permanent result.

James Aho then describes how the sacred power of the Bomb, at its very inception, created a new religious community devoted to its worship. The elites of this cult responded to the first atomic test as if a new god had appeared on earth, investing nuclear construction and test sites with the prestige of sacred places, the home of sacred mysteries. The saving knowledge contained in these mysteries could only be discerned by those scientific experts chosen to constitute the nuclear priesthood. Some ordinary believers participated in the cult by celebrating the blessings of the "fundamentalist" Bomb, with its attendant erotic imagery.

Robert Benford and Lester Kurtz continue to focus on the sociology of the Bomb's veneration by examining its ritual dimension. Military rituals surrounded the development and continued refinement of nuclear weapons. Political leaders reiterated familiar incantations about the crucial role the weapons played in ensuring the survival of the nation. Ritual denunciations created and reinforced images of "the enemy." Rituals of mystification developed that made these weapons seem necessarily the arena of the expert. Consequently, Benford and Kurtz suggest that we need new images and rituals to help us redefine the nuclear dilemma by expanding our vision in order to redefine the culture's core symbols.

Are the symbolic responses described in these chapters the only possible responses to the Bomb? Must one hold to a stance of dread or veneration? How else might one live under the nuclear shadow? The final five chapters in this collection speak to these questions. John McDargh warns that the greatest danger from the Bomb is its ability to cripple humanity in a unique way: the image of extinction throws into question our ability to adequately symbolize life and death. This "disease" prevents us from being nurtured by traditional images of connection. McDargh describes his study of students involved in protesting nuclear weapons, inquiring into the kinds of symbols that sustain them. He finds that symbols of generativity—of concern for the connectedness of past, present, and future generations—are central in their motivations. This sense of intimate connection, he argues, might be instructive to all those wishing to build an ethic of life in the nuclear age.

Daniel Noel then recounts his own journey through nuclear symbolism. He has encountered images of hunting, capturing, and caging nature as recurrent themes in the literature of the nuclear age. Interpreting this pattern from the perspective of archetypal psychology, he urges us to listen to our own innermost images, which have been caged by the literalizing spirit of modern technology. By releasing archetypal images into conscious awareness, we may come to understand the deepest psychological wellsprings of the nuclear age: modernity has hounded both the powers of nature and the archetypal imaginings at the core of human nature into the core of the nuclear Bomb. The mere act of listening to our images can free those powers, Noel concludes, and free us to choose a different way of life.

The last three chapters in this collection are written by students of religion whose roots are in reflective religious and theological thought. They confront the power of the Bomb from within the context of the Christian traditions, which have already had to grapple with that power and the problems it raises. Both Protestant and Catholic deliberations about nuclear weapons began shortly after the use of the Bomb in World War II. Many Protestant denominations have moved toward total rejection of the use of nuclear weapons. However, there is still a spirited debate in evangelical circles over the possibility of limited use. Roman Catholic deliberations were spurred by Pope John XXIII's interest in renewing discussions of war and peace during the Second Vatican Council. Catholics have slowly moved toward a "radical suspicion" of the possibility of using nuclear weapons, and the American Catholic Bishops' Pastoral Letter focused on the need to develop resources for constructing a "theology of peace."

G. Clarke Chapman responds to this widely sensed desire for religious traditions to enter into the process of reconstructing a symbolic vision of peace. He labels the veneration of the Bomb as a heresy and believes that contemporary Christians—indeed contemporary humankind—must begin to stop this process of veneration by unmasking the poverty of its symbols and the cultural edifices it supports. He criticizes as heretical the notions that power must be equated with violence, that international relations must be modeled after zero-sum (we win, you lose) games, that the image of the future must be based on worst case scenarios, and that faith can be reduced to the cheerful mood of "official optimism." To all of this, he contrasts a biblical imagery that suggests a radically different posture—one that he believes is appropriate both for individuals and for a reorientation of public policy.

Susan Thistlethwaite pursues the search for a viable theology in the face of the nuclear threat from a feminist perspective. She criticizes liberal Protestant theology as a white male tradition, whose vision of God is detached from the material matrix of human biology and history. White feminist theologians have taken important steps to transcend this narrow vision, she contends, by returning to the Goddess as a symbol of reconnecting mind with body and spirit with nature. Yet she urges a closer attention to the fiction of black women writers, whose religious vision grapples with the problem of survival and finds an answer in the ties binding the individual to past and future generations as well as to the endlessness of nature.

Walter Noyalis concludes these religious reflections by interlacing them with psychological and practical concerns. He argues that thought and contemplation can be practical forms of action in pursuit of peace if they are approached metaphorically. Metaphor discovers its truth and concrete application only in the course of action. This hopeful stance can bring reconciliation and peace because it allows the future to shape itself without force or violence. War, by contrast, rests on a hopeless kind of thinking that tries to predict the future precisely and then tries to force the future to fulfill those predictions. Noyalis contends that those who express true faith and hope are those who do truth, acting today in creative ways that open up new possibilities for a more peaceful tomorrow.

In conclusion, we sketch some of the common themes that bind these essays together. Drawing on these themes, we invite the reader to consider some further ideas that arise from the collection as a whole. We have been most gratified to work with the eight other contributors to this book. Together we have begun a journey of exploration into the religious dimensions of the nuclear age. We appreciate all of the assistance, support, and encouragement the contributors have given us and each other in making this book possible. Now we invite readers to join us in this journey, with the hope that all of us will emerge with an altered perspective, one that will generate creative insights and responses to the paramount issue of our time.

Part I

History of Religions

IRA CHERNUS

Chapter 1

Nuclear Images in the Popular Press: The Age of Apocalypse

The many rituals and myths that surround nuclear weapons remind us that these weapons are much more than mere physical objects: they are perhaps the richest and most emotionally charged symbolic realities in America's public life. When we speak or even think of such immensely powerful weapons, we cannot avoid speaking and thinking in symbolic images. Abstract concepts can never express our deepest responses to the Bomb. When historians of religion address the nuclear issue, they therefore find themselves on familiar ground, for their principal concern is the interpretation of symbolic images and the myths, rituals, and cultural contexts in which those images occur. Historians of religion trace the changing configurations of images, hoping to uncover clues to the changing patterns of human experience. At the same time, they inevitably discover enduring constants in the experience of communities, nations, and perhaps even humanity as a whole.

In modern America, nuclear imagery forms a chaotic collage of beliefs, fears, hopes, hunches, and fantasies. While all of us have our own unique kaleidoscope of images, there are common threads running through the national experience. How can we find these unifying threads? We have no sacred scripture, no official body of doctrine or myth to articulate them. Yet we do have a widely shared store of public imagery—the popular media. An unending stream of films, stories, TV shows, comic books, and the like has depicted nuclear themes since 1945 (and even earlier). These are important and instructive for understanding nuclear imagery, but they are usually written off as mere entertainment. Our more serious images occur in the news media, both in current news reports and in feature stories and editorials offering deeper background to the news. A study of these sources using the methods of the historian of religions can illuminate aspects of the nuclear age that might otherwise remain obscure.

There is, as yet, little systematic study of the images of nuclear weapons and nuclear war that appear in the popular media. As a first step toward such a study, this article offers a preliminary survey of the most widely read national magazines treating the subject during the first two decades of the nuclear age: *Life* and *Reader's Digest*. The themes that recur in these sources suggest, among other things, that the power of the Bomb touches deep recesses of the psyche, recesses that are the breeding ground of religious symbols, myths, and rituals. Images of damnation and salvation, omniscience and omnipotence, faith and infinitude, transformation and rebirth, and many other familiar religious motifs abound in this material. There are recurring allusions to traditional apocalyptic imagery; that is, imagery of a violent cataclysm in which the forces of good permanently vanquish the forces of evil, ending the present era of existence and inaugurating a radically new world situation. The "numinous" quality that James Aho defines in his essay in this book (Chapter 4) is as pervasive in the popular news magazines as it is among atomic scientists. And there are new forms of religious symbolism spawned by the Bomb and its numinous aura. Readers can judge for themselves whether the themes and images described here are indeed the nation's common heritage and basic vision of the nuclear issue.

I

When *Life* reported to its readers the bombing of Hiroshima and Nagasaki, it added a lengthy editorial on the true meaning of "The Atomic Age."[1] This editorial prefigured many of the basic motifs that would dominate popular perception of the nuclear issue at least until 1963. The great atomic "bang," readers learned, signals the birth of a radically new age. It is as if the world has awakened from a long sleep into "a strange new land . . . an entirely different country." The Bomb is clearly a numinous power; "this uncontrollable new secret [is] the miracle" that certifies "the inherent mystery of things." Although we properly feel like ants, "in awe before the harnessed infinite," the crucial point is that the infinite has indeed been harnessed. Invoking the image of Prometheus, the cunning hero of Greek legend who gave fire and hence civilization to humankind, the article asserts that "no limits are set to our Promethean ingenuity." America, with sole possession of this unlimited weapon, is "the most powerful nation perhaps in all history."

It may seem, the editorial admits, that this new age is one of moral chaos. We have emerged from World War II "with radically different practices and standards of permissible behavior." Atomic science itself has proven that everything, including morality, is relative. Thus there is "the very real danger of a reversion to barbarism." Our bulwark against barbarism is firm adherence to traditional moral values. President Truman himself said that, as always, "the basic proposition of the worth and dignity of man is the strongest, most creative force now present in the world." This means the dignity of the individual who can choose the right and the good: "The individual conscience against the atomic bomb? Yes. There is no other way." Just as scientists have harnessed the infinite, individual conscience can harness the nation's "Jovian impulse," its urge to emulate the unfettered power of the ancient Romans' supreme deity. If omnipotent America can restrain itself, it "can abolish warfare, and mitigate man's inhumanity to man."

The whole editorial is riddled with contradictions: All things are new yet little has changed; we are gods and ants; the Bomb is harnessed yet uncontrollable; moral standards are abolished yet they endure unimpaired. The subliminal message may be the incomprehensibility of the new weapon and the new age it brings. What is the best response to our bewilderment? The editorial's true message may be buried in its recurring imagery of being underground. We have "emerged from the tunnel," but "the really terrifying questions are not under the bed but in the cellar." The lesson of the ants is that despite endless warfare the species survives: "Constructing beautiful urban palaces and galleries, many ants have long lived underground in entire satisfaction."

This lesson is relevant now because "if there is no defense, then perhaps man must either abolish international warfare or move his whole urban civilization underground." One way or the other, a weapon of limitless destruction must portend some radical transformation of human life— perhaps a return to our origins in the womb-like cave. But such a drastic conclusion may be just "wild speculation." It is better to be "cool and unimaginative." In a similar vein, *Reader's Digest* advised that the damage to Hiroshima and Nagasaki had not been nearly so bad as we are led to believe.[2] The hysteria over the supposedly dreadful new weapon is therefore uncalled for and should be avoided.

Life was apparently unable to heed its own call for calm, however, in the face of infinite power. A few months later, it ran a most imaginative article describing World War III as "The 36-Hour War."[3] Accompanied by large science fiction cartoons, the brief article describes a Soviet nuclear missile attack that leaves American cities in rubble. American missiles retaliate in kind; the concluding sentence is an unexplained assurance of American omnipotence: "The United States wins the war."

Our sole possession of the Bomb permitted such naive confidence for just a few years. By 1950, as the Cold War reached its first peak, Americans had to absorb both the Soviet Union's successful atomic bomb test and their own government's decision to build hydrogen bombs. The nuclear issue was now framed within an overarching East-West dualism and an unquestioned need to maintain U.S. military superiority.[4] Although many Americans, *Life* lamented, respond to the news of the H-bomb by "looking for a hole to hide in," they should stand up and face the awesome challenge of "the elemental fact of 1950: The enemy of the free world is implacably determined to destroy the free world." This "godless opponent . . . cannot surrender and cannot make peace. . . . There can be no compromise and no agreement with Soviet Communism."[5] The February 27, 1950, issue of *Life* , adorned with a cover photo of a mushroom cloud in brilliant colors, carried seven separate articles on the Bomb.[6] The title of one, "War Can Come; Will We Be Ready?" captures the apocalyptic spirit of the ensemble.

"This is the age of obliteration," readers are solemnly informed. "The hydrogen bomb reeks with death. . . . A burning, searing death." Scientists, moralists, and politicians wrestle with its problems, but, as one title puts it, "The Soul-Searchers Find No Answer. In the face of the world crisis and the H-bomb they foresee annihilation but not how to forestall it." In fact, there may be no way to forestall a catastrophic war: "All-out war is never predictable. But it is always possible." Therefore, as in the past, we must know what to expect and learn to accept it: "Horrible as it may sound, we must be prepared to lose 10 to 15 million people on the first day of the superblitz." Though the numbers are much larger than ever before, the basic principles of war have not changed. The evil enemy will, of course, start the war. We must be prepared to finish it with superior power, whatever the cost. "Every effort must be pressed to maintain our overwhelming advantage in the development of atomic weapons," as Bernard Baruch says. The bottom line is the spiritual wisdom of General Eisenhower: "Every invention of mankind has been capable of two uses, good and evil. It is up to the moral fiber of mankind to decide to which use an invention is put." Even obliteration, it seems, can be harnessed to serve the forces of good in their cosmic struggle with the forces of evil.

No doubt Eisenhower would have endorsed Baruch's stirring proclamation in the *Reader's Digest* a year later: "Spiritual Armageddon Is Here—Now."[7] As in all apocalyptic crises, the article said, the true battle is not between weapons but between values. The freedom, individualism, and peace of one side oppose the tyranny, communism, and war of the other. Yet good cannot defeat evil unless it temporarily adopts some of evil's tactics; if the citizens of "heaven" will not voluntarily choose guns over butter, their government must somehow control their selfishness and enforce "voluntary" self-discipline. Peace can be maintained only through economically painful preparation for war: "No outside enemy can defeat us. We *can* defeat ourselves. Yours is the decision. Which shall it be—discomfort or defeat? The spiritual Armageddon is here."

The crisis atmosphere may be unwarranted, however. We have "Our Triple-Threat Atomic Weapons"[8] to protect us: "Conventional A-bombs, the kind that can pulverize an entire city in an instant, still are a mainstay in the U.S. arsenal." But now all three military services have smaller versions for tactical as well as strategic use. War is still war as we know it; troop advances must be stopped, submarine bases bombed, and ground attacks supported by air forces. All of this can be done even more efficiently with "baby" atom bombs. So if Russia "insists on picking a fight" and "wants an atomic war, she will get it." There is little to fear. With our superior moral power and superior military power, we are bound to be victorious.

Defense is the other side of war as we know it, and here two important advances have been made. By mid-1950, an "Atomic Handbook is a Best-Seller: New government handbook tells what will happen and what to do if A-bombs fall on U.S. cities."[9] Laden with facts and figures, this article shows that experts have the answers. They know that an atomic blast is awesome. It begins with a "blinding flash of terrible light brighter than a hundred suns." But the light, heat, shock wave, and radiation can all be translated into scientific terms. And understanding means the possibility of protection: "Inevitably casualties will be heavy; but the precautions suggested by the AEC may make the difference between life and death to thousands." "The elements of atomic defense" are illustrated in two sets of cartoons. "This is how you can protect yourself": crouch behind a tree, dodge into a doorway, fall flat on the sidewalk. "This is what must be done" following an attack: fighting fire, detecting radioactivity, treating burns, giving transfusions, and so on. Trained experts are pictured efficiently handling these tasks. "An air blast will leave little residual radiation . . . and those parts of a city that are still standing will be usable very soon after the blast." So a well-coordinated civil defense program, following the experts' advice, will ensure that we can meet the challenge of all-out war. If we must endure obliteration, with proper preparation we shall rise and live again.

After 1950, nuclear concern faded for several years. When it returned in 1953, defense was still on *Life*'s mind. "Outcasts of Yucca Flats"[10] tells us how "Mannequins are martyrs for science in a 'nuclear diagnostic shot'" at the Nevada test site. This "experiment," with soldiers and civilians watching at close range, "confirmed a foregone conclusion: that foot soldiers, prudently disposed and properly equipped, have no particular reason to fear the atomic bomb more than any other weapon . . . . The A-bomb [is] something between a heavy hand grenade and an artillery shell." While some test houses were destroyed, the damage was nothing more than a normal three-alarm fire. One mannequin survived in a $40 basement shelter (as a picture shows), though "radiation effects were not determined." As a spectator event, a nuclear explosion no longer makes the grade:

> When the first nuclear device exploded at Alamogordo, observers had the sense of being close to the infinite. Now it is depressingly plain that the bloom is off infinity's rose . . . . Hardly had the mushroom cloud gained its full height before it became apparent that the audience was disappointed. A middle-aged woman in a lumberman's shirt remarked to a colleague, "I really don't mind it at all. I rather expected something much more violent."

Life's ostensible conclusion is the need for more public apprehension and "sensible" civil defense. But the real message is made clear: "Atomic weapons are not necessarily the terrifying devices that some have painted." If the Bomb is so benign, why not think of its infinite might as a trustworthy ally? And even if nuclear war comes, you can meet death both as a martyr and as a mannequin—already dead.

The air of tranquilizing nuclear boredom was shattered by news of the first H-bomb explosions. The grotesque irrationality, mystery, and unpredictability of "the Super" was the central theme in a sequence of three articles in *Life*'s March 29, 1954, issue.[11] The main article, "First Casualties of the H-Bomb," "translated the awesomeness of the H-bomb into human terms all Americans can comprehend"—and all Russians as well, who are meant to comprehend that the United States might indeed unleash this "limitless weapon" upon human beings. But how and where and when, and with what effects, no one can really say. That is the key to our supremacy.

The "first casualties" were the unfortunate crewmen of a Japanese fishing boat (ironically named the Fortunate Dragon) that was 71 miles from Bikini atoll when the United States detonated the biggest H-bomb blast to date. As the crewmen tell their story, the numinous power of the Bomb is evident. At first they mistook it for the sun rising eerily in the west, but then "the sun was obliterated" by the mushroom cloud that seemed to billow infinitely high, raining down "ashes of death." The crewmen tell of radiation sickness (amply illustrated in lurid photos), intolerable itching and swelling, and feelings of panic, confusion, anger, and depression. The Japanese people, like the crewmen, believe that radiation's danger is omnipresent and inescapable. Accompanying articles confirm the implications of these images: the United States has "the psychological—and military—advantage of possessing the most devastating weapon in the world . . . several hundred times as terrifying as the Hiroshima bomb." Although it still leaves the United States "a good deal short of omnipotence," it is only "the biggest so far"; the mere mention of omnipotence offers something to think about for the future.

The sense of grotesque terrifying power is tempered, as so often, by contrasting images. A U.S. medical expert found the irradiated fishermen "in better shape than I had thought." The Japanese "welcomed assurances of their recovery, but they were still worried." Similarly, "Tokyo University specialists agreed that the danger from the 'hot' fish had probably been overemphasized. But the average Japanese was dubious." Apparently the average person lacks sufficient respect for the experts' expertise. To encourage proper respect, another article explains the basic scientific principles of the H-bomb but confides that "the details are known only to a few top scientists [who] grapple with the 1,001 details of perfecting the hydrogen weapons." Military experts are also accomplishing impressive feats: "The atom has been tamed to a wide variety of nonsuicidal uses, including battlefield tactics." Despite the nuclear priesthood's grasp of the Bomb, however, the layman must see it as the ultimate in irrational mysterious power.[12]

And this is the key to a successful American military posture. We had to develop the H-bomb to "move the U.S. ahead another big notch" and ensure "adequate power to deter Soviet bloc aggression." Yet, as Secretary of State Dulles put it, the way in which we would retaliate against aggression "is a matter as to which the aggressor had best remain ignorant." "Uncertainty is our own and our enemy's lot." Diplomatically, "we can never regard the present boundaries of the Soviet world as fixed." Militarily, "peace will remain as precarious as freedom." The one thing we know for certain is that war may come, and if it does, "there is no longer any doubt that we will use atomic weapons when and where they promise to be effective." As we perfect our weapons and move toward omnipotence, the Bomb's inscrutable irrationality is a powerful tool in the hands of our leaders who resolutely save us from the Communist menace.

Just two weeks later, *Life* ran another large spread featuring numerous pictures of the fireball and mushroom cloud at Bikini atoll.[13] The photographs speak more eloquently than words of the Bomb's wondrous might. But there are plenty of words, too, helping to shape the reader's response, and this time the emphasis is on reason and restraint. The introduction to the issue admits that the pictures of the

> frightening holocaust mushrooming up . . . resemble nothing else on earth because there has never been anything like it on earth . . . but we were not among the doom-shouters who wail that this means the end of everything, so we note that such easily recognizable journalistic symbols as kids, dogs, and pretty girls are still around. P.S. As this issue went to press we were still alive.

The mushroom cloud was obviously becoming an "easily recognizable journalistic symbol" itself. By 1954 it seems to have been mainly a symbol of the ambivalent feelings, the fear and fascination, aroused by limitless power. Indeed, the issue informs us that in an H-bomb blast "there is no known practical limit to the area of destruction. . . . Although it is inconceivable that any nation would try, it is possible to make doomsday come to pass."

The dominant theme, however, is to mute the cries of the doom-shouters. "A mood of alarm and bewilderment [is] the worst of all moods in which to pass sweeping judgments or to take fateful decisions." Similarly, the greatest hindrance to civil defense planning is the threat of widespread panic: "To achieve discipline an urban population would have to be drilled like an army," the magazine asserts, without passing judgment on the possibility it has raised. In "this desperate world of survival," with "the whole world worried," the best advice is obviously to "keep cool." So we are challenged to develop a philosophy of "adjustment to the constant presence of this vast *memento mori* [reminder of death]." A series of photos indicate scientists' impersonal objective attitude toward the H-bomb explosion. Why should we not all feel the same way? Although a policy of massive retaliation is still necessary to deter Soviet aggression, our attention should return to our main task—calmly building prosperity for the free world. "The avoidance of hydrogen war is merely a precondition of civilized life, not a substitute." Once the experts have harnessed the infinite in the service of freedom and prosperity, there is no limit to America's prospects for progress.

The image of an infinite, ambiguous, incalculable power sustaining good in the war against evil is hardly new in human history. Religious traditions around the world, and certainly in the West, have been built on just such foundations. So the *Reader's Digest,* in its principal nuclear article of 1954, intertwines political and religious themes in issuing its own challenge to the nation. "The Road Ahead in the Light of the H-Bomb" is subtitled "Provocative gospel on today's major problem."[14] The question is really spiritual salvation, defined here as peace, international harmony, and the brotherhood of all humanity. The road to salvation is a pilgrimage of the spirit, following the Star of Bethlehem up the Lord's mountain. On this road we must "toil through rough realities, with the hydrogen bomb our companion—and peace our compulsion."

The Bomb is ambiguous. It leaves us "poised in dread on a hairline between life and death. . . . Many of the ancients made the sun a god. We have made him a devil. How shall we chain that devil? No man can answer surely." But the very need to "chain the devil" is the force propelling us on the road to salvation. We are "searching in the horrendous glare of the H-bomb" for peace. Its saving light brings together scientists from around the world, prophesying the coming time "for making the atom the friend of the whole human race." Even if there is a war, "the world is not going to disappear. Enrico Fermi informs us authoritatively that science knows no way of destroying the planet. And life will persist on it." Religious wars in the past often destroyed whole nations. Yet the world survived and enemies often became friends: "Someday the Russians may again be allies. . . . When that day comes we shall see that our true enemies were not the millions of Russian people but the handful of men who ruled them."

We should be busy preparing for that day, the article continues. Yet few of us work for peace earnestly enough. The true challenge of the nuclear age is the spiritual challenge to overcome our own deficiencies and travel the long hard road to saving peace. The H-bomb, with a moral ambiguity mirroring our own, lights our way, leads us, and compels us on that eschatological journey. So we must do more than merely chain the nuclear devil. We must use it to purify and redeem ourselves from evil. Doing so, we redeem the Bomb from its own evil, transform it, and render it divine: "We want *permanent* peace. Let us follow the light that can lead us to it. . . . Since the stars gave us the hydrogen bomb, we can call it the saving Star of Bethlehem."

II

The nation seems to have needed time to absorb these new challenges, for nuclear imagery subsided again, reappearing as a pressing concern in 1958. This time the stimulus was the debate over fallout from atmospheric tests. *Life* saw both sides of the matter. Reassuring us that scientists and legislators were undertaking "A Searching Inquiry Into Nuclear Perils ,"[15] it warns that "the danger point could be reached in five years." Above the article, a large surreal photograph shows bronze mannequins arrayed in rows wearing "plastic masks, which are designed to protect their wearers against gas or radioactive particles in the air. . . . Six basic sizes will fit everyone from a child to an adult. Masks weigh eight ounces, are not yet in mass production." Once they are in mass production, the caption implies, this scene of death-in-life may depict our technological salvation. Other articles illustrate scientists' studies and the impressive progress they have made, although "out in the far west some citizens, less well informed, were openly worried." They may have been better informed after reading Edward Teller's reassuring words: fallout risks are overrated, and further nuclear tests can perfect "clean" weapons that will spare civilian lives in war. Tests will continue, *Life* concludes, since the United States "must continue to perfect its stockpile of nuclear weapons until a world-wide agreement on controls can be reached." The Bomb is still the way to safety and salvation, though its path remains darkened by shadows of numinous peril.

By this time, *Reader's Digest* had less patience for the complexities of nuclear issues. Under the heading "Soviet Union vs. U.S.A.—What Are the Facts?"[16] it offered a recitation of classic Cold War images, as presented by "three distinguished Americans who have unsurpassed opportunity to know the facts." The "authorities" are a triumvirate of well-known cold warriors: Admiral Arleigh Burke, SAC General Curtis LeMay, and AEC Chairman Lewis Strauss. The "facts" fall into a flawless pattern of moral dualism. "The United States has never seriously been labeled as an aggressor." Ever since 1946, the United States has made "the most earnest and persistent efforts to achieve real atomic disarmament, inspected and controlled." We are a hard-working, honest people whose industriousness gives us the high standard of living that all freedom-loving people desire. The Soviet Union, on the other hand, is the polar opposite of all that we value. "Their purpose and intention is to conquer and destroy the free world. That means, first and foremost, us." Their promises of peaceful intention are worthless, as are any agreements they might sign. (An accompanying article documents "the Reds' shocking record of violating every important promise they have ever made.") The Soviet leaders compel their people to forego basic consumer goods so that they can build up their war machine. Although it is not likely that they would be foolish enough to attack us, "there is always the possibility that a mad or irresponsible person or government in possession of nuclear weapons could start a war."

This possibility compels the United States to keep on building nuclear weapons. We have maintained peace until now because we are omnipotent.

> *As of today,* our defensive shield comprehends a vast complex of ground, sea, and air units superbly equipped and strategically deployed around the world. The most powerful deterrent to war in the world . . . presents to any potential attacker who would unleash war upon the world the prospect of virtual annihilation of his own country.

The key phrase is *as of today.* If we have the will to build bigger and better bombs tomorrow, and the day after, the Bomb will continue to be our savior.[17] Our superior technology and industrial capacity can keep us ahead of the Soviets forever. "If, however, we let them get ahead of us—well, I never have thought Communists the sort of people you should offer a shot at a sitting duck." The challenge remains as clear, and as urgent, as ever.

Popular concern about nuclear war reached its pinnacle in the great bomb shelter craze of 1961. "As the warlike rattle rolled out of Moscow and as small amounts of fallout from the daily succession of Soviet nuclear tests floated over the U.S., the people woke up to the fact that they ought to be doing something to protect themselves." War with all its horror is still an everpresent possibility, so there is the "grim reality of the necessity to prepare for the worst." But the good news is that we can prepare. The September 15, 1961, issue of *Life* offers a five-article spread to help us.[18]

Nuclear war is not "too terrible to contemplate. . . . The best-informed estimates deny that maimed survivors would be fighting for burned crusts amid the ruins of civilization." The nature of nuclear attack and its fallout is now well understood. Although people may still be worrying, "parades of sober statistics also bring them relatively hopeful facts." Fallout, for example, loses 99 percent of its radioactivity within two days. "Prepared, you and your family could have 97 chances out of 100 to survive."

Protection is not very difficult. One article offers a quick "Rundown of Things to Remember in Case Attack Should Come." The Russians will probably attack at night, which means you will be at home where you can have your own fallout shelter. Otherwise, you can take shelter in a subway tunnel or "dig a cave in a hillside." "You can live for several weeks without food," though it is necessary to have a water supply. After the war the government "will provide food and medicine [and] rebuild a going economy," in ways to be revealed later on. Knowing that shelters can do the job, we should set aside moral qualms. Some 5 million people might die in a nuclear war, "but you have to look at it coldly." Though shelters cannot guarantee survival, "they will increase the odds." The man who builds a shelter "is actually a solid, sensible man—and a responsible citizen." Responsibility means a prudent, rational approach to the irrational; it means gambling intelligently. As readers learn in "A Message To You From The President," "we must prepare for all eventualities. The ability to survive coupled with the will to do so are essential."

Responsible citizens not only know how to prepare for disaster—they have the will to prepare, endure, and survive. The imagery of the shelter craze offers a communal celebration of all the nation's traditional values. Americans are optimists with an eye toward a better future, but they are also hard-headed realists. If an emergency arises, "there can be no doubt that it will be met as America has met past emergencies with speed, know-how, and calm efficiency." Americans pool their funds and work in off-hours to build communal shelters; they pull together to make sure that everyone is protected. Fortunately, there is enough excess wealth to make shelters available for all. In fact, shelters fit in nicely with the affluent American life-style. *Life* offers instructions on a variety of shelters, including "A $700 Prefabricated Job to Put Up in 4 Hours." One family is pictured relaxing on the patio alongside "an attractive addition" to their home; another is seen "In the Shelter, Snug, Equipped, and Well Organized." Beneath a photo of a teenager on the telephone, laughing and drinking Coca-Cola, the caption reads: "At the moment the shelter is her clubhouse. But the air-blower is ready for serious work."

The leitmotif of *Life*'s campaign is captured in the headline: "Pioneers of Self-Protection in Barnyard and Patio." Although shelters can form an attractive addition to the home, they are fundamentally a symbol of Americans' will to prevail through every trial.

> Life is still as full of danger as it was for the pioneer who plowed with a musket in his hand; we must now guard against dangers infinitely magnified above those of the marauding Indians, but with the same threat of sudden and violent death to the unwary. . . . [Shelters] will give all Americans the hope that they, like their forebears, can some day abandon the stockades to cross whatever new mountains of adversity or trial may lie ahead.

Like the frontier days of old, these are stirring times. They offer an opportunity to join with the whole nation in surmounting a great challenge. A headline trumpets its message: "A New Urgency, Big Things To Do—And What You Must Learn." For once, the nation can visibly act out its faith in itself, its values, and its Bomb.

A few months later, *Life* was a bit less ebullient but still enthusiastic.[19] Now, it appears, "shelters are *not* a direct military deterrent against Soviet attack." But "under certain ghastly circumstances, they *might* save millions of lives—and the nation." The key to survival has become mass shelters: "Group shelters would probably provide the best guarantee that the largest number of Americans could survive a nuclear attack, fight back, and carry on." More studies are needed by the most competent people using computers; "neither individual citizen nor local officials are competent to make these highly sophisticated studies." But the ordinary person can still muster the pioneer spirit. As an example, *Life* offers its Picture of the Week: "With Strength and Love a Family Goes On." Beneath a heart-wrenching photo of a young family walking away from their burnt home, the caption calls it "a classic portrait of sober human courage. . . . They are alive, their precious children are alive, their life will go on. . . . A breath of the kind of grass-roots invincibility which the U.S. respects and understands."[20] With enough group shelters, we can all become similarly invincible. Then we can look forward to obliteration as an opportunity to gather together, withstand the trial, rise from the ashes, and be born again.

The *Reader's Digest* was a bit more skeptical than *Life*, running an article on "The Case against Fallout Shelters."[21] When it comes to nuclear war, "the variables and the unknown factors are so numerous as to defy any rational attempt to fill them in or limit them. . . . In the confusion, the government appears as mixed up as its citizens." Despite this familiar air of irrationality, however, the article continues, it is both possible and necessary to analyze the situation rationally. Experts who have done the most logical calculations conclude that some 90 percent of our people would die in a war unless the shelter program were much more massive and massively expensive than now proposed. With "no perceptible limit to the power that can be produced by a thermonuclear explosion," the concept of defense is meaningless. Yet this article stays within the bounds of acceptable orthodox belief. To criticize government shelter plans is not to criticize nuclear weapons—something *Reader's Digest* would never consider. In fact, the Bomb can still be our savior as long as it can "force any aggressor to face certain devastation." The obvious conclusion is that weapons, not people, should be sheltered and secure against any attack.

As the shelter campaign bogged down in inconclusive public debate, attention switched in 1962 to the continuing atmospheric tests. *Life* reluctantly endorsed continuation of "this job that must be done."[22] We would readily give up such tests, it averred, if the Soviets would agree. But they, the only threat to world peace, insist on testing bigger bombs merely for propaganda value, "to terrify the world into submission." Perhaps more is at stake than propaganda points, however. In Edward Teller's "Plan for Survival," "A preeminent authority suggests that the Soviets, by clandestine testing, may have taken the lead in nuclear weapons. Further U.S. tests are vital—for the sake of peace."[23] The backdrop is classic moral dualism. The United States, supporting peace and freedom in an open society, is self-reliant and prepared for anything. The USSR, a closed society fomenting illegal acts, is the potential aggressor who robs us of our freedom. Worst of all, the Soviets are so dishonest that disarmament and international law are now impossible. Nuclear weapons are the sole guarantor of our security, freedom, and peace—and we need more of them.

> We now have enough nuclear weapons to devastate all the cities in the Soviet Union. But we are not appropriately armed to survive an initial attack on the United States, strike back precisely, or to engage in limited nuclear warfare. . . . We can never be sure that our existing military strength is sufficient. We cannot keep abreast by standing still.

For limited war, we can develop "tactical nuclear weapons which are lightweight, transportable, and 'clean'. . . . Some of the most interesting tactical explosives produce blasts of under 1000 TNT tons." Political and military progress goes hand in hand with scientific progress; so we need more atmospheric tests for science, national security, and peace. Ultimately they can lead to a workable world government, sustained by "physical [presumably nuclear] force—a world government capable of enforcing world-wide law." Better bombs are the path to fulfilling all of humanity's highest aspirations. They can lead us to limitless horizons.

Lest readers doubt its own commitment to the value of nuclear weapons, *Life* offered a similar hymn of praise to progress and the Bomb.[24] Three huge pictures of a test blast filling the Pacific night sky with brilliant colors are followed by a lyrical description of the sight and poetic musings on its meaning. The vision of the Bomb is like a vision of god. It was "the greatest rainbow in history. . . . But it left something behind I'd never felt with rainbows: elation, awe, and an unearthly fright." A photo of gaping spectators illustrates this mixture of emotions. Fear and awe seem to predominate; "It Was As If Someone Had Poured Blood On The Sky" a headline exclaims. It was "the awesome night when we set the sky on fire" with our "man-made inferno." "Man looked up in awe and wonder at what he had done . . . in the bright fury of the blast." "People afterward groped for words to describe it."

There is elation, too—at the beauty of the Bomb and at its manifold benefits. "It was a crucial part of our effort to deter a nuclear war by keeping our nuclear superiority. The Pacific blast may lead to better weapons for us—and perhaps even a defense against enemy missiles." As part of our endless technological advance it "has also the promise of untold reward." And it seems so benign. A nuclear explosion is a thrilling spectator event, "safely remote." Some spectators in Hawaii, "seemingly undisturbed by the symbolism, watched from a cemetery." Of course, there are dangers in the nuclear age. The religious emotions evoked by this awesome blast include "prayers across the world that man's headlong mastery of his universe would always stay as wondrous, and as safety remote." But human progress always has its risks. When man first discovered fire and burned his thumb, "he chose, in his moment of anguish, to keep the fire—and all its benefits—and to take the risks. . . . Since then it has been his nature to go on burning his fingers. . . . The beauties and bounties of the ages have been his reward."

This greatest of all human-made fires is primarily a symbol of our wondrous mastery of the universe. "Now man was no longer an observer of his sky. He had tumultuous lightnings of his own. Last week he loosed them. . . . We set the sky on fire. . . . We seemed to be triumphing wholesale in tests of strength and skill with nature." Inevitably, a headline tells us, "Man Pursues His Fiery Destiny." Now man is

> making plans still more vast. . . . It is foolhardy to predict what these things may some day mean. . . . In rising so far so fast, man has pursued his roving destiny, accepting both the risks and the rewards. The fire that once could only warm his food . . . now propels him, as he knew intuitively it one day must, toward the stars.

Though we must go through fire and blood, "occasionally be hurt, even to death," we shall one day rise to the heavens—propelled by the Bomb—and assume our rightful place as masters of the universe.

The religious response to nuclear weapons was equally prevalent, though in a very different context, in *Life*'s coverage of the 1962 Cuban missile crisis.

Under the headline, "Heads Down—But Not The Spirit,"[25] a photograph of a woman praying in church is juxtaposed with one of schoolchildren crouched in a corridor. The article leaves no doubt that "across the U.S." calm prayer was the universal response to the crisis. People knelt, crouched, bowed their heads, went to church and listened to clergymen. They took cover, shielded and braced themselves, watched alertly. They "gave way to neither panic nor jubilation." Inwardly, though, they were standing proudly erect. "Clergymen of many faiths . . . exhorted their congregations to stand united with the President," and they did. Although the government was far away attending to the crisis, the people, left on their own, supported their leaders with national unity. (The only permissible doubt was whether the President "had gone far enough.") A machinist from Illinois sums up the article's message: "Before it was just like putting your head between your legs. Now you know you can hold your head up." The familiar image of descending to the ground to survive numinous danger is applied here to a real, rather than a fantasy, crisis. But the result is the same—the nation weathers the storm and arises reborn, taller and stronger than ever.

Yet the mood of this article is distinctly subdued. There are no stirring calls to wipe out the enemy's evil, no praises of the Bomb and its beneficent power. Perhaps the nation had come too close to an actuality that would belie its naively confident imagery. In fact, this closest brush with nuclear reality had a profound impact on America's nuclear images: the images virtually disappeared, at least from the popular news media. In 1963, the press reported the Limited Test Ban Treaty. After that, the nuclear issue made only rare appearances for over fifteen years. The nation occupied itself with other concerns and other images.

This brief excursion into the first phase of nuclear imagery has led through a rather chaotic maze. Although nuclear war was obviously not "the unthinkable," popular thinking about it seems to have been a patchwork affair. The images reflect a wide variety of conflicting policies, ideologies, feelings, and fantasies. No logically coherent sets of concepts underlie these scattered pieces. But a psychologically meaningful pattern comes into focus once we realize that the Bomb was essentially a religious reality. At the heart of the nuclear issue lies a quest for salvation. With good and evil locked in mortal global combat, we—the forces of good—can only be saved from the threat of evil by making ourselves invulnerable and omnipotent. We must be prepared at every moment for the final apocalyptic battle in which we will vanquish evil forever. We must possess the infinite saving power that only the Bomb can offer. As we bring its unlimited power and possibilities under our control, we can look forward to political mastery of the world and along with it a technological mastery that promises limitless prosperity. So the fear inspired by the awesome weapon should be outweighed by feelings of security, trust, progress, and hope. With the Bomb as our savior, there is no limit to the ways in which we can transcend ourselves.

Just as the Bomb can redeem us, so we redeem the bomb. It is an incomprehensible mystery, radically alien to our ordinary life and capable of unprecedented mass destruction. Yet every religious symbol is marked by the same moral ambiguity. The uncanny irrational terror of the numinous always makes it a potential source of evil, while its beneficent, rational, and familiar qualities make it the ultimate source of all good. When salvation is conceived as apocalyptic transformation, this ambiguity is resolved with little difficulty. The redeemer makes all things new precisely by enacting the old familiar pattern; good defeats evil one last unalterable time. Nuclear irrationality is redeemed by serving as the instrument of omnipotent rational order. It unleashes its infinite destructiveness precisely to secure the triumph of the constructive and the good. It brings us to the edge of terrifying danger only to save us from danger forever.

In these apocalyptic times, however, the saving graces of the Bomb are not simply given to us. If we are to redeem the redeemer and make it a force for cosmic good, we must be willing to face difficult trials, endure them, and prevail. We are challenged to be strong enough both to prevent a war and to win it. Indeed, the challenge of a "hot" war would only be an extension and intensification of the challenge currently facing us in our Cold War. The same kind of nuclear strength is necessary to meet both tests, so the way to succeed, no matter what the future brings, is to build more and better bombs. The true challenge, though, is spiritual. We must uphold traditional values, especially the discipline and self-sacrifice required to build military invulnerability. We must trust our experts, following their example of calm rationality. Simultaneously, we are summoned to the deep emotional commitment and intense excitement of joining in the nation's battle. There may be pain to endure— perhaps even the pain of nuclear war—but America can survive and triumph over every obstacle. Indeed, every threat and test is a blessing in disguise—a chance to feel transformed and revitalized, as if we had risen to new heights and entered a greater world. It is only by meeting challenges that we can transcend ourselves, be born again, and realize our unlimited possibilities. Ultimately, as the Bomb offers us its power, it allows us to feel released from all our limits; it allows us to feel infinite.

If one analyzes this imagery looking for logically coherent attitudes, fundamental contradictions turn up everywhere: the Bomb is dangerous yet benign, incomprehensible yet comprehensible, a technological weapon yet a spiritual symbol, evoking responsibility along with helplessness, chaos along with order, a need for preeminence and a need for compromise, a radically new world and a reassuringly familiar world, and so forth, and so on. Yet these contradictions actually reinforce the Bomb's persuasive potency as a religious symbol. In all religious traditions, the central symbols encompass such opposites in profound paradox. They project the believer beyond the realm of finite human reason into a realm where opposites live side by side in harmony. They resolve the dualities of life on the far side of logic.[26] The contradictory imagery of the Bomb indicates that it, too, was such a symbol from 1945 to 1962. Its unlimited physical power was matched by its unlimited symbolic power. In nuclear imagery all of our ambivalences toward order and chaos, life and death, good and evil, and their manifold relationships were mirrored, synthesized, and harmonized. In the same breath we could affirm absolute dualism, perfect unity, and an infinite power transcending and incorporating both dualism and unity.

EDWARD TABOR LINENTHAL

Chapter 2

War and Sacrifice in the Nuclear Age: The Committee on the Present Danger and the Renewal of Martial Enthusiasm

The power to blow all things to dust
Was kept for people God could trust,
And granted unto them alone,
That evil might be overthrown.
—*Edgar Guest, September 17, 1945*

War that is very strong and very hot ends
either with death or peace, whereas cold war
neither brings peace nor gives honour to the
one who makes it.
—*Don Juan Manuel, Fourteenth Century[1]*

Americans hoped that victory in World War II would bring about the creative transformations necessary to end war. Douglas MacArthur expressed this hope during the ceremonies concluding hostilities in September 1945: "It is my earnest hope and indeed the hope of all mankind that from this solemn occasion a better world shall emerge out of the blood and carnage of the past."[2] For many Americans, what emerged from the blood and carnage of the war, however, was the transmutation of a perennial evil from the guise of national socialism into the guise of communism. Enduring suspicion of the Soviet Union, muted during much of World War II, reappeared during the latter stages of that war. The seeds of the Cold War were planted as the fragile coalition of Allies felt the stresses and strains of postwar competition to gain political and strategic dominance in a war-weakened Europe. Many Americans easily transferred the hatred of Hitler and the ideology of national socialism to a hatred of Stalin and the "Red fascist" ideology of the Soviet Union. Soviet actions in Eastern Europe, the fear of Soviet subversion in the United States, the perceived sellout of Roosevelt at Yalta, all contributed to the image of a Soviet Union ready to attack the nations of Western Europe, deterred only by American nuclear weapons.[3]

Speaking before Congress on March 12, 1947, President Truman portrayed the bipolar world that confronted the United States in the early years of the Cold War:

> At the present moment in world history nearly every nation must choose between alternative ways of life. The choice is too often not a free one. One way of life is based upon the will of the majority, and is distinguished by free institutions, representative government, free elections, guarantees of individual liberty, freedom of speech and religion, and freedom from political oppression.
>
> The second way of life is based upon the will of a minority forcibly imposed upon the majority. It relies upon terror and oppression, a controlled press and radio, fixed elections, and the suppression of personal freedoms.[4]

As America emerged from the war as the preeminent world power, it was easy for Americans to perceive the nation as a nuclear-armed savior standing between war-weakened nations and the relentless evil of communism. Writing in the *New York Times* in early 1947, military editor Hanson Baldwin expressed this popular perception. "We alone," he said, "may be able to avert the decline of Western Civilization and a reversion to nihilism and the Dark Ages."[5] For Baldwin and many others, traditional images of American exceptionalism could register in even more persuasive ways, for now the nation could be, according to Truman's Lincolnesque interpretation, the "last best hope of earth."

The Committee on the Present Danger (CPD) was one group that contributed mightily to the creation and persistence of Cold War orthodoxy. The CPD functioned as a prophetic minority in the early 1950s, when it was first formed, and again in the 1970s, when it came together again to warn Americans of the "present danger." It declared that the nation was beset by a crisis of conviction, which called for a revival of certain national virtues. Only by awakening to the degenerative processes at work in the nation could Americans be led to recognize the true nature of the "present danger" and then enact the different prescriptions of the CPD, which made use of traditional revivalist declarations of decline and doom as well as expressions of revitalization and restoration.

The CPD saw itself as a significant actor in the great cosmic battle between good and evil in the nuclear age. It was motivated by an apocalyptic view of history and sought to awaken Americans from their spiritual bondage caused by the degenerative processes at work in the nation. Further, the CPD sought to outline the proper plan for a total reconstruction of the national spirit and, consequently, to motivate the public action that was crucial for the life of the nation. Certainly, the CPD functioned as a restorationist group, designed, as William McLoughlin wrote, "to alter the world view of a whole people or culture."[6] It has been able to shape profoundly the symbolic environment of the nuclear age within which all of us live.

The CPD asked Americans to become attentive to the continued existence of the Cold War world described by President Truman. The committee worked out of certain historical paradigms, sought to revive old mythologies, and wanted to reconstruct a certain vision of America, a vision perceived as necessary for the resuscitation of American patriotic will. Craving a strength and determination that was perceived to have been lost, its warning and its corrective program was designed to reverse the process of physical and spiritual degeneration at work in America. The CPD set forth a program of cultural restoration that it believed was the last chance for the life of the nation and the life of civilization, and nuclear weapons played a crucial role in this program.

By 1950 the bipolar nature of the world was entrenched wisdom in Washington. In that year a joint State-Defense Department analysis of military policy (NSC-68) became the major statement upon which American foreign policy has since been based. The document went much further than George Kennan's celebrated "Long Telegram" that had outlined a policy of containment. NSC-68 stated unequivocally that the Soviet Union was bent upon worldwide conquest, and this threat was projected as an immediate crisis. The Soviet Union was in an "advanced stage of preparation" and could almost certainly attack and overrun Europe and deliver a nuclear attack upon the United States. Despite the ominous revelations of Soviet military might, NSC-68 declared that the real crisis was internal: the nation must learn to maintain vigilance in the face of the enemy, and the nation's "fundamental purpose is more likely to be defeated from lack of the will to maintain" such vigilance.[7]

Responding to this perceived crisis, a group of prominent citizens formed the original Committee on the Present Danger to help legitimate the goals of NSC-68. The members came from the ranks of government, business, and education. In their initial statement on December 12, 1950, the cofounders of the CPD, James Conant, president of Harvard; Tracy Vorhees, former undersecretary of the Army; and Vannevar Bush, who had served during the war as head of the Office of Scientific Research and Development and then as head of the Carnegie Institution, proclaimed that the current crisis and the American response to it were caused by the "aggressive designs of the Soviet Union." Disbanded in 1953 after its members were satisfied that the nation was alerted to the danger, the committee was reconvened in 1976 in the midst of a growing sense of "injured innocence" in America. Unreconstructed Cold War liberals, contemptuous of the McGovernite triumph of 1972, had finally clothed the visceral anticommunism of the New Right with intellectual respectability. The intellectual elite of the CPD consisted of Paul Nitze, a former secretary of the Navy, who had been active in government service since the mid-1940s; Eugene Rostow, former undersecretary of State; and Harvard Sovietologist Richard Pipes. Two journals served as the intellectual organs of the CPD—*The Public Interest,* edited by Irving Kristol and Nathan Glazer, and *Commentary,* edited by Norman Podhoretz.

The dilemmas and frustrations of the postwar world were clear for members of the CPD. They believed that absolute evil, far from being destroyed in World War II, persisted, indeed in an even more hideous form—but could not now be destroyed without cataclysmic effects to American society. The conflict was present but there seemed no path to an emotionally satisfying ending—the final purification of the world. J. Robert Oppenheimer, the scientific father of the atomic bomb, captured the nature of the dilemma in 1953: "We may anticipate a state of affairs in which the two Great Powers will each be in a position to put an end to the civilization and life of the other, though not without risking its own. We may be likened to two scorpions in a bottle, each capable of killing the other, but only at a risk of his own life."[8]

The CPD understood that Cold War was now pervasive and the context within which all life must be lived. Eternal vigilance needed to be nurtured in what previously had been called "civilian" life. While the nation must maintain this vigilance toward the enemy outside, it must also demand internal purity against the enemy within.

The memory of post-World War I Europe haunted CPD members. They feared that America, too, was morally tired and militarily weak after its failure of nerve in Vietnam. Desperate for peace, the committee feared that Americans would fail to appreciate the danger from the Soviet Union, an implacable and brutal foe whose ultimate aim was the destruction of Western civilization. Failing to realize that the Truman Doctrine provided the proper strategic and moral orientation and accurately expressed the terms of the clash between civilization and barbarism, the American loss of will combined with its own innate goodness—a Billy Budd kind of innocence—kept the nation from awakening to the danger. The nation would, then, fall prey to a nuclear age Munich that would lead either to the Finlandization of America or to the terminal war no one wanted.

Consequently, the CPD's purpose was to sound the alarm and awaken the country to the danger and to unwise national security policies (SALT II, for example). But beyond these concerns, this sense of danger touched deep fears among many people that the nation had indeed been victimized—by the war in Vietnam, by the hostage crisis in Teheran, and by the Soviet invasion of Afghanistan. For many Americans, the warnings and the prescriptions of the CPD were coherent and allowed them to make use of historical paradigms, such as Munich, that seemed appropriate.

In order to reveal clearly the plan of Soviet "global hegemony," CPD members were successful in influencing the famous Team B National Intelligence Estimate of 1976. Unhappy with CIA figures, conservative military and political elites persuaded President Ford to allow CIA Director George Bush to appoint an alternate team from outside the CIA to assess Soviet military strength and intentions. Not surprisingly, Team B claimed clear Soviet superiority in conventional and nuclear weaponry. Leo Cherne, chairman of the President's Foreign Intelligence Advisory Board, commented on the social utility of such "revelatory" knowledge: "We are in the midst of a crisis of belief and a crisis of belief can only be resolved by belief. 'Will' depends on something most doomsayers have overlooked—crisis, mortal danger, shock, massive understandable challenge."[9] The nature of the CPD's world was certainly one in which crises were imminent. The external crisis was dangerous not only because of aggressive Soviet intentions but because of the "fallen state" of the United States. Elite members of the CPD began sounding the alarm about the inner disorder the nation faced.

Norman Podhoretz, one of the chief theoreticians of the CPD, asked if the nation had become a "culture of appeasement." For Podhoretz, the legacy of Vietnam was bitter. As the critical event in the contemporary loss of will in America, it engendered internal disorder and tempted the totalitarian impulse. It led to an insidious pacifism that thought *nothing* worth dying for, and produced a loss of clarity in foreign policy, a loss of confidence in American power, and a "national mood of self-doubt and self-disgust." This "spiritual plague" had moved through the protest of the 1960s, and then found its contemporary home among the "kind of women who do not want to be women and . . . those men who do not want to be men."[10]

These gender confusions—the loss of the masculine principle that was the basis for the will to sacrifice—were important, for they reminded Podhoretz of the spiritual malaise that swept over post-World War I England and led to a similar abdication of "proper manhood among homosexual writers of the

20's." This abdication had, Podhoretz believed, "an inescapable implication in the destiny of society as a whole." Certainly, Podhoretz would have approved of the spirit of a member of the Roosevelt administration who said during the early years of World War II: "In an America grown magnificently male again we have the chance to fight for a homeland. . . . Here is the time when a man can be what an American means, can fight for what America has always meant—an audacious adventurous seeking—for a decent earth."[11]

For the CPD, the period of detente only contributed to the inner malaise that gripped the country in the post-Vietnam years. Podhoretz spoke contemptuously of "Nixon's doctrine of strategic defeat." Detente, he argued, did not allow for clarity of purpose in a dangerous world. As evidenced by the trauma of Vietnam, it did not allow meaningful sacrifice to inspire the nation to acts of courage. Podhoretz stated that detente took from the Soviet-American conflict "the moral and political dimension for the sake of which sacrifices could be intelligently demanded by the government and willingly made by the people."[12]

The inner confusion brought about by the war in Vietnam and "spiritual Finlandization" caused by the policy of detente terrified Podhoretz and his contemporaries. In 1978, Eugene Rostow compared the years of detente to the European situation before both World Wars, and his perceptions revealed the continued relevance of the Munich paradigm for members of the CPD: "Since the final bitter phases of the Vietnam War, our governments have been preaching with the fear, passivity, and inadequacy which characterized the British and American policy so fatally in the Thirties, and British policy before 1914."[13] This kind of gloom pervaded the ruminations of the CPD. Sociologist Peter Berger, in his famous mea culpa regarding his once critical stance of American involvement in Vietnam, looked into the future and saw only a "long, long age of darkness," in which "American society may be swallowed up."[14]

The perceived loss of will and abdication of global responsibility were all the more significant because of the external crisis that was upon the nation. The 1976 policy statement of the CPD declared, "our country is in a period of danger, and the danger is increasing." The danger was, of course, from the Soviet Union's desire for world domination. As the crisis grew worse, the CPD stated in 1980 that the Soviet Union was pursuing a policy "even more ambitious than Hitler." Nowhere, however, was the reassertion of national will more significant than in the will to nuclear superiority. Eugene Rostow declared that unless the strategic deterrent was strong, "unless the adequacy of our second-strike capability is clear—our position in every lesser conflict is in peril." Doubt regarding American will to use these weapons stemmed not only from what the CPD perceived as nuclear inferiority but also from debilitating debate at home. Hence, the CPD was wary of domestic dissent. Verbal policies, its members well understood, could be misinterpreted in the symbolic world of perception that was so crucial to deterrence theory.[15]

Nowhere was the sense of American weakness greater than in the CPD's analysis of the strategic balance—a weakness (ironically enough) that it chose to proclaim loudly, which could be construed as a destabilizing act in itself. In 1982, the committee stated that the Soviets had a clear margin of nuclear superiority and knew how to use it. "The United States has become second best," and a respectable second-strike capability was not foreseen until *perhaps* the 1990s. Soviet superiority had immediate implications, Richard Pipes claimed, because the Soviet Union had never followed the philosophy of Mutual Assured Destruction (MAD) and was making plans to fight and *win* a nuclear war. Further, even if nuclear war never came, Pipes believed that nuclear superiority was part of the Soviet plan of global hegemony. This superiority would be translated into nuclear blackmail—"armed suasion." In 1984, seven years after writing his celebrated article on Soviet nuclear strategy, Pipes declared that Soviet leaders "believe that nuclear weapons are the means of quick and decisive victory." The chances for change were slim, Pipes believed, because the trouble was in the very roots of Russian culture. The Communist Revolution had installed in power the Russian peasant *(muzhik)*, and wrote Pipes, "the *muzhik* had been taught by long historical experience that cunning and coercion alone ensure survival: one employed cunning when weak, and cunning coupled with coercion when strong."[16]

The message of the CPD went beyond depictions of the internal and external crises that the nation faced. The committee also offered its plan for recovery. The first stage of national rehabilitation was the resuscitation of national courage—the realization that the enduring struggle might be endless. Podhoretz declared that Americans could no longer simply wish a different world into being. While "liberals are dreaming the dream of a new intellectual order," he complained, the Soviet Union is in a period of "active, imperialist, expansion."[17]

The path toward redemption led through the recovery of the American spirit that had supposedly been lost in the 1960s. Speaking before the platform committee of the Democratic Party in 1976, Eugene Rostow marveled that slowly, almost intuitively, public opinion "has come to realize that the Cold War is far from over." In that same year, Podhoretz offered a Wilsonian call to righteous battle, declaring that the nation's leaders must "use American power to make the world safe for democracy." In 1980, after the Soviet invasion of Afghanistan, when the Carter administration had reverted to orthodox Cold War anticommunism, Podhoretz thought it quite likely to be too late. The only salvation was for the United States to spend billions more on new nuclear weapons systems, "which alone can prevent the Soviets from achieving nuclear superiority and thus an unobstructed road to domination."[18]

For the CPD, commitment to weapons modernization and restoration of moribund systems (the B-1 bomber, for example) were unmistakable signs of the recovery of the American will. Failure to do this would only bring about Podhoretz's ultimate nightmare, the Finlandization of America. In this vision, the Soviet Union would gain economic and political leverage in Western Europe through nuclear blackmail, and American politicians would be forced to work "toward a socio-political system more in harmony with the Soviet model." Podhoretz remained cautiously optimistic, however. He saw the hostage crisis and the invasion of Afghanistan as triggering the end of America's period of self-doubt. He looked to the 1950s as the period that should serve as the paradigm of American patriotism, for this was a time when Americans were willing to "pay the price in blood to fight Communism." Those like George Kennan, who should have known enough to look back to this period as a time when perceptions of the enemy were clear and national will inspired blood sacrifice, had failed to do so, a sign that they had obviously "grown weary and fearful over the years."[19]

For the CPD, the election of Ronald Reagan, a CPD member, signaled a "new consensus" on the threat from the Soviet Union. In spite of this internal patriotic awakening, the committee thought the external crisis grew even more desperate. Podhoretz envisioned a "Cuban missile crisis in reverse . . . staged in the Persian Gulf, with the Finlandization of the West following inexorably in its wake." Others also constructed invasion scenarios to ensure that the hopeful signs of national recovery would not lessen perceptions of the danger. Robert Conquest's *What to Do When the Russians Come* offered a detailed picture of what would happen in America when the Russians invaded. Based on the experiences of Eastern European countries and the postwar occupation of South Vietnam by North Vietnam, Conquest painted a vivid picture of the gradual "Sovietization" of American life—a scenario that would become reality, he said, only if the United States became weak militarily and misperceived the intentions of the Soviet Union. Americans *were* often misled, Conquest believed, but they may "yet wake to the problem." Time, however, was on the side of the Soviet Union, and the bleak scenario Conquest painted was designed to awaken Americans to this present and ominous danger. At the same time as these apocalyptic scenarios were being vividly portrayed, others spoke of the hopeful seeds of recovery. Jeane Kirkpatrick echoed the theme of the rebirth of America, suggesting that our "dark night of the soul" was over; Reagan's election symbolized the end of a "national identity crisis through which the nation has been passing for some ten or fifteen years."[20]

The vision of the apocalypse—descriptions of the terrors that await, the inner degeneration by which the terrors will conquer, but the persistent hope for final recovery—was a part of the awakening process. It motivated the true believer to a sense of missionary fervor, for with the advent of nuclear weaponry, apocalyptic fantasies were readily believable, and the invigoration of living in the last days provided a sense of cosmic importance to the task of awakening to the end-time crisis.

For the CPD, there were only mutually exclusive choices regarding the future. One could believe that it was better to be "Red than dead" or better "dead than Red," and the choice once made governed all future individual value decisions and public policy decisions. Podhoretz's hope for the future rested with the bulwarking of American military might and, with the strength of such martial will in the face of the danger, the eventual breakup of the Soviet Union. Otherwise, he envisioned a gloomy future: an endless war, an "eternity of confrontation . . . without hope of victory in the end." He also foresaw a "universal gulag and a life that is otherwise nasty, brutish, and short." To forestall this process and to bring about the only palatable future, the United States must roll back communism, not just Soviet power, and this meant hearkening back to John F. Kennedy's crusading message: "Let every nation know, whether it wishes us well or ill, that we shall pay any price, bear any burden, meet any hardship, support any friend, oppose any foe, in order to assure the survival and the success of liberty."[21]

The success of the CPD's campaigns lay in its ability to construct a milieu of crisis at a time when the perplexing memories of Vietnam and more current foreign policy dilemmas made Americans susceptible to the comfortable, if not comforting, symbols of the Cold War. Sorting out the "proper" perceptions of the enemy offered at least social orientation, and as the CPD offered the logic of its analysis of the present danger, latent anticommunism arose quickly. The crisis, some believed, was a time of unprecedented opportunity. Perhaps, it *was* possible to resolve the inevitable frustrations of the "scorpions in the bottle" without living forever in the cold situation that allowed for no sense of a redemptive ending.

To resolve this unsatisfying balance of terror, the CPD pointed beyond containment to a reassertion of traditional images of heroic war and the renewed power of redemptive sacrifice in a holy cause. A crucial part of the agenda was the committee's attempt to perceive nuclear war as potentially decisive and purifying. As always, this was accompanied by rhetorical denials that Americans were at all warlike. Podhoretz wrote, for example: "The idea of war has never been as natural to Americans as it used to be to the English or Germans or French. We have always tended in this country to think of war as at best a hideous necessity."[22] The development of generations of nuclear weapons had not—any more than had the development of the machine gun—brought humanity to the realization that war might at last be obsolete.

The fear of the power of nuclear weapons was matched by the fascination with the opportunity for final victory using the ultimate weapons. If Cold War was so intolerable, perhaps the last hot war might bring about the final fundamental transformations that had been dreamed about for so long.

These millennialist fantasies usually were not expressed crudely, except in fundamentalist visions engendered by apocalyptic models in scripture. More often they were construed in the dispassionate language of nuclear strategists. Nuclear war-fighting scenarios and plans for civil defense were part of the desire for a way out of MAD, for they allowed people to dream once again of conditions that could allow for final victory, a new birth of freedom, and millennial peace. Colin Gray, consultant to the State Department and member of the General Advisory Committee of the Arms Control and Disarmament Agency, expressed this hope:

> The United States should plan to defeat the Soviet Union and to do so at a cost that would not prohibit U.S. recovery. Washington should identify war aims that in the last resort would contemplate the destruction of Soviet political authority and the emergence of a postwar world order *compatible with Western values.* (emphasis added)[23]

The Minuteman was now a missile, but its purpose was apparently the same as that of those original embattled farmers—protection, salvation, and the transformation of the world.

The CPD correctly understood that the debates surrounding nuclear weapons were part of the ongoing debate about what it meant to be an American in the nuclear age. For many, Richard Barnet's comments on the early 1960s seemed appropriate: "What characterized America was now its power, and the citizen's sense of belonging was somehow related to the vicarious exercise of national power. More and more an American came to mean someone who identified with the struggle against America's enemies."[24] As one shared in the tremendous power and promise of nuclear weapons—either in fantasies of their use or fantasies of their potential political utility—one presumably shared in the only experience that linked all Americans together. The CPD's call for a revival of the crusading spirit of World War II and the 1950s reflected the yearning for a new beginning.

The statements of many CPD members on the character of nuclear war made it clear that nuclear war was perceived as different in *degree*, but not in *kind,* from other wars. Because no fundamental discontinuity existed between the nuclear age and previous ages, no fundamental discontinuity existed between war in the nuclear age and previous wars. Richard Pipes, for example, described "realistic" scenarios for nuclear war fighting and argued that "victory is quite feasible *exactly as it is in any military conflict* [emphasis added], i.e., one side disables the other and inflicts its will upon it." Pipes dismissed the arguments that nuclear weapons, by their very nature, precluded rational use in a battlefield situation. These arguments, he believed, served the purposes of the Soviet Union. Pipes believed that the Soviet Union was primarily interested in keeping fear of nuclear weapons at the center of Western thought so that the West would desire good relations with the Soviet Union *above all.* Hence, nuclear anxiety, according to Pipes, was part of the Soviet plan for global hegemony: "it is designed to translate the natural dread that most people have of war in general and nuclear war in particular into an overwhelming anxiety that paralyzes thought and will."[25] In other words, the rise of fear of nuclear war in American culture in the late 1970s was mainly due to Soviet-constructed anxieties, designed to make Americans think that there was nothing worth dying for. It was *this* insidious degeneration of the will to sacrifice that the CPD feared would lead to the surrender of the West.

It is not entirely clear whether the millennialist ethics of the CPD called for the will to consider global human sacrifice in the final battle between the forces of good and evil. The justification for global sacrifice has been discussed for some time. In 1961, Sidney Hook declared that "survival at all costs is not among the values of the West." More recently, President Reagan communicated this sense of global sacrifice to the National Association of Evangelicals on March 8, 1983. The message came anecdotally. The president was reflecting on a speech that he had heard a "prominent young man" give on the subject of communism before a "tremendous gathering" in California during the Cold War:

> "I love my little girls more than anything—" And I said to myself, "Oh no, don't. You can't—don't say that." But I had underestimated him. He went on: "I would rather see my little girls die now, still believing in God, than have them grow up under communism and one day die no longer believing in God."
>
> There were thousands of young people in that audience. They came to their feet with shouts of joy. They had instantly recognized the profound truth in what he had said, with regard to the physical and the soul and what was truly important.[26]

The CPD's call to recovery seemed to balance precariously between a desire for the final battle in which the national will to preserve sacred principles would be expressed by a willingness to die for them, as a country and perhaps as a world, and a desire for a recovery of American will necessary to maintain the contest of wills with the enemy that could continue for the foreseeable future. Without question, the CPD called for America to awaken to the dangers that it faced from within and without. The will to nuclear superiority and the stoic determination to sacrifice whatever was necessary was, in its view, the unmistakable sign of the vitality of cultural renewal.

The Committee on the Present Danger set forth a powerfully articulate statement about the risk the nation faced, the proper identification of internal and external enemies, and the prescription for American recovery. The CPD perceived that the moment of truth was drawing near and that its restorative work was the last chance for the nation and for Western civilization. The CPD made use of the familiar rhetorical pattern of the jeremiad: it spoke both of decline and doom and of revitalization and exaltation. Cultural restoration would begin with a tactical revolution of feeling, a required shift of the affections. The CPD worked out of a dominant historical paradigm: the memories and lessons of Munich.

The CPD knew that national recovery would begin with a kind of spiritual discipline: an inner transformation, the restoration of the will to sacrifice, would precede, but be directly related to, the public policy decisions that would spring from a rejuvenated nation. Nuclear weapons played a crucial symbolic role in the restorative process. For the CPD, the will to modernize the arsenal and to plan soberly for the possible use of nuclear weapons revealed that Americans had recovered the sense of millennial destiny they had abandoned only recently. The CPD had great success in revitalizing Cold War orthodoxy in the late 1970s, and yet, ironically, Cold War fears engendered not only fears of the Soviet Union and *their* nuclear weapons, but fear of nuclear weapons in general. Consequently, the eruption of the fierce ideological civil war in America over the function of nuclear weapons can be partly traced to the fervor of the CPD. For Americans who thought the world view of the Cold War dangerously archaic, the CPD's message was *itself* the "present danger," and American nuclear weapons, far from being symbols of protection and ultimate salvation, were symbols of ultimate destruction. Consequently, in the late 1970s and early 1980s, Americans battled over the proper symbols with which to interpret the dangers of the nuclear age.

Antinuclear activists argued that the threat of nuclear weapons made nuclear war the real danger and entered into the realm of symbolic politics by proposing a "freeze" on the research, testing, and production of nuclear weapons. The assumption of those enamored of the Freeze Movement was that the nuclear threat could be measured by numbers of weapons not specific crisis situations. Hence, the way out of the nuclear dilemma was first to freeze, then to reduce, and then to do away with nuclear weapons. Like the CPD, antinuclear activists sought to utilize fear as a prod to public awareness and action. In a 1983 article in *Science,* several scientists, including the popular Cornell professor Carl Sagan, argued that even a modest detonation of nuclear warheads could bring about a "nuclear winter," in which the earth would suffer catastrophic environmental damage, and life on earth might come to an end. Antinuclear activists hoped that such a dramatic symbol would have a profound impact on people's consciousness and force the superpowers to reduce nuclear arsenals, which would, in their view, make nuclear war more unlikely.[27]

In response to the symbolic politics of the Freeze and nuclear winter, those more fearful of the Soviet Union than of nuclear weapons maintained their belief in the contours of the Cold War world and argued that a sturdy deterrent and the revival of traditional American patriotism would safeguard the nation. Yet, by the mid-1980s, these same cold warriors who often sneered at the political naivete of antinuclear activists offered the nation the most dramatic example of utopian politics: on March 23, 1983, President Reagan offered his vision of a missile defense designed to make nuclear weapons "impotent and obsolete." In the ensuing years, members of the CPD helped articulate the ideology of strategic defense. This ideology was rooted both in the world view of the Cold War *and* in the belief of antinuclear activists that the threat of nuclear war called for a dramatic transformation in the status quo. Those who shaped the ideology of strategic defense told the American public that the Cold War *was* still being waged, for Americans would have to conquer the final frontier of space or else risk losing the war in space to the Soviet Union. Yet, these same spokesmen also told Americans that strategic defense would dramatically alter the nuclear age, eventually bringing about a world free of nuclear weapons.[28]

The Committee on the Present Danger could take credit for helping arouse both anticommunist activism and antinuclear activism in American culture. Like every other group that enters the public forum to shape opinion on these issues, the CPD had to contend, it seems, with two conflicting impulses—the popular desire to be nourished by the patriotic enthusiasm that has given coherence to the postwar world and a fear that these tribal allegiances might lead the nation into the abyss.

Chapter 3

Nuclear Images in the Popular Press: From Apocalypse to Static Balance

Nuclear imagery had lain dormant for some fifteen years when it emerged again in the late 1970s. By 1982, it had reached a crescendo of concern rivaling that of 1962. Although much had changed over two decades, much remained the same. *Reader's Digest* was still by far the most widely read magazine in the country. Time-Life, Inc., was still the leader in the news category, although *Time* had replaced *Life* in the number one slot. And the arms race spiraled on, unabated. While the nation seemed to rest from nuclear anxiety and "the nightmare of actual war receded somewhat into the subconscious of civilization . . . in the '60s and '70s, both sides increased their nuclear firepower by several orders of magnitude."[1] There was one momentous new reality, however: by the beginning of the 1980s, the United States could no longer claim nuclear superiority. Indeed, *Reader's Digest* warned that "the United States is already running second in important aspects of military preparedness,"[2] and *Time* concluded that "the two nations are in rough parity—meaning essentially that each could destroy the other."[3]

Whether our position was perceived as parity or inferiority, a major shift in nuclear imagery was inescapable. With military victory no longer a meaningful concept, images of omnipotence and readiness for apocalyptic war could not be sustained. Some new context was needed to give meaning to the Bomb and the arms race. The media apparently realized this before the Reagan administration. Although the Reaganites spoke freely and easily about fighting a nuclear war, *Time* assured its readers that

even those in the Administration who sincerely believe that the U.S., if it had
to, could fight and win a nuclear war agree that the primary goal of U.S.
weapons and policy should be preventing one. . . . The best way to prevent a
holocaust is to prevent any kind of nuclear war in the first place. On that
everyone agrees.[4]

As for the USSR, "the preponderance of the evidence is that the Soviets just do
not want to fight a war."[5] The premise of nuclear imagery in the 1980s was that
no one intends to use these weapons to fight a global war: "Nuclear war
remains a special kind of nightmare, threatening an apocalypse for the whole
human race."[6] "The only thing harder to imagine than a permanent
reconciliation between the U.S. and the U.S.S.R. is a rationalization on the
part of either nation for taking the risk of all-out war."[7]

Visions of apocalyptic battle had to recede into the background, but the
Bomb remained front and center in the nation's consciousness in the only
meaningful role left to it—guarantor of safety and peace. How could the
Bomb keep the peace? The new image turned out to be a very old one,
refurbished for the nuclear age: "While balance of power may be an old
fashioned idea, it can be argued to be all the more valid now that power is
nuclear. Precisely because these arsenals must not be used, they must keep
each other in check."[8] The image of stable balance—rationally achieved and
rationally maintained—became the unifying thread tying together all the
nuclear imagery of the 1980s. The central message was that nuclear weapons
can still be our savior, because they play a crucial role in moving the world
toward perfect and immutable balance.

Despite this new vision, the Cold War still rages on in all its cosmic
importance and intensity. "The Russians say plainly, over and over again, that
they are in an ideological war with us. . . . Most Americans believe that the
war of ideologies will determine the future of the world order."[9] The NATO
military commander contrasted himself with his Russian counterpart: "I'm
defending liberty and all the values we hold so dear in the West. He's fighting
for secret police, censorship, labor camps and the suppression of individual
freedom."[10] In sum, "the values of the U.S. and Soviet society are too starkly
contrasting to permit for the foreseeable future anything friendlier than a more
cautious competition."[11] The competition must be more cautious because the
stakes are so much higher; balance must be maintained at all costs.

And this is now seen as the overriding threat and crime of the Soviet
Union—its irresponsible and unpredictable destabilizing behavior. "Nothing
did more to destroy detente than the Kremlin's insistence throughout the 1970s
on piling up weapons far in excess of any legitimate Soviet defensive need."[12]
Even if the Soviet leaders do not intend to attack us directly with those
weapons, their buildup is still dangerous; any "gross imbalance" in the arms

race "would raise the danger of a political crisis turning into a military one, inadvertently but catastrophically."[13] "They might be tempted to try to get the drop on the U.S. in a *High-Noon*-type showdown over some crisis in the Third World or Europe."[14] The confrontation "would probably be related to political instability in some region or the competition for scarce resources, or both."[15] If "the nuclear arms race has reached a point that no one could really have wanted," and the United States must prepare for a war it does not want to fight, "the fault for these deepening dilemmas lies largely with the Soviet Union. If the Soviets were truly interested in restoring stable mutual deterrence, they could scale down their military machine and desist from international behavior that provokes crises."[16]

They could also negotiate arms reductions in good faith. Although Soviet leaders loudly proclaim their desire for peace, they are simply "trying to enhance their bogus claim of championing disarmament."[17] When both sides do sit down at the bargaining table, "The United States tends to enter negotiations in a spirit of good will and fair play. This is hardly the Soviet approach. . . . We failed in the SALT negotiations because we continued to believe that the Russians would or could think like us."[18] Indeed, the contrast in thinking could hardly be more complete. Whereas they talk of peace without meaning it, we talk of war without meaning it. As is often the case in the realm of the sacred, there is a deeper truth hidden beneath superficial appearances. If the president lets slip some "loose talk" about limited nuclear war, this is just a "tiny tempest" that should "stay in the teapot."[19] "Reagan, according to his closest aides, believes fervently in reducing nuclear arms."[20] If he enthusiastically builds up our nuclear arsenal, he is merely evincing his commitment to balance and peace. He has no other choice, in the face of the destabilizing Soviet buildup: "The 'lengthening shadow' of Soviet power. . . . The Soviet threat. It is the driving force behind the administration's major rearmament program."[21] "Any U.S. President elected in 1980 would have had to continue and enlarge the counterbuildup that Carter had already begun."[22]

Plans for limited nuclear war in Europe have nothing to do with warmongering either. They are just a necessary component in "NATO's deterrent strategy of flexible response, which creates real uncertainty as to what our reaction to any attack by them will be. . . . This uncertainty is presently the biggest deterrent to war."[23] Plans for fighting a "protracted nuclear war" reflect the same benign motive. As the Secretary of Defense explains, "We see nuclear weapons only as a way of discouraging the Soviets from thinking that they could ever resort to them. That is exactly why we must have a capability for a protracted response."[24] Nothing that the United States does indicates any desire to conquer the enemy force. Everything grows out of "the theory of deterrence, the main canon of U.S. nuclear doctrine for nearly

40 years. . . . Ronald Reagan has relied on the same doctrine of deterrence as his predecessors."[25]

This perception (or misperception) of history is now a cornerstone of our nuclear imagery. Every new weapon is justified as another step toward peace through deterrence. An article entitled "Trident: Deadly New Deterrent" opens with the claim that "our new Trident sub will help restore the balance of power" and closes with a solemn affirmation of "that basic rule of the nuclear age: deterrence must not fail."[26] The strongest argument in support of deterrence strategy is that so far it has not failed: "It is acknowledged by most authorities in the field that peace over the past 40 years has been maintained by the controlled use of horror. . . . If nuclear weapons did not exist, the U.S. and the Soviet Union might have gone to war at least once since 1945."[27] Once we penetrate to the truth of the matter, we know that the irrational power of the Bomb, ruled by the hand of reason, is still our savior.

This commitment to deterrence is part and parcel of the new emphasis on rational balance. It conjures up the image of a world safely frozen in a permanent stalemate. As long as both superpowers keep using their weapons to build inviolable magic walls around themselves, neither can harm the other and everything remains status quo. If deterrence has always been the "main canon" of U.S. policy, this benign stability—not superiority—has always been our goal. Certainly, it requires skillful balancing of many complex factors; but the problems are not insurmountable:

> Avoiding nuclear war depends on keeping a balance between the imperatives of American policy and various factors of international relations, particularly the U.S.-Soviet rivalry. While those international tensions cannot be eliminated, they can be, and have been in the past, kept in a state of overall equilibrium. . . . But it is an equilibrium with an underlying paradox.[28]

One side of the paradox undermines the old image of apocalyptic warfare, as we have noted: "By their very nature, nuclear weapons are military instruments too powerful and destructive to 'solve,' in any meaningful sense, political problems that confront the U.S. and the Soviet Union."[29] But the arms race must continue anyway because of the other side of the paradox: nuclear weapons "are also too powerful and destructive for one superpower to relinquish as long as its rival has them."[30] Indeed, the quest for balance demands that each side keep building new weapons until it believes it has achieved the elusive goal of parity. Even if we long ago had more than enough weapons to deter the Russians from attacking us, we need more weapons to deter them from continuing a destabilizing arms race. Ultimately, our purpose is to deter destabilization itself.[31] Perfect equilibrium is now the accepted definition of peace—and salvation.

Of course, the media insist, we do not really want to build more weapons. We want to reduce our nuclear arsenals. But this must be done in a balanced way—through mutual and rational negotiation. "Progress in arms control has always depended on a degree of civility and a broader context of cooperation, or at least jointly regulated rivalry, between the superpowers."[32] Such a context cannot be created simply by good intentions, however. In the first place, the issues to be negotiated are overwhelmingly complicated: "There is no simple nostrum, no simple solution."[33] No disarmament proposal is helpful unless it "does justice to the complexity of the problem, and steers clear of simple-minded pseudo solutions."[34] This is the principal objection to the nuclear freeze campaign: "The very simplicity of the freeze idea—stop building bombs now—makes it inadequate to the technical and diplomatic rigors of arms control."[35] Only the experts, with their highly specialized and highly logical minds, can meet these rigors. Clearly, they should be left to negotiate their way through the wilderness of complexities without undue interference from the public.

Yet even the best of America's experts may be stymied by the biggest stumbling-block of all—the intransigence of the Soviets. So, as they go to the bargaining table, they must be backed up by an awesome and growing arsenal, "for unfortunately it is strength alone that the Soviets understand and grudgingly respect."[36] As the only force able to compel the Soviets to bargain in good faith and accept true parity, the Bomb is once again the path to peace. It is now deployed in Europe in hopes that "the new U.S. missile presence will pressure the Soviets to bargain more seriously in Geneva."[37] Although the Soviets seem to have dashed this hope by breaking off the Geneva talks, *Time* echoes the president in remaining "optimistic that the NATO missile deployment will, if anything, make a negotiated arms agreement more likely."[38] At the same time, of course, the "Euromissiles" are also seen as effective deterrents to the Kremlin's designs on the West: "The U.S. must ultimately rely on the big stick to deter Soviet aggression."[39] A new weapons system like the MX is also promoted for both functions: "At stake is our ability to deter Soviet aggression—and war. . . . It should also convince the Soviets of the futility of continuing arms competition."[40] Along both lanes of the "dual track" of deterrence and arms control, more bombs are the path to equilibrium.

The "dual track" approach deserves its name not only because it deftly balances deterrent strength and negotiating flexibility but also because it weaves together old and new imagery with similar dexterity. The new imagery of rational balance has served as a screen behind which much of the old imagery could survive and still appear meaningful. Of course, additions and alterations were necessary. We have already seen that the Cold War continues as a contest of cosmic proportions, with the awesome power of the Bomb providing the key to victory; yet we have also seen how the understanding of victory has changed. Defeating the Russians now means primarily defeating the instability and threat of war that the Russians are held to represent; the two enemies become one. Given the pervasive fear and rejection of nuclear war,[41] there is much less focus on the destructiveness of the Bomb itself (although pictures of weapons continue to be customary). So the contest, like the whole nuclear issue, comes to have an air of familiarity and, thus, of safety. As long as we are on the way to the protective shelter of perfect balance, we can accept— and perhaps even enjoy—the thrill of a competition with infinitely high stakes. *Time* uses appropriate terms from the sports world quite often in reporting the nuclear issue: *players, playing the game, strategy, scoring, next move, stalemate*. Gambling terms such as *betting, ante, odds* are equally common. A spectator sport is also a spectacle, and so diplomatic events are described with words like *acting, oratory, stances, cues, delivering lines, interludes in the drama*. The Cold War is perceived as a play—both in the sense of a game and of a theatrical event.

The principal actors are the experts, driving the nuclear train along the "dual track" to security and salvation. Their favorite and most important show, it seems, is the "show of resolve."[42] Challenge and willingness to meet the challenge are still key elements in the nuclear drama: "They must see . . . that we *are* the leaders of the free world and that we have the purpose and strength to carry out that role."[43] "The first half of the '80s may well be the most critical period that the West will have to face for many decades to come. It will be a time of testing and perhaps of crisis."[44] The public, of course, is encouraged to be a deeply involved audience, identifying with its leaders as they do whatever is necessary to demonstrate our resolve to meet the test.

The show of resolve is equally important in both lanes of the dual track. We must show a willingness to use the terrible weapons that we claim no intention of using: "If the use of nuclear weapons is renounced, they lose their utility not only as weapons of war but as instruments of peace. If deterrence is to work, an aggressor should not be able to dismiss entirely the possibility of nuclear retaliation."[45] "For the American threat to be credible, there must be widespread acceptance of the proposition that the U.S. forces would be 'survivable and enduring.'"[46] Resolve is just as crucial in diplomatic negotia- tion, where words can be almost as potent as bombs in demonstrating strength. An "East-West War of Words"[47] reached new heights during the "Euromissile" crisis: "It loomed as a fundamental test of wills between the Soviet Union and the 16 members of the NATO alliance."[48] The Soviets'"chill blasts" and "barrage of threats" "appeared to signal an increased willingness by Moscow to push its war of nerves with Washington to the breaking point."[49]

With the USSR finally breaking off negotiations, "the overall climate of U.S.-Soviet relations has reached poisonous intensity . . . but there was an important positive consequence: the oft-fragmented Atlantic Alliance had, contrary to many predictions, responded to its most stringent test in more than 25 years by affirming rather than weakening its resolve."[50] In the global theater, a proper show of resolve is apparently more important than improved relations with the foe; a resolute will is the path to peace, because only firmness can deter instability. The Cold War remains a war and a test of the nation's spirit.

All of these intertwined themes are evident in the media response to Ronald Reagan's "Star Wars" proposal. There is nothing radically new here, *Reader's Digest* points out: "A U.S.-Soviet 'space war,' undeclared and veiled in secrecy, has been going on for over 20 years . . . to see who will perfect a new generation of weapons of blinding speed and destructiveness. . . . And while the Soviets lost the race to the moon, they seem determined not to lose the grim cosmic race of orbiting weaponry."[51] The challenge of combat is combined here with the challenge of technological progress and conquering the heavens. Yet, now victory is urged in the name of peace through deterrence; *Time* headlines its major article on the subject "Reagan for the Defense."[52] As always, *Time*'s concern is stability: "A missile defense system could undermine the very foundation of strategic stability, namely, the concept of Mutually Assured Destruction (MAD)."[53] But its final word is an affirmation of faith in unlimited progress through competition and will: "We must in our own interests pursue it, if only to find out what our adversaries may be doing. . . . Once challenged, and once convinced, this nation has been able to do just about anything it wanted to do. . . . A determined, skilled President who captures a nation's imagination, energy and know-how can work miracles."[54] Perhaps we can still aspire to omnipotence by imposing the immutable order of a pax Americana, in heaven and on earth, without firing a single shot. And we might just do it by reenacting a "Star Wars scenario" that was once only a motion-picture show.

The recurrent theme of play and show serves a vital role in tying together old and new imagery. It allows us to accept the persistence of old images by suggesting that the whole nuclear issue is nothing more than high drama and, therefore, fundamentally unreal. We can live with apocalyptic images that might otherwise be terribly frightening by distancing ourselves from them and seeing them as part of the show. On that level, they become quite appealing. The show is intensely exciting, holding cosmic significance yet touching each of us individually, and it is even tinged with comic relief in its black humor. Both as actors and as audience we get to participate vicariously; we get to step into a larger, richer world, imbued with infinite power and ultimate meaning.

Yet we feel safe, for no one seems to seek anything other than peaceful stability through this show. Indeed, the nuclear drama offers much the same appeal as religious ritual: a play staged by experts, offering safe contact with numinous power, and aiming at the restoration of balance on a cosmic scale. But when political realities become so thoroughly imbued with ritual play, the line between theatrical play and everyday reality threatens to disappear, and an air of unreality hangs over all we think and do.

                                        II

The air of unreality helps to sustain the most terrifying of all the old images, the actual waging of a nuclear war. Here again, though, the new modifies the old. Despite the explicit affirmations that no one can win a nuclear war, there are implicit claims that nuclear war will be fought much like traditional war—the familiar contest of challenge and response, offense and defense, with a winner and a loser. "Many features of the American defense plan greatly increase confidence that the U.S. could mount a potent nuclear counterattack even if the Soviets were to strike first."[55] Pentagon war-fighting plans "describe what has for some time been U.S. strategy: ensuring a second- and third-strike capability that would allow the country to continue fighting the Soviets after an initial nuclear exchange."[56] The commander of a Trident submarine "will have at his fingertips the power to bring a total of 192 targets under nuclear attack."[57] "If the vital interests of the Atlantic Alliance are involved," the NATO commander stoutly asserts, "we'll fight."[58] For the average reader, the obvious implication is that we are ready to fight—and win—now as we have always been.

In hot war as in Cold War, however, winning no longer means quite what it used to mean. Of course, in the media's view, only the Soviets could be destabilizing enough to launch a war. If they do attack us, then deterrence has failed, and our goal is to reestablish deterrence: "War fighting makes sense (and rather shaky sense at that) only as an extension of deterrence—deterrence by other means, as Clausewitz might have put it."[59] So our goal is not primarily victory over the attacker but victory over the true enemy—instability: "Whatever the Soviets do or threaten to do, the U.S. must be in a position to do something worse, and to do it with such speed, precision and force that the Kremlin will not escalate the conflict."[60] Fortunately, we have both the rational plan (the Single Integrated Operating Plan) and the technological capacities to keep control of any situation, even a nuclear war. The SIOP "would theoretically allow for a limited nuclear war, in which a Soviet attack could be answered with surgical retaliations that would conceivably be halted before a full-scale missile exchange occurred."[61] The president is at the helm: "The SIOP is intended to give the President an elaborate array of carefully calibrated choices for retaliation."[62] The assumption is that the president would remain cool, logical, and precise. Yet even if tempted to respond emotionally, "there is no way a President could succumb to reflexive nuclear revenge. . . . The President must deal with an impersonal and coldly rational chain of command."[63] In war as in peace, only balanced rationality and the Bomb can be our salvation.

Could this combination in fact save us? The answer remains unclear. "Even some distinguished American strategists. . .concede in private that a so-called selective flexible response would be likely to unleash a chain reaction out of either side's control."[64] Others, apparently, disagree. If full-scale war came, *Time* sees only the gloomiest prospects. It labels civil defense proposals "Planning for the Unplannable."[65] *Reader's Digest* joins *Time* in using a litany of familiar terms to describe nuclear war: *horror, holocaust, devastation, terror, annihilation, extinction, apocalypse, catastrophe, the end of the world.* *Time* spices up its reporting with vivid images of a postwar world: *universal fire, the abyss, freezing cold, mass death,* and the like. Yet *Reader's Digest* also reports the sanguine views of Edward Teller: "Our survival can be considered certain. . . . Civil-defense planning in the United States could save 100 million more lives. . . . Were the Soviets aware that the American people are able to survive an attack, they would be much less likely to take the risk of initiating a conflict."[66] As always, planning for war can be seen as the path to peace.

These conflicting views on all-out war echo the complexities that run through all nuclear imagery. The resulting bewilderment adds to the air of unreality. "Understanding and making nuclear policy are like stepping into a wilderness of mirrors."[67] This does not mean, however, that the issue must end in confusion. "There is one given in the debate: nuclear weapons cannot be disinvented, so ways must be found to ensure that they are never used."[68] "Living with nuclear weapons is our only hope. It requires that we persevere in reducing the likelihood of war even though we cannot remove the possibility altogether."[69] It is obvious by now that the media see only one way to do this—unflagging pursuit of rational balance. To that end, the prime virtue of the nuclear age is to remain calm and reasonable amidst the terror. *Time*'s chief criticism of the disarmament movement is its tendency to get emotional: "In an open society, legitimate movements based on valid ideals, like the arms-control crusade, have the potential to be manipulated in such a way that passions and emotions override rational judgments."[70] This is also *Time*'s criticism of the nationally televised film, *The Day After.*

> Real events, unlike TV scripts, keep demanding not just emotion, not just
> fear, but answers. . . . If the film's lasting impression is one of fright, then no

purpose has been served save to boost ABC's ratings. But if by looking at the unlookable, millions of Americans start thinking about the unthinkable and appreciating the complexities of coping with atomic arsenals, then the show could prove to be a public service.[71]

Appreciating those complexities, we are likely to realize that only the experts have the sufficient skill and understanding to stay in control of this "wilderness of mirrors." So, the safest course is to follow the advice and example of our leaders:

> The horror of nuclear war has greatly troubled every President, and yet all of them since 1945 have conditioned themselves to plan nuclear strategy coolly and prudently. The experts tend to agree that too much fear in the Oval Office would warp judgements and make crises more likely. . . . Presidents have all become tempered, cautious, and properly fearful stewards of our destructive might. But none has had nightmares over his nuclear responsibility.[72]

The dual track of deterrence and arms control, of old and new images, is also a dual track of trustworthy experts and a calm rational public. Riding this dual track toward the heaven of unending stability, we have reason to be hopeful: "Like all the complex interactions within the atom, the volatile human forces at work on the planet earth may be able to maintain their dynamic equilibrium indefinitely. That will unquestionably require ever increasing wisdom and skillful management," *Time* optimistically opines. Yet it cannot avoid adding: "as well as luck.[73] But isn't a little bit of unpredictability and risk the ingredient that makes every game exciting?

By the middle of the 1980s, the imagery of rational balance had become nearly universally triumphant. Its appeals are many and varied. It demands no choice between an arms race and arms control, for it sees the two as partners aiming toward a single goal. Just as important, it sees the two as partners in a ritual reenactment of fundamental American values: faith in technological rationality and in the technical experts who implement that rationality to give us an everimproving way of life. The Bomb has become our prime symbol of abiding faith in human ability to master and control all realities, no matter how complex or forbidding. The numinous power of the Bomb has been joined to the numinous power of the experts who claim to have it safely in hand. As the average person participates vicariously in the journey down the "dual track," there is a growing conviction that "we, the people" are indeed omnipotent. For if we can in fact harness the atom and its dangers in an immutable stability, then we can do anything.

This wonderous achievement is evidence of our strength—and of our right and obligation to remain strong. For if we can forge a perfect world equilibrium, it is a victory for and tribute to our national strength; but it is also a victory for the world. What more could anyone, anywhere in the world, desire? We are exercising our firm resolve just as much for the benefit of the Russian people as for our own, though they do not realize it. So we can justify the imposition of those values we celebrate through our nuclear arsenal. Reason tells us that truth is one and the same for all people. The technological reason we enshrine in the Bomb is equally valid in every nation. Just as it has given us unparalleled abundance and ease, so we would offer this to all other peoples. The image of a single salvation and a single savior for all is still very much alive. But, if we are to use our weapons for universal salvation, we must be strong and unyielding in the Cold War struggle. We must form an immovable center around which the world can gather and ultimately revolve. Our Bomb and our resolve can make us the sacred center of human life—if we remain strong enough. So there is no need to choose between nationalism and universalism; like the arms race and arms control, the two go hand in hand.

Immovability is a basic theme in all this imagery. In a world encircled by nuclear weapons, we can be safe only if the weapons are immobilized. Safety comes to be equated with stasis, yet stasis has a deeper meaning. The transcendence or cessation of time is an age-old dream embodied in the myths and rituals of virtually every culture. In a time when the rate of change seems so dizzying, we are ever more strongly drawn to this dream. But we must express it in modern terms; immutable balance achieved through technological reason is the perfect solution to the problem. If the most potent power known to us can be fixed in this static state, so can everything else. As we move toward nuclear equilibrium, using the Bomb itself as our vehicle, we may believe that we are moving toward a time when change and the passage of time itself will cease. As long as we have the Bomb, then, every day brings us a bit closer to this eternal end-time. The Bomb itself redeems the passage of time by giving it a transtemporal meaning. Yet, this whole process must occur, the images tell us, carefully and gradually; the complexities must be worked out one by one. There will be no sudden cataclysmic transformation, no great rupture with the known and the familiar—and so we are safe.

This is the one crucial point at which the imagery of the 1980s departs from its predecessor of the early Cold War era. Both agree that our values must be ritually reenacted by nuclear means. Both agree that we have become, and must remain, awesome and omnipotent. Both agree that our victory will be a victory for all humanity, and that time must work toward its own elimination by means of the saving Bomb. But, once the hope for a sudden apocalyptic redemption is gone, conflict no longer has the same overwhelming appeal. Gradual amelioration takes its place, and along with it a professed willingness to work with and for the enemy, if the enemy is tractably willing.

When images of balance replace images of conflict in the forefront of our minds, stasis comes to be prized more than change. The world we work toward is in fact the world pictured by technological and scientific reason: a world that is wholly predictable and wholly manipulable because it is inert.[74] This immovable world is the terminus at the end of the "dual track." It is our salvation.

So we are called to act out this value, too, in the nuclear issue, by remaining emotionally stable, rational, and passive. We can aid our redeemers, the experts and their weapons, by allowing them to pursue their course unimpeded. We can adopt this supine posture confidently, for we are assured over and over again that the experts have only our best interests at heart. Their only goal is to build a rational order, using the Bomb, that will protect us forever from the chaos of the Bomb. So, although the new imagery does differ in significant ways from the old, its deepest appeal is the same. It offers an infinite power that symbolizes both life and death, order and chaos, good and evil, and the harmonious synthesis of all in a single universal equilibrium. Because this equilibrium works on many levels—military, political, technological, ideological, emotional, and more—it assures us that beneath the apparent fragmentation and disorder of our world there is a fundamental unity.

This all-encompassing unity has room for every contradiction. Everything can be affirmed; nothing need be denied. Indeed, the more contradictions it must face, the stronger is its appeal, for each is further evidence that balance and static synthesis can in fact be perfectly achieved. So the new image welcomes the old apocalyptic images, giving them an enduring place while buffering their frightening impact with its aura of impregnable safety. We believe ourselves to have mastered the apocalypse; we have taken the place of our ancestors' God.

Do we really believe that such salvation through balance and the Bomb is possible? Perhaps it is only a smokescreen, a way to go on holding the old apocalyptic images that are so central to Western civilization without going mad from terror. But, if these images are sincerely held and affirmed, we must reckon with a new kind of religious experience. The aspiration to rational balance is not new; it grows out of the Enlightment dream that human reason and order could eliminate chaos forever. What is new, though, is the embodiment of this vision in an unlimited technological power that serves as the vision's symbol and vehicle. Because this unlimited power threatens to unleash unlimited chaos, chaos now returns to a central, although paradoxical and hidden, place in our image of perfect order. And this may be the key to the widespread appeal of static rational balance. Although we crave order, we have an equal craving for the power that can destroy every order. Our ultimate desire is for the paradoxical unity of the two that our ancestors enshrined in their images of God. Today, images of static rational balance tell us that we can have that unity. They tell us that we need make no choice. As long as we have the Bomb, we can have it all.

Part II

Sociology of Religion

JAMES A. AHO*

Chapter 4

"I Am Death. . . Who Shatters Worlds": The Emerging Nuclear Death Cult

Sociology acknowledges for itself a number of different tasks: the collection of raw data, the empirical evaluation of social policy, theory construction, and the critical exposure of significant cultural and historical trends. This chapter is in the last genre. It inaugurates a sociological critique of an emerging religious cult fraught with profound significance for our time. We shall call this cult, with some initial intent at emotional impact, the *nuclear death cult.*

American cultural criticism has always been concerned with "new religions," and in recent years much attention has been given to the notion of an American "civil religion." Yet the cult with which we are dealing has so far largely eluded sociological purview, although it is a new religious form that must be seen in the context of, and indeed as a manifestation of, American civil religion. To be sure, the disturbingly friendly fascination with nuclear holocaust on the part of the religious right has not entirely escaped the notice of journalists and social scientists.[1] But this chapter addresses a similar awakening, not just among those who might be dismissed as extremists, but also among more intellectually respectable types: nuclear physicists and engineers. Although we typically treat the alleged prophets of new cults with disdain, these fathers of the nuclear death cult are often approached as objects of admiration. By critically exposing the religious imagery and mythology of both the nuclear establishment and of ordinary folk, we can make our own conventional attitudes toward the Bomb a bit more conscious. Once compelled to view the authentic religious roots of our peculiar attachment to a

*This paper was read at the plenary session of the 46th annual meeting of the Association for the Sociology of Religion, San Antonio, Texas, August 25, 1984. The author would like to thank Ken Westhues and John Lofland for their supportive comments on earlier versions of this paper, and particularly Margaret Aho for her critical reading and editing.

49

weapon of mass destruction, we may be momentarily freed to address the problems it brings in a more profound and clear-minded way.

But what could possibly be "religious" about the Bomb? Those of us raised in the benign comforts of intellectualized western religious traditions— where God is seen as the epitome of goodness—perceive religion as integral to the development of the humane life. We forget that religion is first and foremost a response to manifestations of power, and these can take many forms, humane and inhumane. Rudolf Otto considered religious experience as quite unlike the everyday emotions of trust, submission, hope, humility, or contentment. The experience of the numinous, the sacred, is a feeling of frightening mystery that either slowly envelops the soul or bursts in upon it.[2] In either case, it is ineffable, inexplicable, and unforgettable: it demands a response. Its power to transport the subject to wholly unfamiliar psychological regions is unmistakable. The experience of the sacred is not, then, in its most elementary sense a vision of a specific God, a certainty of salvation as prescribed in a particular theology, nor a compelling example of sacrificial moral uprightness. While after long periods of systematic rationalization holiness may be overlaid with ethical, aesthetic, and cognitive attributes, it is not itself derived from these.

The unearthly power of nuclear weapons has engendered responses of awe and allegiance among members of the nuclear cult. Human beings have, in both their primal fears and primal attractions, responded to the Bomb as laden with otherworldly power. It is among the very physicists and engineers who design, construct and test nuclear weaponry that we can chart these responses. These are men and women presumably immune to irrational flights of imagination and emotion, practitioners of the experimental method and operational definition, disciplined to ignore personal fancy or fear in generalizing from facts, and, above all, professionally imbued with an attitude of ethical and emotional neutrality.

THE BOMB AS HOLY

We are fortunate in having as matter of public record the pronouncements of a considerable number of witnesses to the first nuclear explosion conducted at Alamogordo, New Mexico, on July 16, 1945. Given the remarkable congruence of these reports, an inference can be safely made about the responses produced in the minds of those present. In the words of William L. Laurence, the resident journalist who would later win the Pulitzer Prize for his account of the affair.

> it was like being witness to the Second Coming of Christ! . . . [I]t then came to
> me that both 'Oppie' [the affectionate title given J. Robert Oppenheimer,

director of the Los Alamos Laboratory] and I, and likely many others in our group, had shared in a profound religious experience, having been witness to an event akin to supernatural.[3]

It is July 1945 in the wasteland west of Alamogordo, New Mexico. All reports testify to mounting tension among the scientists at the site. The summer heat of the desert merely aggravates this. Never before has the government invested such treasure on a project with such an uncertain outcome. The repute not only of the scientific community is a stake—the "long hairs" as they are derisively called by their military commanders—but of each individual. Will it work? Will it, perhaps, work too well, igniting atmospheric nitrogen and engulfing the whole world in one vast conflagration?[4] Already zero-moment has been set back several times because of lightning, the flashes of which have come tantalizingly close to prematurely igniting the "gadget."

Countdown begins. The first streaks of dawn have yet to appear over the Oscuro Hills to the east; it is still pitch-dark. Among others, General Farrell prays fervently to himself that the test be a "boy" rather than a "girl," a success rather than a dud: "Lord I believe: Help Thou mine unbelief." "Five. . . . Four. . . . Three. . . . Two. . . . One. . . . Now!"

> And then, without a sound, the sun was shining; or so it looked. The sand hills at the edge of the desert were shimmering in a very bright light, almost colourless and shapeless. This light did not seem to change for a couple of seconds and then began to dim. I turned round, but that object on the horizon which looked like a small sun was still too bright to look at.... It was slowly rising into the sky from the ground, with which it remained connected by a lengthening grey stem of swirling dust. Then, as the cloud of hot gas cooled and became less red, one could see a blue glow surrounding it, a glow of ionized air.... It was an awesome spectacle; anybody who has ever seen an atomic explosion will never forget it. And all in complete silence; the bang came minutes later, quite loud though I had plugged my ears, and followed by a long rumble like heavy traffic very far away. I can still hear it[5].

As a precaution, witnesses had been supplied acetylene goggles and those at 5-mile station told to protect themselves from the shock wave by kneeling in trenches with their backs to the blast. Several skeptics ignored this advice and, like Saul of Tarsus on his way to Damascus, were hurled to the ground by the force and sight of the explosion.[6] Victor Weisskopf describes it this way:

> The visual impression of that explosion was enormous. I think it was probably the most impressive experience I ever had in my life. How this hemisphere increased and increased, and then as the whole sphere detached itself from the earth, white and then yellow, and then orange. And most impressively, this big sphere was surrounded by a halo of blue light, caused by radioactivity.

> And at that moment, I was reminded, of a picture by Matthias Grunewald, *The Ascension of Christ to Heaven.* He also pictured Christ in a ball like this, even with the blue halo around. And I was almost scared by this contrast, between this instrument of death and the symbol of faith in Grunewald's picture.[7]

Henry De Wolf Smyth, official historian for the project, quotes another observer saying of the blast that it was "unprecedented, magnificent, beautiful, stupendous, and terrifying."

> It was that beauty the great poets dream about but describe most poorly and inadequately. Thirty seconds after the explosion, came, first, the air blast, pressing hard against the people and things, to be followed almost immediately by the strong, sustained, awesome roar which warned us of doomsday and made us feel that we puny things were blasphemous to dare tamper with the forces heretofore reserved to the Almighty. Words are inadequate tools for the job of acquainting those not present with the physical, mental, and psychological effects. It had to be witnessed to be realized.[8]

Terror, fascination, ineffability, unforgettableness, and above all, a vague feeling of unworthiness and sin in the face of a transcendent vision: in a word, the very elements Rudolf Otto depicts as constituting the experience of the numinous. And other even more telling examples can be cited: for example, when his imprecation to the Lord (quoted earlier) was answered, General Farrell felt "the sensation turned into a thrill of realization and dread";[9] Oppenheimer stunned by the "shattering effect" whose words Laurence would never forget;[10] the words of Charles Thomas,[11] Carson Mark,[12] or of Isador Rabi—"The experience was hard to describe. I haven't got over it yet. It was awful, ominous, personally threatening. I couldn't tell why." Gooseflesh would appear on the backs of his hands, just as for Otto Frisch the sight would induce nausea;[13] the words of Samuel Allison;[14] of George Kistiakowski— "This was the closest to doomsday one can possibly imagine";[15] or finally, those of the journalist Laurence, written, as he tells it, "without full awareness . . . feverishly, like one awakening from a dream, in a frantic effort before the return of full consciousness":

> It was as though the earth had opened and the skies had split. . . .
>
> The big boom came about a hundred seconds after the great flash—the first cry of a newborn world.
>
> It was like the grand finale of a mighty symphony of the elements, fascinating and terrifying, uplifting and crushing, ominous, devastating, full of great promise and great forebodings.[16]

"Now we are all sons of bitches," Kenneth Bainbridge muttered to himself. Oppenheimer would later come to feel that this was the best thing anyone said after the test.[17]

But not all present that morning were so moved. For at least three of the witnesses the Alamogordo experience was entirely devoid of religious meaning: General Leslie Groves, the chief of security of the Manhattan Project, a highly authoritarian if brilliant bureaucrat; Enrico Fermi, who was preoccupied at the time with measuring the size of the blast for purposes of judging the bets on its energy yield; and Edward Teller, the flamboyant Hungarian emigre who would later father the hydrogen bomb. In Fermi's lottery, Teller was one of the very few to significantly *over*estimate the eventual explosive power of the first atomic ignition. "I clearly remember the feeling of disappointment," he later revealed to his biographer, when the actual yield of the experiment fell far below his expectations. "This is all?"[18] "Is this what we worked so hard to develop?"[19] (Teller would later become the basis of the perverse Dr. Strangelove in Peter George's novel *Red Alert* and the movie script *Dr. Strangelove*, written by George, Stanley Kubrick and Terry Southern.) For his part, General Groves' "first impression was one of tremendous light, and then as I turned, I saw the familiar fireball. . . . As I look back on it now, I realize the shock was fairly impressive."[20] He was to learn "later" that the effects of the test, particularly on the scientists, "were quite profound for a number of days."[21] When someone cheerfully turned to him declaring the war to be over, he sullenly disagreed, saying, not until "one or two of those things" are dropped on the Japanese.[22]

For some, then, the first nuclear explosion was simply a continuation of the ordinary routine of everyday "profane" existence. Perhaps Fermi (who, it might be noted, also had a distinct distaste for music and other things artistic) and Groves may be grouped among them. It should be pointed out, however, that Fermi was evidently so shaken by Alamogordo that he was unable to drive his own automobile back to Los Alamos.[23]

For others it meant awakening from a life of innocence to the reality of God. None of the security forces had more than an inkling of the nature of the preparations feverishly undertaken at Alamogordo. And one unnamed guard had returned to his barracks just three hours before ignition. Still feeling the effects of a weekend of carousing in Albuquerque, and noticing all his comrades absent, he fell onto his bunk and into an uneasy, alcohol-induced slumber. Suddenly he was thrown to the floor and blinded by the blast. When discovered about an hour later his buddies found a raving madman, "speaking incoherently about the 'wrath of the Lord,' and the 'Day of Judgment,' and about the sin of getting drunk on the sabbath."[24] Swearing off drink forever, the soldier was institutionalized for some time in a mental hospital before recovering his senses. At least for this anonymous soul, then, the atomic bomb had occasioned the vision of the Almighty.

THE NUCLEAR DEATH CULT

Religious experience is the beginning and end of religion, but it is not identical to religion. Religion is a social enterprise, one analyzable from at least three distinct viewpoints: its body of myth, its ritual ceremonies, and its organizational structure. Sociologists claim an ability to crudely rank religions on a scale of relative complexity and size, the most primitive being called cults and sects, the most advanced, denominations and churches. Only in this sense is the word *cult* used in this chapter. It is understood to be socially the most elemental, simplistic, and least articulate of the forms of organized religion. Our intention in the remaining pages is to describe some basic myths, rites, and organizational features of the nuclear death cult.

Myth

Religious experience by its very nature is incomprehensible, ineffable, inexplicable. Yet human beings struggle for words to give it meaning. And always the most satisfying language is metaphor and poetry, especially what Otto calls "numinous poetry." What strikes the attentive reader of the pronouncements of the nuclear physicists and their popularizers such as Laurence and Jacob Bronowski, the celebrated television commentator, is the frequency and evident naturalness of their resort to numinous poetry when describing their work and its products.[25]

It will be impossible here to exhaustively reconstruct the entire mythology of the nuclear death cult.[26] Instead, we shall focus on the mythical consecration of two places of singular moment in the cult's history: the plant within which the first bomb was assembled—"Omega" (the last letter of the Greek alphabet), and the site where it was tested—"Trinity." Of course, the canyon where Omega was built was already long known to local natives as *Formiga*; this was the location where the Manhattan Project was brought to completion. As for "Trinity," Oppenheimer himself has said that "this code name didn't mean anything.[27]

However, it is clear from the revelations both of the scientists who entered the building and those who observed their work in it that Omega had more than unconsciously intimate ties to what the letter symbolizes in Greek mythology—death. For it was there that the test known colloquially as *tickling the dragon's tail* was conducted, on an apparatus called, furthermore, the *guillotine*, its operator called the *executioner*. The details of what seems to have amounted to something close to a sacrificial rite will be described later. Here it is sufficient to point out that this macabre language was far more than an empty embellishment. On separate occasions at least two young physicists experienced excruciating deaths from radiation poisoning as a result of the dragon test, a number of others barely escaping a similar fate, including Otto Frisch, the one who invented it.[28] In other words, in naming the critical assembly unit *Omega,* the staff was cognizant not only that here an instrument of incalculable destructive power was being devised, but also, as the fairy tale teaches, that he who dares tickle the tail of a sleeping dragon may himself be struck a mortal blow.

The designation of *Trinity* for the first fission explosion is even more telling. Let us accept at face value Oppenheimer's claim that nothing was consciously on his mind when asked by General Groves to provide a code name for the experiment. And yet just prior to this request, Oppenheimer had learned of the suicide of his long-time acquaintance and one-time lover, Jean Tatlock. For consolation he had turned to the sonnets of John Donne, at least two of which deal directly with the Christian trinity.[29] "Trinity," Oppenheimer says, "was just something suggested to me by [these sonnets], which I happened to be reading at the time."[30] In examining this off-hand comment more closely, Oppenheimer's enigmatic personality and the strange charm the Bomb had for him become more coherent.

What consolation might a modern physicist find in the work of a seventeenth century writer? Donne is not only a poet obsessed with the subject of death, but with the possibility of *mortem raptus,* a death of rapture and ecstasy. And at least one critic considers his psychology to anticipate Sigmund Freud's theory of the death instinct.[31] For Donne, earthly life itself is but a form of death, "our common grave," as he calls it; birth but issues into a series of little deaths; the embryonic sac is a funeral shroud. So many are the calamities befalling us at every turn, he tells us, that far from being timidly approached, death should be welcomed joyfully as a release of the soul from its sorrows.

However, Donne does not merely prefigure Freud. In any case, this hardly explains Oppenheimer's interest in him. Much more to the point, Donne reiterates the ancient wisdom of the Upanishads. Many of his sonnets[32] teach lessons analogous to the Hindu doctrine of spiritual transmigration. Perhaps here, then, was the consoling appeal of Donne to Oppenheimer. For Oppenheimer, too, as translator of Sanskrit and avid student of Hindu myth, was intrigued by the doctrine of transmigration of souls.

In the *Bhagavadgita,* Prince Arjuna arrives in his chariot on the field of battle. Seeing his cousins arrayed against him in the enemy ranks, he balks at the thought of the upcoming slaughter. Limbs quaking, mouth dry, hair standing on end, he pleads with the god Krishna to release him from his onerous caste duties as a warrior. It is not far-fetched to think that Oppenheimer saw in Arjuna a parallel to the tragedy of his own status at Los Alamos. By nature a morally sensitive individual and a practitioner of the Hindu ideal of nonviolence, he found himself paradoxically duty-bound to devise the most violent and morally revolting of all instruments. And like Arjuna, Oppenheimer might silently have entreated his own god—whom some have suggested was Krishna himself—to spare him this terrible task.

In the Hindu tale, Krishna refuses the request of his devotee, telling him that the opposition between enemies, between slayer and slain, between good and evil, indeed between life and death, are mere illusions produced by a mind still attached to material things. This argument has the immediate effect of precipitating in Arjuna a fantastic vision of the god Vishnu, ravenous, skull-crushing, and blood-lapping, devouring men as fire might a moth.[33] And with it comes a conviction of the inevitability and necessity of Arjuna's work.

What does all this tell us about Oppenheimer? Mercilessly driven by a politically dictated deadline, discouraged by Tatlock's death, doubtful of the correctness of his own work, yet consumed by the possibility of its failure, he desperately needed an equally direct and indubitable certification of his role at Los Alamos. For this he prayed to the Christian trinity in the words of John Donne's "Batter My Heart." For Oppenheimer, *trinity* may have symbolized the impending violent consecration of his labors, and the annihilation of fatigue, disheartenment, anxiety, and doubt.

> Batter my heart, three person'd God; for you
> As yet but knocke, breathe, shine, and seeke to mend;
> That I may rise, and stand, o'erthrow mee, and bend
> Your force, to breake, blowe, burn and make me new.
> I, like an usurpt towne, to'another due,
> Labour to'admit you, but Oh, to no end,
>
> . . .
>
> Take me to you, imprison me, for I
> Except you'enthrall me, never shall be free,
> Nor ever chast, except you ravish me.[34]

Oppenheimer would await the Day of Trinity at Alamogordo to have his prayer answered. Words neither from the Bible nor from Greco-Roman fable crossed his mind when his face was illuminated by the awesome majesty of the Bomb that dawn on the plain of the Jornada del Muerto (the journey of death). They were instead the very words uttered by Arjuna at the sight of Vishnu.[35]

The radiance of a thousand suns
Which suddenly illuminate the heavens.
All in one moment. Thus,
The splendor of the Lord
I am Death, who taketh all,
Who shatters worlds . . .[36]

Rite

All those in Trinity blockhouse at zero-moment testify that Oppenheimer's countenance visibly relaxed when the brilliant fire of Vishnu lighted
the sky. For the whole community as well, the successful blast meant release
from the tension under which they all had been living. "A loud cry filled the air.
The little groups that had hitherto stood rooted to the earth like desert plants
broke into a dance—the rhythm of primitive man dancing at one of his fire
festivals at the coming of Spring. They clapped their hands as they leaped from
the ground."[37]

Religious ritual is not consciously invented. Instead it emerges out of
reverential gestures automatically called forth by a religiously charged
circumstance and then formalized, evoking humility, attentiveness, quiet, and
above all, care: care in speaking of its profound mystery, care in avoiding its
paradoxically fascinating danger, care in positioning the sacred object in
surroundings appropriate to its majesty. We will deal here only with one
example, the rites of Bomb assembly and testing.[38]

Why was Los Alamos chosen as the place where the Bomb would be
devised? True, it was then isolated enough to be safe from spying eyes and was
far enough inland to be immune from air attack, but that did not exhaust its
attraction to Oppenheimer, who recommended the site to General Groves.
Los Alamos sits atop a mesa, the abutment of a crumbling volcano,
approximately 7000 feet in altitude at the northern tip of the Jemez Mountains
directly northwest of Sante Fe. In the aspen and pine forests of the Sangre de
Cristo range on the far side of the Rio Grande Valley, Oppenheimer's family
had owned a ranch. There, by hiking its trails and exploring its peaks, he had
rewon his health from tuberculosis. The mountains of the southwest, then,
would always have a powerful attraction for Oppenheimer.

Oppenheimer was gifted with a poetic imagination. Like religious men of
other times, he sought a ground equal to the task he was about to undertake.
His closest friend Haaken Chevalier, says it this way:

> As dumb animals, when they sense that their hour has come, look to a dark
> hole to die in, so man, in those supreme moments when he must face his
> destiny and make ultimate choices for good or evil, seeks out the high places.
> A mountaintop was selected as the birthplace of the Thing.[39]

Adding to the mystique of Los Alamos was an adobe hut, a tea house of sorts, "perhaps the loneliest in the world," inhabited by an old poetess named Edith Warner and her Indian servant, Tilano. According to Neul Pharr Davis, "to Oppenheimer, old Edith seemed the genius of the place and the place itself the heart of the desert country he loved.[40] Others were similarly struck by the disturbing eeriness—the "something weird and deathly"—of the mesa. Samuel Allison, for example, "felt it was of a piece with Oppenheimer's exotic predilections for the Mahabharata, 'nasty gory' [one of his culinary concoctions] and physics at night." Leo Szilard went even further. "Everybody who goes there," he warned, "will go crazy."[41]

One of the deepest canyons off the cottonwood mesa of Los Alamos was chosen for Omega, the precinct wherein uranium and plutonium would be assembled for the Bomb. Assembly involved proving that the two or more subcritical pieces of radioactive material would fit together snugly enough, to create a critical mass at the instant of firing. The most well-known variation of the assembly was the dragon experiment, so-called because Richard Feynman, one of its technicians, had received it with a chuckle saying, it's "like tickling the tail of a sleeping dragon." In it were two subcritical pieces, both harmless by themselves, one shaped like a doughnut, the other like its hole. When the core successfully negotiated the entry, there would occur in a split-second a large burst of neutrons and an increase in temperature of several degrees. At this exact moment the executioner, as he was called, had to quickly withdraw the core. For that split-second was tantamount to a stifled nuclear explosion. The explosion itself could not occur because the experiment was conducted with a metal shield to deflect the neutrons back into the critical mass. For this reason the assembly unit was known as *Lady Godiva*. However, if the core were not withdrawn at the precise moment that critical mass was reached, the executioner would receive a fatal dose of radiation from the escaping neutrons.[42]

The analogous experiment today is conducted behind lead and concrete walls from a console one-quarter mile from the assembly unit, using robotic arms and computerized sensors. At Los Alamos, however, it was originally done entirely by hand with screwdrivers and "feel." It was, in other words, a highly risky and fascinating exercise, one to which we need not hesitate applying the adjectives *numinous* or *religious*.

The risks of the dragon rite were well known and thus only certain kinds of men were recruited to conduct it, men like Louis Slotin, a thirty-one-year-old bachelor and, at least in Davis' mind, sociopath who reveled in estimating blast and radiation casualties from fantasy explosions of the Bomb.[43] Even Enrico Fermi, who otherwise showed very little moral sensitivity to the work at Los Alamos, was so "enraged" by the way Slotin's eyes gleamed when talking about the dragon that he escaped to the Sangre de Cristos whenever an assembly was scheduled.[44]

Already Harry Daghlian, a like-minded spirit and Slotin's superior, had been killed by the dragon. As a precaution against future accidents, therefore, a number of safety features, including a spring-activated release mechanism, had been improvised. But Slotin refused to have anything to do with these. In his last and, as it turned out, most fateful experiment, he planned instead to employ a pencil to separate the two subcritical pieces at the moment of highest tension. Did he really think a pencil was a safe support? Or did something deep down in his mind tempt him to play atomic roulette? Whatever the case, in the burst of radioactivity that followed the pencil slip, the air around Slotin's body ionized, giving off a blue aura. He immediately threw himself on the unit to protect the others in the room. Within hours he was seriously ill and in nine days dead of acute leukemia.

Organization

A mountain peak, a tree-shadowed glen, a charismatic person, or any object or event that occasions religious experience is, ethically speaking, beyond good or evil. Instead it is mysterious and powerful, hence dangerous, as the Slotin case proves, to be approached, if at all, with caution. Our word *religion* comes from the Latin infinitive *relegere*, (to take care, to be cautious). The essence of all religious rituals, the rite of Bomb construction included, are "covering acts," gestures undertaken to protect communicants from being contaminated and perhaps even killed by the sacred power. But covering acts have the effect of increasing the enchantment of that which is forbidden. We all may wish to transgress the very thing tabooed. This naturally increases the danger of the power to its devotees, adding incentive to make it even more forbidden.

Given this we can understand the impetus behind two organizational attributes of any cult: a closed priesthood with exclusive responsibility for the cult proper, and secrecy surrounding their affairs. By training, test, inheritance, or some other criterion deemed relevant, the priest attains sufficient holiness himself to be relatively free for safe intercourse with the sacred. This is confirmed by his formal ordination to office, his initiation into the cult mysteries, and his bestowal with sacramental powers. Although it may be stretching the analogy to insist that the nuclear scientist granted security clearance is formally consecrated into a priesthood in the strictest sense, it is important to acknowledge the most glaring tendencies in this direction. There are the years during which the suitability of the candiate is studied, not only in terms of substantive skill, but more crucially on lines of discreteness, political reliability, propriety of friendships, and teamwork. From the infamous "Oppenheimer Case" we know that only those who demonstrate the utmost care, which is to say the proper reverence when dealing with material and ideas of measureless danger to the community, within a context of political orthodoxy, are awarded entry into the closed circle and access to the terrible powers.[45] Those who do not—as the examples of Frank Oppenheimer (Robert's brother), Giovannni Lomanitz, David Bohm, and Bernard Peters demonstrate—may find themselves blacklisted even from university employment.

In 1972 Alvin Weinberg, then director of the Oak Ridge Laboratory, indicated that a technological "priesthood," as he called it, may in the future be necessary to administer this country's nuclear energy programs because of the problems of long-term, continuous storage of hazardous wastes. He went on to say that it might be organized on lines similar to what he argued was an already existing "military priesthood" that controls nuclear weaponry.[46] (Cf. Kurtz and Benford's discussion in Chapter 5 of Edward Luttwak's proposal for a fourth branch of government—a so-called Supreme Nuclear Council). After evidently giving the idea further thought, Weinberg repeated the proposal a year later, this time more explicitly and emphatically. The problem, he said, is that one of the most carcinogenic isotopes of plutonium has a half-life of 23,000 years. That is, it still retains half its toxicity after a period two times longer than the span from the beginning of the age of agriculture to our time. But, as no government has survived more than 1000 years, how can the human species even hope to monitor hazardous wastes for a period of twenty-three millennia? The answer, Weinberg happily suggests, will not be found in a government at all, but in a religiouslike body. Only an organization like the Catholic Church possesses the institutional "resiliency" to remain alive for the length of time at issue. "The Catholic Church is the best example of what I have in mind: a central authority that proclaims and to a degree enforces doctrine, maintains its own long-term stability, and has connections to every country's own Catholic Church."[47]

Lest this be dismissed as a "charmingly naive musing," as one critic called it, it should be pointed out that the first clumsy steps toward the establishment of such a priesthood have already been undertaken. A recent technical report, commissioned by the Department of Energy and written by the renowned semiotics professor Thomas A. Sebeok, has proposed a number of "rituals and legends" to warn the next 300 generations (up to *A.D.* 12000) against the dangers of the nuclear waste deposits now being planned. Given the likelihood that earthly inhabitants ten millennia from now will no longer speak present-day languages, the issue, says the report, becomes one of how to communicate. Among the proposals entertained are the creation of a "modern Stonehenge" to ring various waste dumps, passing the warning message through surgically initiated genetic coding, making the wastes "repulsively malodorous" so that the stench will drive people away, erecting archetypal cartoon narratives depicting the dangers of the deposited material, or the most "reasonable" of all: through a myth composed by a "Nuclear priesthood," passing to each successive generation an "accumulated supersitition to shun a certain area permanently." "A ritual annually renewed can be foreseen," the report bouyantly assures us, "with the legend being retold year by year."[48]

Implementing the Weinberg-Sebeok program faces enormous hurdles, not the least of which is the seeming absurdity of scientifically engineering religious belief. Furthermore, it faces a structural impediment associated with any fully evolved priesthood: secrecy. As early as 1935 Leo Szilard was expressing concern about the uses to which neutron experimentation might be put by naive or ambitious politicians and industrialists. He proposed that those doing nuclear research voluntarily refrain from having its results published.[49] By 1939, with Neils Bohr and Fermi publicly theorizing about neutron-initiated chain reactions, the alarm among physicists had generalized. P. W. Bridgman, Victor Weisskopf, Eugen Wigner, and others all began to see the wisdom of scientific censorship. What makes this both noteworthy and ironic is that these same men were fully cognizant of the centuries-long struggle by science to wrest itself from ecclesiastical control. But new circumstances called for a reassessment of the ideal of unrestrained inquiry and information sharing. Similar efforts were undertaken by the Curies in France[50] and by the German Uranverein to keep the Bomb from Nazi hands.[51] Carl Freidrich von Weisacker, a member of the last group, would say, "perhaps we ought to have been an International Order with disciplinary powers over its members."[52] In an age of rampant nationalism, he sadly concluded, this was probably impractical.

THE FUNDAMENTALIST BOMB

Sociologists of religion speak of religions for the elite and religions for the masses. Although this is not a hard and fast dichotomy, the first is said to be based on intellectually satisfying, esoteric understandings of scripture, the second on anti-intellectual, literal interpretations of sacred words and a belief in sacramental magic to promote health, fertility, happiness, and immortality. Likewise, it can be argued that the nuclear death cult is somewhat different for its priests, those physicists and engineers granted security clearance, than it is for uninitiated and uninformed folk. For both the Bomb constitutes the most profound mystery, but the manner in which it is approached, spoken of, and paid obeisance differs. On close examination, even the cult of the folk is no one thing,[53] but a shifting complex of contradictory stances, from moral revulsion to outright advocacy of nuclear war, or more commonly, a despairing political paralysis, a "psychic numbing," in the face of its enormity. Unraveling these dynamic and intertwined attitudes will entail considerable research. Here we will deal only with the most frightening of the responses: the Christian fundamentalist Bomb.

As Norman Cohn has demonstrated in his classic history of millenarian thinking,[54] end-times prophecy runs deeply through occidental religious literature, from the advent of Zoroastrianism, through Judaic prophecy, appearing in Islam and in both Protestantism and Catholicism. Modern enthusiasm for the Second Coming and the millennium (1000 years) of divine rule is nothing new. This prophecy is often accompanied by imagery of the most bloodthirsty sort. Consider these words of the Great Reformer, a man for whom the apocalyptic vision was an intimate acquaintance, Martin Luther, and his sermon on Exodus, Chapter 20:

> Yes, for the world it seemeth as though God were a mere yawner, with mouth ever agape, or a cuckhold, who lets another lie with his wife and feigneth that he sees it not.
>
> But He assaileth man, and hath such a delight therein that He is of His jealousy and wrath compelled to consume the wicked. Then shall we learn how that God is a consuming fire. . . . That is then the consuming, devouring fire. . . . Wilt thou sin? Then will He devour thee up. . . . For God is a fire, that consumeth, devoureth, rageth, verily. He is your undoing, as fire consumeth a house and make it dust and ashes.
>
> Yea, He is more terrible and frightful than the Devil. . . . In his majesty He is a consuming fire.[55]

If this warning can be considered typical of the genre of millenarian writing, and if attention is given to Luther's constant return to the image of God-as-devouring-fire, then it can be understood how virtually from the moment of that first blinding flash at Trinity in 1945, millenarian theologians have seen in the Bomb God's terrible judgment. And, not without significance, these same theologians who otherwise wax eloquently about the inaccuracies of modern science frequently invoke the honorific *physics* to bolster the authority of their forecasts of Doomsday-by-Bomb.

The popularity of end-time literature as a way of deciphering present dilemmas is clearly seen in the reception of Hal Lindsey's *The Late Great Planet Earth*,[56] now in its 83rd printing. In Lindsey's book, which is touted as the hottest selling *non*fiction book of the 1970s, two of the epigrams at the beginning of chapter 12, "World War III," are by physicists, the remaining one by a bona fide religious leader. In a competing work, *Arming for Armageddon*, by John Wesley White, an associate of the Billy Graham Crusade, particular pleasure is taken in drawing theological lessons from modern science. The recent discovery, says White, of Quasar PKS 2000-300, 18 billion light years from earth, supports the contention that the universe was created by a Big Bang. "So what relevance has the 'Big Bang' to the second coming of Christ, to Armageddon, and to the end of all things? It is almost unanimous among astrophysicists that as physical creation came into existence with a 'Big Bang,' so it will go out of existence with a 'Big Bang'.[57]

Modern millenarians claim an ability to find in biblical prophecy explicit, if understandably clumsy, anticipations of nuclear weaponry employed in the war of Armageddon (the final battle of good against evil). These, too, are used to enhance the credibility of their doomsaying.

Such prophecy teaches that in the Last Battle, "The Main Event" as Lindsey cheerfully titles it, Jesus Christ together with His chosen ones will return in clouds to the earth to smite nonbelievers, apostates, and heretics. The Mount of Olives on which, we are told, oil company seismologists recently discovered an enormous fault, will split, and into it the prophesied Jewish Remnant will flee as into a bomb shelter.[58] And well they might, for on that day nuclear fury will be poured out on the inhabitants of the earth. "Their flesh shall consume away while they stand upon their feet, and their eyes shall consume away in their holes, and their tongues shall consume away in their mouths" (Zechariah 14:12). "A frightening picture, isn't it?" Lindsey unnecessarily asks. "Has it ever occurred to you that this is exactly what happens to those who are in a thermonuclear blast?"[59]

But many instruments besides nuclear weapons can effect similar results to these. John Wesley White, for example, mentions huge microwave ovens. Lindsey therefore feels a need to further substantiate his argument. "But the day of the Lord will come like a thief, in which the heavens will pass away with a roar and the *elements* will be destroyed in intense heat, and the earth and its worlds will be burned up" (II Peter 3:10-13). We italicize *elements* because Lindsey himself stresses its pivotal revelatory significance. The "basic element (GK. *stoicheiov*) of nature," says Lindsey, "the smallest building block of nature" is the atom. This being so, Peter's prophecy may, he insists, be retranslated as follows: "In other words, Christ is going 'to loose' the atoms of the galaxy in which we live. No wonder there will be a great roar and intense heat and fire.[60]

White takes issue with this interpretation, but comes to an even more inventive conclusion. The "basic elements" to which Peter alludes, he argues, are not atoms; otherwise, the Greek Bible would have used that very term, *atomos*. Rather, the word *element* must refer to "the letters of the alphabet." But we all know, don't we, that "scientists describe a nuclear explosion as 'the radiation of alpha, beta, gamma, and delta rays'—the letters of the Greek alphabet."[61] Again, "The powers of heaven will be shaken—with obvious nuclear warfare, for the word used by our Lord in Luke 21:26 for heaven *(ouranos)* is the one from which we derive uranium."[62]

In other places, White evinces less certainty about the actual nature of the weapon with which God and His saints will enjoy satisfaction over unbelievers. Might it be, perhaps, "a multiple-prodded laser beam?" "enriched plutonium?" or a "neutron bomb?" Scripture does not specifically say. "What it does tell us is that our God is a consuming fire—just as He is light."[63] By the end of the book, however, White has returned to his original conviction that indeed our Last Days will be atomic. To prove this he undertakes what can only be marvelled at as a remarkable effort at paralleling scriptural utterances with modern events. In Luke 17, Jesus warns the Pharisees to "remember Lot's wife," who was turned to a salt pillar for her infidelity. White continues:

> The first atomic bomb . . . killed one hundred thousand. That was in Hiroshima, Japan. Scientists note there is a substantial resemblance between the ashy soils on the site where Sodom and Gomorrah were incinerated and those where Hiroshima and Nagasaki were vaporized. It was said that some who were fleeing Hiroshima and Nagasaki turned back to see them going up in mushroom flames. But alas, in exposing themselves to the nuclear quietus, they were turned into saltlike—or ashy pillars resembling burnt, unsnuffed cigarettes.[64]

The full significance of nuclear holocaust for these fundamentalists must be understood in the context of its complementary theme: the joys of Rapture. Rapture is the coming of Christ for the Church when He instantly "catches up" all the believers and "translates" them into immortal bodies.[65] The word "rapture" is a fundamentalist rendition of the Latin translation of the Greek *harpazo*. Says Hal Lindsey: "It literally means "to seize' or 'to snatch away.' If I had my way, I would call the Rapture 'the great snatch.'"[66]

Herman Kahn, the late physicist and apologist for the cost-effectiveness of limited nuclear war, was one of the first unapologetically to use sexual metaphors in the course of his briefings on nuclear strategy. In one of his most widely read books, *On Escalation*, he describes a possible scenario with the Soviet Union over an imaginary crisis, and depicts 44 steps on a ladder of successively dangerous hostile acts. Rung 44 he calls *spasm* or *insensate war*, terms that, he proclaims, are "now almost standard jargon" in decision-making and journalistic circles. The terms originated, he tells us, to caricature the vision of nuclear exchange as a blind, overwhelming fury, "a function of the central nervous system, so to speak, rather than of the brain," resulting in "orgiastic spasms of destruction": a fair representation of the fundamentalist Bomb.

> During one of these briefings, I said to the audience, "you people do not have a war plan. You have a 'war-gasm.'" These expressions were put forward with no particular reference to their sexual implications, but some of my colleagues, more conversant with Freudian concepts and literature than I, argue that "spasm war" is more accurate and descriptive than one might think.[67]

Is it true that beneath the nuclear fire and radioactive brimstone of the evangelical apocalypse can be found a more earthy and beguiling erotic message?

There is considerable debate among fundamentalists concerning whether the Rapture of the believers will occur prior to or immediately following nuclear Tribulation.[68] This is not the place to detail the debate; it is only important to observe that in both schools the two events are inextricably related. There can be no ecstatic seizure of the soul by God without also His total annihilation of the infidel by the Bomb. The height of erotic craving by the believer can only find satisfaction in its opposite: *thanatos*, death to the Other.

The argument that it is incorrect to see in the fundamentalist Bomb promises of erotic fulfillment does not entirely stand up to close scrutiny. Conscious intention aside, Lindsey's extremely popular writing on the Rapture is filled with erotic imagery but never more obviously than in the concluding comments of *There's A New World Coming*. The words *snatch* and *come* in colloquial English have well-known sexual connotations. When describing the irresistible delight of the Rapture, Lindsey plays on this semantic ambiguity. This is clearly indicated by his use of quotation marks whenever the word *come* is mentioned. In this way the veiled eroticism of biblical passages from the Song of Solomon, for example, becomes vulgarized and transparently sexual. "The word 'Come,'" says Lindsey, "is a favorite of the Lord." When the "spirit" and his "bride" are betrothed and the marriage consummated in the house of the groom's father, they say "come." And "'come' is an offer you can't refuse." "The eager bride . . . sends forth her 'Come' as she awaits her groom." The believers "add their 'Come' to the upward chorus." "The final 'come' is an invitation from Jesus for the person who is still thirsting for fulfillment." "All you need do," therefore, "is 'Come.'"[69]

While the evident crudity of Lindsey's erotic metaphors may be unique, the association of religious rapture with erotic ecstasy and these with physical mortification, violence, and death is traditional in mysticism, both East and West.[70] John Donne himself, the so-called poet of the death-wish, already cited in speaking of Oppenheimer's Trinity, earlier in his life was considered the erotic poet of his age. He frequently resorted to symbols of sexual consummation to characterize the strange allure of death. Freud is merely one of the most recent to rediscover these ancient psychic connections.

Certainly, we should not expect Christian literalism to fully develop the thematic tie between sexuality and violence, for the simple reason that, although fundamentalism enthusiastically embraces the idea of God's terrible justice, it sets its face squarely against worldly pleasure. In this regard it is similar to both Islamic and Judaic fundamentalism. And in this very fact may be hidden a significant truth that deserves much closer attention than it has yet received. Depth psychology teaches that although erotic cravings may be repressed the energy behind them does not disappear. Instead it is redirected into more emotionally acceptable channels, manifesting itself with an intensity equal to the force of the original repression. Might not this "acceptable" channel be *thanatos*, the instinctual urge to death? And might not this urge find fulfillment in a craving after a glorious death for God or country—cross, star, or crescent—or in a crusade to eradicate the "infidels" or "unbelievers"? It is striking how often religious communities deem themselves "righteous" principally because they have visibly repressed their own eroticism, whereas the "unbelievers" are often accused, above all other sins, of failing to control their erotic urges. Is it not likely that crusades and wars often begin when one group projects its own tabooed desires onto another group? Setting out to punish the supposed sinners, the group may actually be punishing itself for its sinful desires and simultaneously releasing repressed energy by unbridling its urge for destruction and death. Although this is an hypothesis, not a demonstrated proposition, we may be close to identifying the peculiar fascination, the "strange love," of Kahn's "wargasm." And this fascination lures not only fundamentalists but all of us, and perhaps even the highest priests of the nuclear death cult.

CONCLUSION

With his acute sensitivity to romantic institutional facades, Max Weber was able to discern the distinguishing characteristic of the nation-state: violence. The *State*, as he defines it, is the corporation that monopolizes the legitimate use of violence over a territory.[71] The crucial word in this definition is *legitimate*. Weber appreciates that the great challenge facing the State is not just to direct killing, raping, and looting. It is instead to *legitimize* these activities to those who perpetrate and suffer them. Every State therefore erects an altar, and around it emerges a cult of the dead, with martyr legends, festivals, monuments, and in the most extreme cases, a public confessional. Among its most important festivals are those of symbolic power regeneration: execution and holy war.[72]

The nuclear death cult is just one such cult, different in kind but not in nature from the ancient altar of Joshua on Mount Ebal or the high temple to Huitzilopochtli in Tenochtitlan, Mexico. It has its initiation rites and cult masters, its succession of chambers hiding the innermost altar where the power over life and death is wielded (the Cheyenne Mountain war room), its secret twelve-digit codes and double keys that can unlock that power, silent attendants who bear the mechanisms in attache cases, perpetually hovering like angels of death at the right shoulders of the priests. It has its white vestments donned by the Bomb builders and its "white trains" (now painted dark to present a less surrealistic aspect to the public) transporting their gruesome product across the country at night. It has its arsenal christened after the Greco-Roman gods: Poseidon, Hercules, Atlas, Hermes, Vulcan, and Jupiter. And terrorists beware! The Department of Energy recently committed over $100 million to beef-up security at Oak Ridge, Hanford, and other national nuclear engineering laboratories.[73] Have we in the new Uzi machinegun-armed special response teams (SRT) a parallel to the order of acolytes whose original role was to guard the sanctity of the altar? As the ancient acolyte was selected for his devotion to Christ (the word comes from the Greek *akolouthos*, "follower") so these black-garbed, ski-masked, helicopter-riding SRT recruits are proudly spoken of as exemplifying "the ultimate in patriotism." Finally, the nuclear death cult has "theologians" as they are known in the Pentagon, grand nuclear strategists like Herman Kahn, who after reflecting on the teenage game of chicken, advocated its strategic use in American-Soviet confrontations.

The atomic bomb is God's gift to America, so Phyllis Schlafly is alleged to have said. Rightists have always had better instincts for these things than liberal intellectuals. Sociologists have recently expressed concern that the "civil religion," as they call it, that once bound Americans together "today... is an empty and broken shell," shattered by material greed, contempt for nature, and an obsession with technical success.[74] On closer view, however, this concern seems far from justified. There is an American civil cult flourishing at this very moment—the nuclear death cult—rich in mystery, tradition, and ritual. True, it is in part horrifying. Indeed, it may be, as G. Clarke Chapman convincingly argues in Chapter 8 that nuclearism is a heresy against which the Christian Church must protest; a transgression against the original Puritan covenant from which the idea of America as a humble, family-based, biblically ruled Christian commonwealth emerged; a transgression, furthermore, that Providence will most certainly punish. It may even be, as Robert Bellah has suggested, that our punishment, ironically, lies in our (very technological) "success" of which the bomb is, of course, a diabolical symbol. But "'Religion' began with devil-worship, and... at bottom the devil is more ancient than God."[75]

Unwilling to see our own devil, have we been looking in the wrong direction for the American civil religion? Have we fallen victim to an anachronistic innocence that has frightful consequences? Here the old cliche that the devil you know is better than the devil you don't know takes on new meaning. The devil we don't know seems to be a basic part of our individual and national selves, repressed and hidden from view. Surely we cannot understand the nuclear dilemma until we know this devil better.

Sociologists of religion, like all academics, have difficulty looking into the dark, diabolical, irrational depths of the self. Academia is inherently biased toward the clarity of precise analysis and lucid reason. But perhaps the academy's most valuable contribution in this dark time of nuclear terror is to bring all the available sources to light, subject them to careful rational analysis, and thereby draw a clearer, sharper picture of the devil that lurks within. Perhaps the academy is uniquely well situated to help us get to know that devil better. And know it we must, if we are to escape its deadly grip. The lesson we must learn again today is the same lesson expressed by Ukrainian poet and physicist Vitaly Korotich. Speaking of Babi Yar, an abyss outside Kiev where countless Jews were murdered and entombed by the Nazi SS, he said: "Each man on earth must have Babi Yar inside. When we have it, it will be something against the repeating of Babi Yar."[76]

ROBERT D. BENFORD and LESTER R. KURTZ*

Chapter 5

Performing the Nuclear Ceremony: The Arms Race as a Ritual

> In a ritual, the world as lived and the world as imagined, fused under the agency of a single set of symbolic forms, turns out to be the same world.
> —*Clifford Geertz[1]*

When humans are faced with difficult situations, crises, or uncontrollable forces, they develop rituals that provide socially constructed responses. The most important rituals are those associated with boundary activities and radical changes of status: death, birth, marriage, puberty, and so on. Perhaps the boundary situation *par excellence* is the thoroughly modern problem of the possibility of the annihilation of human life by means of nuclear warfare. In this chapter, we examine the nuclear arms race in terms of ritualized behavior, suggesting that to frame an analysis of the arms race in terms of ritualization increases our comprehension of its dynamics.

THE SOCIOLOGY OF THE NUCLEAR THREAT

Despite a nearly universal consensus that the nuclear threat constitutes the archetypical social problem of our era, perhaps of human history,

*We are grateful to Steven Dubin, Sam Marullo, Joel Sherzer, Gregory Urban, and Louis Zurcher for comments and suggestions. An earlier version of this paper was presented at the meetings of the American Sociological Association in San Antonio, Texas, August 1984.

sociologists have all but ignored the issue. A recent study by Kurt Finsterbusch found that of the 6500 articles published in the *American Journal of Sociology*, the *American Sociological Review*, and *Social Forces* since 1945, 11 are about nuclear issues, only 4 of which deal explicitly with the nuclear arms race.[2]

Given the sociological neglect of the topic, this chapter represents an attempt to develop a framework within the sociology of culture encouraging further research. Our goal is not to test a hypothesis, nor even to devise systematic propositions; rather, our purpose here is to provide a broad analogy for the examination of one aspect of the arms race—the symbolic dimension.

Our analysis of the rhetoric justifying the nuclear arms race and its attendant behavior suggests that there are a number of parallels between the nuclear arms race and the patterns found by sociologists and anthropologists who have examined ritual. In this chapter we shall examine some of these parallels and construct a conceptual perspective for further study of the symbolic aspects of the nuclear arms race.

In the final analysis, the sociological explanations of the arms race will have to consider a number of levels of analysis, including the social-psychological, the symbolic, and the institutional dimensions of the phenomenon, as well as the interrelationshps among these levels.[3] In this effort, we focus on the symbolic element, which serves as a bridge between ths social-psychological and the institutional elements of the arms race.

Within the symbolic dimension of the nuclear arms race, the crucial issue is, How do people "know" that their actions will help to facilitate "national security"? The knowledge at issue is a set of symbols that strategic planners, politicians, and military officers use to define what will make us secure.

Our concern is the relationship between actions designed to provide security and their symbolic underpinnings. Consequently, we will examine four characteristics of rituals that are relevant to the nuclear arms race. Rituals (1) provide solutions to problems, especially concerning difficult situations and uncontrollable forces; (2) are rooted in experience; (3) identify evil and mark boundaries; and (4) reify social processes and reenforce social structure.

THE NATURE OF RITUAL BEHAVIOR

Ritual refers to "a regularly repeated, traditional, and carefully prescribed set of behaviors intended to symbolize a value or a belief."[4] It consists of actions that are "symbolic expressions of sentiments"[5] that are frequently duplicated.[6] Rituals are social forms that constitute celebrations and affirmations of values, world views, and the social organizations that sustain and are legitimated by them. Thus, ritualization is a neutral process that supports whatever values are celebrated and legitimates the institutions with which they are associated. The *content* of rituals, therefore, can be distinguished from their *form*, and the critique of ritualization that follows is not intended to assess the value of the ritual form but to analyze the implications of the content of a particular kind of ritualization which has emerged in the nuclear age.

Many recent scholars use the concept of ritual in a very general way, quite divorced from established religions,[7] as in Goffman's discussion of "interaction rituals"[8] or Moore and Myerhoff's discussion of "secular rituals."[9] Goffman, following Durkheim and Radcliffe-Brown, used *ritual* to refer to "a way in which the individual must guard and design the symbolic implications of his acts while in the immediate presence of an object that has a special value for him."[10] Whereas Goffman was dissecting face-to-face interaction, we discuss a more abstract phenomenon: nuclear weapons are objects with "special value" toward which people are oriented, whether or not they are in one's immediate presence. The very nature of nuclear weapons and their deployment requires that most people treat them as if they were real and immediate, despite the fact that few people have ever actually seen them. That absence of the object in question may enhance, rather than diminish, the value of rituals related to them, as the weapons themselves are mystified.[11]

RITUALS AS PROBLEM SOLVING

Social crisis is usually a precondition for the ritualization of behavior, which is often an effort to provide solutions to social problems. For example, the establishment of the Manhattan Project and the subsequent development of nuclear weapons were responses to Hitler's efforts to produce an atomic bomb. The earliest stages of the nuclear arms race involved the use of the common military ritual of developing more powerful weapons in order to counter an adversary. Ostensibly, nuclear weapons were first used to bring a swift and certain end to the war with Japan; they were later institutionalized as a political instrument in an attempt to prevent Soviet aggression.

Ironically, however, the development of nuclear weapons precipitated a new crisis requiring an additional response. It was just a matter of time before the Soviet Union would develop nuclear capabilities as well. No longer could a simple military buildup provide a sense of safety. No longer did the oceans, or any amount of conventional forces, offer any guarantee of security. Nuclear deterrence emerged as an apparent solution to the problem confronting those who realized that the nuclear genie could never be returned to the bottle.

Rituals provide solutions to problems on a number of levels. They relieve social and psychological tensions by focusing attention on ritual details rather than uncontrollable aspects of a crisis situation.[12] Rituals also link those detailed activities to broader world views and provide participants with a series of rationalizations that enable them to escape the anxiety associated with the crisis.[13]

A funeral ritual provides a constructive example of the process. When confronted with the death of a family member, friend or important person, those affected by the death not only confront the loss of a significant other but a breach in the ongoing flow of life. The need for immediate behavioral responses to uncomfortable social situations, on the one hand, and for answers to broader questions of meaning, on the other, are provided by ritual prescriptions. What is to be done, said, and thought are ritually defined and those caught in the crisis are reassured that their fundamental world view somehow answers the questions raised by the situation. By following socially approved rituals for such situations, the individual can avoid social blunders and at the same time be assured that his own identity is secure. Responses to the crisis are thus rooted in behavior that affirms broader values of the culture and is employed in problem solving.

As Goffman suggests, "the ritual order seems to be organized basically on accomodative lines."[14] The ceremony allows individuals and groups to confront problematic situations by prescribing a detailed set of appropriate behaviors. The nuclear arms race is a paradigm of ritual detail from calculation of megatonnage and throw-weight to potential casualties, survivors, and so forth. Many aspects of the nuclear threat are fraught with uncertainty,[15] and the ceremonies give participants something to do that can be controlled somewhat.

When the focus shifts to ritual detail and repetitive behavior, the larger, disturbing aspects of the situation recede into the background. People who are charged with the task of selecting targets for nuclear weapons, for example, can avoid thinking about the broader implications of such activity. One person engaged in that aspect of the ceremony recalled a day when a colleague and his wife came into his office

> to find me sticking different-colored pins—representing different-sized wea-
> pons—into a map of the Soviet Union. Add a pink pin for Minsk—another
> 200,000 dead. My colleague's wife was horrified. But when the pin went into
> Minsk or Moscow, I didn't see people working or children playing. I assumed
> that someone above me in the system thought about those things. I just stuck
> in the pin.[16]

In addition to diverting attention to detailed, prescribed activities, rituals also link such activity with broader world views, placing the crisis in a larger framework that in turn lends legitimacy to the ceremony. Leaders of the ceremony invoke images of the society's broader world view in order to justify the continued military buildup. A Reagan administration report, for example, blended national security issues with patriotic imagery:

> Because of a major campaign by the Soviet Union to spread lies and half truths about the United States policy and our democratic free enterprise system, . . . third world countries and our industrialized allies must be given a better understanding of the principles for which the United States stands and of the benefits to us and to them of our whole way of life.[17]

As Geertz put it, ritual involves the "symbolic fusion of ethos and world view"; the life-style and behavioral norms of the culture are linked to its larger picture of the universe.[18] One's behavior within a ritual context is believed to have not only immediate but also cosmic and historical significance.

Rituals move people beyond reality; they provide "not only models of what they believe, but also models *for* the believing of it."[19] To some extent, then, perceptions of a crisis are changed by the ritual itself, moving people beyond the chaos created by the disruption, to a reconstruction of "normal life" on the other side of the crisis. The ritual process accomplishes this transformation by placing the response to the crisis within a rational context that explains away anomalies. In responding to the uncertainties of an actual nuclear war, for example, the event is described in precise, rational terms[20] and the ambiguities appear resolved because of the narrative fidelity of the ritual.[21]

Rituals thus may involve considerable social and self-deception that facilitates the denial of the crisis or ambiguity of the situation. Because there is never a perfect fit, even in everyday situations, between expectations and reality, individuals adapt to their reality by elaborating a definition of the situation that smooths over such discrepancies. An individual will often insulate himself or herself "by blindnesses, half-truths, illusions, and rational- izations. He makes an 'adjustment' by convincing himself, with the tactful support of his intimate circle, that he is what he wants to be."[22]

The nuclear realm provides fertile ground for the propagation of half-truths, self-deceptions, and illusions. Among the most dangerous delusions is the belief that a "limited" nuclear war could be fought and "won."[23] Whereas such beliefs have traditionally been held by only a few "hard-liners,"[24] their ranks would seem to be swelling.[25] Even if one accepts the highly implausible assumption that once a nuclear attack were initiated the two superpowers would be able to "control the escalation" and therefore limit the "collateral damage,"[26] it is difficult to envision the possibility of "victory" in any meaningful sense of the term.

Two congressional studies seriously call into question the notion of a "victory" emerging from a "limited" nuclear war. In 1980, a comprehensive analysis by the Office of Technology Assessment conservatively estimated that a theoretically limited nuclear strike would kill between 3 and 22 million Americans.[27] An earlier computer-generated study by the Joint Comittee on Defense Production[28] concluded that to inflict "unacceptable damage" on the Soviet Union would only require "10% of current U.S. strategic force loadings." The Soviets would require unleashing 30 percent of their strategic forces in order to bring about a corresponding level of destruction in the United States.[29]

Recent scientific studies suggest that these dismal scenarios are too optimistic. Based on computer simulations and data obtained from studies of environmental changes precipitated by volcanic eruptions and dust storms on Mars, more than 100 scientists concurred that even a "limited" nuclear exchange would create a "long nuclear winter" resulting in a "global climatic catastrophe."[30] Such dire conclusions from the scientific community and the dissemination of their findings by the media instigated the Pentagon to carry out its own research. It, too, concluded that a 'nuclear winter" would, in all likelihood, follow even a relatively small-scale nuclear war.[31] Those analyses would seem to support Kennan's assertion that "the nuclear weapon is, for war-fighting purposes, an unusable one."[32]

The fact that many cling to traditional concepts of "superiority" and ultimate "victory" in the face of evidence to the contrary is not so difficult to understand. Let us turn to some theoretical bases for comprehending why it is so difficult for the leaders and militarists of the superpowers to renounce such time-honored rituals.[33]

EXPERIENTIAL BASES OF RITUAL

Rituals are rooted in experience and are therefore, perceived as verifiable. Verifiability is not really possible, however, because negative evidence can be ignored or explained away by the participant who has confidence in the ritual's efficacy. Religious rituals often involve a clear means-ends calculation, or what Weber called "instrumental rationality" (*zweckrationalitat*).[34]

Rituals thus represent an institutionalized form of problem solving, the efficacy of which has been demonstrated by one's ancestors or wise sages and codified in the cultural tradition. They involve habitual responses that can be relied upon when the problem is encountered once again. They are not, therefore, mere fantasies, but solutions tested by experience. If the ceremony does not bring about the desired result, it is not because the ritual *per se* was ineffective but because it was improperly performed or because an enemy evoked a more powerful god or performed the ceremony more effectively. Almost any performance has flaws that can be identified retrospectively, and the participants' efforts must be redoubled in order to ensure success.

Rituals are historically based, habitual, and considered appropriate long after the conditions in which they were developed have disappeared. The historical solution to military threats by an adversary has generally been to build better defenses, more powerful and numerous weapons and armies, and so on. The ceremonial sequences of the nuclear arms race are, in part, new activities necessitated by technologies developed in the age of nuclear weapons. For the most part, however, even the new ritual patterns are based on previously existing behaviors carried over from prenuclear, military-related rituals.[35] An essential component of that ritual is the search for better weapons. Nuclear weapons were part of what Fallows called "the pursuit of the magic weapon";[36] any military deficiencies can be compensated through technological development. The series of developments in the nuclear arms race, from the fission weapon to the hydrogen bomb, from ballistic missiles to MIRVs,[37] from antiballistic missile (ABM) systems to laser weapons, all involve what York termed the "fallacy of the final step."[38] Each measure is taken with the hope that the next development would result in the "ultimate weapon" and guaranteed security.

Various institutional factors such as interservice rivalry[39] and the nature of the research and development establishment[40] are significant arms race catalysts. Although the ritual elements involved are not the only reason for a continued buildup, they are an important and heretofore neglected factor. Empirically, it is virtually impossible to distinguish between ritual elements and institutional factors that perpetuate the nuclear arms race, because the rituals have become institutionalized and the motivations of class interest, fear, nationalism, and profit that sustain the military-industrial-academic complex also motivate the performance of rituals related to the arms race. There is an "elective affinity"[41] between the interests of those who benefit from the institutions of the military-industrial complex and the ideologies that legitimate its ceremonies.

As the search for a technological solution to the nuclear threat has continued, Soviet and U.S. nuclear arsenals have grown exponentially.[42] The rationalization articulated by various administrations for the development, production, and deployment of each new generation of nuclear weapons has been that these instruments were necessary to maintain "deterrence."[43] The ceremony of deterrence, like most rituals, involves a set of behaviors affirmed over time as a satisfactory response to similar problems. According to its theologians, as long as an adversary perceives that any potential benefits that might be derived from initiating a hostile action are outweighed by the probable costs, deterrence will be effective. Consequently, in order to ensure that the ceremony works properly, its participants must possess a sufficient degree of political will and military strength to make the threat appear "credible" to their adversary.

The question of "How much is enough?" has been vigorously debated by the active participants in the nuclear ritual as well as its spectators. Those who have been in a position to have any effect (however minute) on the ceremony have typically concluded that the then-present state of the nuclear arsenal was not sufficient to provide a "credible" shield of deterrence vis-a-vis the Soviet Union. As with the perceived failure of most rituals, the efficacy of the deterrence ritual is not questioned by individual performers of the ceremony. Instead, the standard interpretation has been that the ritual was not performed properly or that the enemy had performed it more effectively. In order to elicit support for redoubling efforts to improve the ceremony, the nuclear experts have consistently frightened the public by claiming that "gaps" existed in our nuclear forces: in the early 1950s a "bomber gap"; by the end of that decade, a "missile gap"; in the 1960s, "civil defense gaps" and an "ABM gap"; in the 1980s, some claim that there is a "window of vulnerability" that must be "closed"; and finally, a "particle beam weapon gap" looms on the horizon. Each of the "gaps" of the past were eventually exposed as fictional, but such rhetoric provided an apparently rational justification for the incessant escalation of the nuclear arms race.

Defense Secretary Weinberger's 1984 *Annual Report* exemplifies this belief in the efficacy of redoubling efforts to improve the deterrence ritual. Weinberger emphasized that to make certain that the Soviets perceive that the "costs" of aggression are higher than any potential "benefits" that they might anticipate, the United States must continue its "strategic modernization program" by striving for a "more immediate enhancement of our nuclear capability."[44]

Although there may be some degree of calculation and instrumental rationality underlying the arms race, there are indications that much of the nuclear buildup is of a purely habitual nature. For example, Admiral G.E. Miller, a former deputy director of the U.S. Joint Strategic Planning Staff, points out that "new nuclear weapons are not produced in answer to military demand; they are turned out and then have to be assigned targets, whether or not there is a requirement for additional destructive capacity."[45] At the Pantex facility near Amarillo, Texas, new nuclear weapons roll off the assembly line on a daily basis. What was once a means to an end has now become the end in itself.[46]

Prior to the dawning of the "nuclear age," similar responses, whether habitual or calculated, to perceived threats were considerably less problematic. The splitting of the atom ushered in the possibility that a small group of people could, in a matter of a few minutes, obliterate everything that billions of people had created over the course of several thousand years.[47]

In spite of sporadic statements to the contrary, military strategists and numerous political leaders generally treat nuclear weapons as simple extensions of conventional weapons. As a consequence, they maintain the belief that traditional war-fighting strategies are applicable in the nuclear realm as well.[48] Due to the sheer destructive capabilities of nuclear weapons, however, and the lack of any conceivable assured defense against such weapons, the efficacy of such a response was immediately called into question by some. Bernard Brodie, in his 1946 discussion, "Implications for Military Policy," was among the first critics. He argued that "Thus far the chief purpose of our military establishment has been to win wars." However, he continued, because the costs of a nuclear confrontation would outweigh any potential benefit, Clausewitz's idea of war as a means to achieve political objectives has become antiquated. "From now on," Brodie insisted, the military's "chief purpose must be to prevent . . . [wars]. It can have almost no other useful purpose."[49]

Brodie's approach to strategic policy, however, does not fit the logic of the ritual or military buildup and has for the most part been denounced, especially by military strategists but also by others.[50] Although strict adherence to Brodie's version of deterrence might eliminate the nuclear arms race ritual, it nevertheless holds sacred the deterrence ceremony. Even in the absence of a nuclear buildup, the rite of deterrence may produce unavoidable consequences of a nefarious nature. As Rothschild observed, "the deterrent threat itself—even in its minimal version—has required the expansion of political hatred."[51] Thus, nuclear deterrence, in any of its various forms, as well as the arms race itself, simultaneously evoke and reenforce another ritual: the denunciation of the enemy as evil.

RITUAL DENUNCIATIONS OF EVIL

A central aspect of the most important rituals in a society is the identification of evil and the marking of boundaries. Such rituals remind people of cherished beliefs and hated enemies, linking the norms of everyday life and the values of a culture with a large picture of the universe. Some rituals provide or imply a theory of evil that is a key to problem-solving: a force or group of people responsible for the difficulty or crisis is identified. Hence, the "social construction of evil"[52] which involves labeling enemies and creating an image of those enemies in the popular consciousness. Human history is replete with examples of the social construction of evil that help to define the boundaries between social groups, societies, and nations. From the Greek-barbarian distinction of antiquity through the saved and the damned of the Crusades (and countless other "holy wars"), the witch-hunts of Europe and New England, to the communist-capitalist dichotomy of our own era, political and cultural divisions have been imbued with cosmic significance.

Social scientists have long acknowledged the role of denunciation in efforts to define norms,[53] create social solidarity,[54] and facilitate social "boundary maintenance."[55] As Simmel suggested, "the resistance which has to be eliminated is what gives our powers the possibility of proving themselves."[56] Group solidarity is seldom strengthened by anything as much as the existence of a common enemy, the identification of whom "shores up the ranks" and reenforces systems of dominance.

Definitions of what is good and acceptable, true and beautiful, are not created *ex nihilo*, but are fashioned out of conflicts with enemies and ritual denunciations of evil.[57] Labeling theories of deviant behavior stress the ways in which social norms are defined and societal boundaries maintained through the public denunciation of alleged transgressors.[58] Certain groups and classes of people are denounced for purposes of social and political control in witch-hunts, both literal and symbolic.[59]

A broad range of activities create and reenforce images of evil in the popular consciousness. By socializing people through the media, jokes, and folktales, such pictures of the enemy are embellished, modified and internalized. As Turner's studies of the "ritual process" reveal, images of evil within the context of rituals are frequently distorted and drawn to monstrous proportions.[60]

A major task of both American and Soviet political leaders in the nuclear age has been to justify the development, construction and deployment of nuclear weapons. To warrant building such weapons, each side has to know that the enemy is outrageous, unprincipled, and out to destroy it. Both sides have inundated their citizens with a barrage of propaganda to convince them that the enemy is sufficiently reprehensible to require new weapons programs.

Justifying the Bomb was, at first, not difficult. Its development was motivated by wartime fears. Similarly, for the Soviets, legitimating nuclear weapons programs was not difficult—the United States had them, there was a history of invasions of their land (including the allies in 1918), and a recent war in which they lost 20 million people. After World War II, an emerging "two world doctrine" helped both countries to justify stockpiling nuclear weapons. Everything that was wrong with the world, according to many in the West, was the consequence of communist aggression; in the East, it was allegedly a consequence of American imperialism. Although the American denunciation of Soviet communism was not a new development,[61] it has been particularly important in the nuclear arms race, especially during the McCarthy years and most recently with Reagan administration rhetoric that identified the "Soviet empire" as the "focus of evil in the modern world."[62]

Finally, ritual denuciation is facilitated by the identification of both external and internal enemies.[63] External enemies are often beyond the authority of elites and cannot be successfully controlled. They are, furthermore, not always as convincing, and therefore as threatening, as are internal enemies who, like Simmel's "stranger,"[64] are near and remote at the same time. Consequently, elites will attempt to link internal and external enemies by suggesting similarities in their ideologies and tactics. Such a strategy facilitates the mobilization of a population in the face of common enemies, both those at a distance and those "within the camp." As Douglas observed, it is often believed that difficulties within a society "can be rectified merely by purging the system of internal traitors allied with outside enemies."[65]

The social construction of evil surrounding the nuclear arms race thus involves not only the identification of external enemies against which the weapons are deployed, but also labeling internal dissidents who are allegedly in sympathy with external adversaries. Opposition to weapons programs is portrayed as either overtly in sympathy with, or unwittingly manipulated by, the external enemies. Barron, for example, argued that the nuclear freeze campaign "thus far has been remarkably successful, for the KGB has induced millions upon millions of honorable, patriotic and sensible people who detest communist tyranny to make common cause with the Soviet Union."[66] Barron went on to detail his charges, contending that the freeze campaign has been "orchestrated from Moscow," through the World Peace Council.

Similarly, in a film narrated by Charlton Heston, "Countdown for America,"[67] Major General Richard X. Larkin (U.S. Army, retired) remarked that "the KGB, I believe, claims this is one of their most successful enterprises, that is, this World Peace Council orchestration of the nuclear freeze movement." He went on to speculate how expensive it is for the Soviet Union to organize such mass rallies as the June 12 (1982) Rally in New York.

Such statements, especially when echoed by the United States president, constitute an important counterpart to the ritual denunciations of external enemies who, for the most part, are identified by the administration as communists. The campaign to identify evil in the world as communist-inspired has been a major goal of the Committee on the Present Danger, an organization whose leaders became the architects and engineers of President Reagan's foreign policy.[68] A major consequence of such ritual activity was to drum up support for a continued military buildup and reliance on nuclear weapons.

THE REIFICATION OF SOCIAL PROCESSES

Because rituals are socially constructed responses to difficult situations, they frequently involve a dependence on a "power outside of ourselves."[69] The institutions that sustain ritual performances are imbued with symbolic significance, as is the expert who directs the ceremonies.[70] Hence, questions of power and control are paramount. If the social consensus supports the efficacy of a ritual that solves a pressing problem, universal compliance with the ritual process is imposed not only by the ritual expert, but also by others in the society who view his or her authority as legitimate. The social arrangements and processes surrounding the ceremony are thus reified—viewed as a concrete and necessary object—and labeled sacrosanct.

Even everyday interaction rituals, as Goffman noted, require a certain degree of control over the participants. People work together to create a ritual performance. Each individual who is willing to be subjected to informal social control in order to maintain the ceremonial order is given "hints and glances and tactful cues" as to what is and is not appropriate behavior for the given ritual being performed.[71]

The more complex and important rituals, such as the arms race, require even more control over the participants, and a greater reliance upon the experts who understand the "mysteries" that lie behind the ritual and know how to direct their performance and identify ceremonial errors. Rituals have a power of their own, but they are supported by and reenforce social institutions.[72] There are built-in sanctions for those who refuse to participate in the rituals. As Turner pointed out, there is considerable mystery involved in rituals, and it is therefore essential to rely upon those who have been initiated into the mysteries.[73]

Ironically, reliance upon the experts is particularly important when the rituals are not "working." As suggested earlier, when a ritual does not bring about the desired effect, it is often believed that it is simply because the ritual has not been properly performed. The problem may therefore lie with those participants who were not sufficiently compliant with ceremonial instructions.

When the nuclear arms race does not bring about the desired security it is supposed to produce, people turn to the experts for advice. The strategists and scientists are summoned to Capitol Hill or the Kremlin to explain what needs to be done to alter the ritual performance. Hence the "mystification of technique" and even the very failure of the ritual reenforces the institutional structures that support it. Like many ancient rites regarding religious mysteries, the nuclear arms race is shrouded in mystery.

As with other ceremonial leaders, many a modern military expert or strategist embellishes the mystery in order to protect his or her special status. The technical nature of both religious and scientific mysteries sometimes makes it difficult indeed for the laity to understand, a situation often exploited by the expert to his or her advantage. Consequently, two simultaneous goals are accomplished: on the one hand, the mystification of technique, and on the other, the desensitization of language by referring to ghastly events through technical acronyms,[74] numbers, and terms. Linguistic manipulations thus serve to reenforce the authority of the nuclear experts and the specialized institutions in which they work.

Some, like Edward Luttwak, a long-time Pentagon consultant, have gone so far as to suggest that the laity in fact have no business criticizing the ritual. Luttwak recommended the constitutional creation of a fourth branch of government to handle a government function not foreseen by our forebears: a Supreme Nuclear Council to make decisions about nuclear weapons. "Our system of government," Luttwak argued, "which was built to cope with ordinary problems, which is run by ordinary men in a rather ordinary way, is now supposed to control nuclear weapons, which are none of these things."[75] The nuclear theologians seem to believe that the people cannot be trusted with such decisions, nor can their "ordinary" representatives.

Russett suggested that such a position is a self-serving belief for the elites who perpetuate it. Nuclear policy, he argued, "is the only area of public policy that is so sharply removed from informed democratic discussion—and it is also probably the most critical area."[76] Similarly, Falk observed that the areas of foreign policy and national defense are the least democratic aspects of governance in the nuclear age. The removal of nuclear policy issues from public discussion through the mystification of technique, the segregation of experts from the public, and the maintenance of strict secrecy all serve to reify the ceremony and to elevate the status of the experts within the hierarchy of the ritual.[77]

Some of the most vocal critics of current U.S. military policies are themselves experts, including such former military officers as Admirals Laroque and Rickover, former defense secretary McNamara, and a large number of scientists, including those who were involved in the actual development of the bomb such as George Kistiakowsky and Hans Bethe. Although few insiders criticize the ritual, the history of the nuclear arms race is replete with those who denounce the ritual after leaving office.[78]

Where any doubts exist regarding the participants' loyalties to the ceremony, measures of social control are introduced in an attempt to ensure that the prescribed roles will be carried out properly. Severe sanctions are imposed upon those within the nuclear order who violate the sacraments of obedience, secrecy, and devotion. In the early 1950s, J. Robert Oppenheimer, who had once directed the Manhattan Project, was excommunicated and denied security clearance because of his opposition to the development of the "Super"—the hydrogen bomb.[79] The Oppenheimer affair made it clear to future nuclear initiates that heresy would not be tolerated.

Although prestige, careers, and even personal freedom are sometimes at risk, the extension of social control is frequently exercised in more subtle ways.

The potential success of these mechanisms is facilitated by the selection process—deciding who will perform which of the myriad of ceremonial tasks. Evidence suggests that the most crucial subservient roles are consciously filled with the most malleable individuals. A vivid illustration is provided by Falk, who, following a visit to the Strategic Air Command headquarters near Omaha, Nebraska, noted that the junior personnel

> seemed to be virtual extensions of the computer terminals they were seated at, as close to robots as I have ever seen. Some years later I read some classified studies of "human reliability" that helped explain this impression. The personnel chosen to operate sensitive equipment associated with nuclear weapons were supposed to be selected, in part, on the basis of their *absence* of moral scruple. The express idea was that individuals with an active conscience might hesitate in a crisis to follow orders leading to nuclear war, that such soldiers would, in this decisive military sense, be unreliable.[80]

The reification of social processes goes hand in hand, in a dialectical fashion, with a tendency for those who construct the reality, as it is perceived, to forget that it is a social construction. When participants are effectively socialized into a role, its institutional context and the world view that legitimizes it are taken for granted. The socially constructed reality becomes "objectivated" or reified to such an extent that it appears to the actor as if it were inevitable and immutable.[81] Extensive investments in the performance seem to precipitate further participation, even in the event of failure, as with the gambler who throws "good money after bad" or the member of a millenarian group whose belief in the imminent end of the world fails to be confirmed.[82] Participants in the ritual forget that the ritual itself is a product of human activity, and it is not the only available response to the crisis but rather the culturally approved one.

As the nuclear arms race "progresses," experts and citizens alike find themselves trapped by the boundaries of the ritual. Adherence to the sacred formulas creates a "nuclear cage"[83] that acts back upon its creators, forcing their activity along seemingly determined lines. Thus, situations are defined and lines of action are planned out within the narrow boundaries of the ritual. Alternatives to nuclear deterrence, for example, are not seriously considered by those at the core of the ritual, and even by many of those at the margins.[84]

Such a blindness to the implications of the ritual context in turn enhances the process of reification. Problem-solving strategies within the ceremony are designed as a response to more than the empirical situation at hand; instead, calculations are based on the problem as it is "set up" by the ritual. In attempting to respond to a potential threat from an adversary, strategic planners habitually develop worst-case scenarios that would enable them to counter not only an anticipated assault, but a greater-than-expected threat.

Over time such worst-case scenarios become reified, as if they were the only valid scenarios, resulting in what some have called *systematic overcompensation*.[85]

Even the commander-in-chief, who is ostensibly directing the entire ritual, is bound by the ceremony's logic. Ball remarked that few presidents "come to office with a deep comprehension of the implications of nuclear bombs, and in their innocence they may find themselves surrounded by advisors who believe their own metaphysics."[86] U.S. presidents and Soviet party chairmen alike are consequently forced to direct a ceremony that was written long before they took office. Because the specifics of the threat continue to change with an ever-escalating arms race, aspects of the rite must be constantly embellished; new generations of weapons are periodically introduced as required by the rules of the ceremony.[87]

Rituals may provide a means for preparing participants to act in a specific manner without questioning the implications of their individual or collective actions. The manufacturing, testing, and deployment of nuclear weapons, and particularly civil defense drills, military training, simulation games, worst case scenario production, and so on, may be viewed as ritual components of the larger nuclear ceremony. Such preparations may, in fact, increase the possibility that the event for which we are preparing would actually occur. Jim Jones prepared his followers for a ritualistic mass suicide by having them rehearse the liturgy. Similarly, the participants in today's nuclear rites are often not informed that the ceremony is only a rehearsal until it has neared completion. Having practiced the ritual countless times, and having survived its consequences, we may become complacent or psychologically numb to the potential effect of our behavior.

CONSIDERING THE ALTERNATIVES

In the preceding analysis, we have demonstrated the benefits of a ritual analysis of several aspects of the nuclear arms race. The conceptual framework has been constructed around four characteristics of ritual behavior: rituals (1) provide solutions to problems, especially concerning difficult situations and uncontrollable forces; (2) are rooted in experience; (3) identify evil and mark boundaries; and (4) reify social processes and reenforce social structure.

Ritual analysis raises a number of questions about ritual behavior that are germane in gaining an understanding of the nuclear arms race. First, what are the *assumptions* upon which the ritual is based? A sociological analysis of the assumptions underlying a ritual would require a study not only of the "texts" of its performance but also of the various adherents to the assumptions and their critics. Here, the symbolic dimension of the nuclear arms race begins to intersect with the social psychological and structural. For example, in what ways are people whose interests are protected by the ritual blinded by false assumptions?

Second, what *conditions* affect the efficacy of a ritual? A study of the conditions within which the ritual is perceived as effective would require a historical analysis of the context within which a ceremony was created and the changes over time of those conditions. We suggested, for example, that because of the habitual nature of rituals, the military rituals constructed prior to the nuclear age may still be performed, despite questions about their appropriateness and the possibility of "winning" or "losing" a nuclear conflict.

Finally, what are the *consequences* of the ritual? The consequences of a ritual's performance must be explored, despite the obvious empirical difficulties in doing so. The question that arises in studying the nuclear buildup is whether it actually makes people more secure.

Systematic research is needed on various specific symbolic aspects of the nuclear arms race, by people with particular areas of expertise and access to the appropriate data. A number of those areas of potential investigation follow: First, to what extent does the research and development of nuclear weapons involve a number of ceremonial sequences? Second, in what ways do the building, testing, and targeting of nuclear weapons, and their deployment in specified sites comprise traditional, regularly repeated behaviors that are meant to symbolize values and beliefs, particularly the logic of deterrence, sacrality of "national interests," and the efficacy of military responses to perceived military threats?

Third, are strategic planning and debates over nuclear policy ritualized? Approaches to defining nuclear policy, the language used in such discussions (e.g., the concern over a series of security "gaps"), and so forth have remained relatively similar throughout the nuclear era. Although there are some shifts in emphasis over time, the debates themselves, as Freedman observes, have a cyclical character: "Much of what is offered today as a profound and new insight was said yesterday."[88] The comparative counting of warheads and missile delivery systems, the juxtapositions of throw-weight, megatonnage, and so on take on a ritual aura related to the value system that legitimates the arms race.

Fourth, are mock battles in preparation for nuclear warfare, training maneuvers, war games, and computer simulations all rituals designed to give participants a sense of security about their ability to fight in and rationally control an actual nuclear conflict? To what extent are public displays of weapons and pronouncements on their characteristics routinized along ceremonial lines? Are the parading of weapons in Red Square, the exhibition of missiles, the aerial gymnastics of the Blue Angels, the open houses at Air

Force bases, and the recitation of Defense Department figures by government representatives similar to the formulas and actions of activities more conventionally considered to be ritual behavior?

Do Civil Defense planning and drills constitute a sixth element that could be viewed through a ritualistic screen? Although the details of such ceremonies have shifted from the "duck and cover" drills of the 1950s to the detailed crisis relocation plans of the 1980s, one of their functions is to offer citizens of targeted areas a conviction that "something can be done" about the threat of annihilation.

Are arms control negotiations ritualized, in as much as they provide participants with agreed-upon boundaries and a sense (or at least an *image*) of "good faith?" Do participants engage in arms control negotiations in order to foster the impressions that they are peace-loving people who would not participate in the arms buildup except for the actions of their adversaries? If so, the parties involved may periodically reach agreements that do not seriously alter the ritual process, followed by occasional accusations that the other side is cheating.

Finally, to what degree do the repeated denunciations of evil enemies— the "social construction of evil"—play a key role in the arms race? Such denunciations appear to be used to justify the stockpiling of nuclear weapons and mark out the boundaries between adversaries.

Human life seems to contain a paradox, in that it requires us to construct rituals that respond to life's crises and inconsistencies. Because the world is everchanging, however, the rituals we construct can never contain it and the very solution to yesterday's problems helps to create tomorrow's crisis.[89] Once reified and institutionalized, rituals may limit the opportunity to examine or develop alternatives to present conditions. The focus remains on the quality of the performance of the ritual as prescribed, rather than on innovation, creativity, and the development of radically different rituals.

The thrust of this chapter is to provide a *critique* of the ritual elements of the arms race, and we believe that such a critique is appropriate to the social sciences. We do not, however, intend to suggest that ritual per se is inherently contemptible. It is not the form of the nuclear ritual we find troublesome but rather its content. Indeed, the ritual form would seem to provide a blueprint for the social construction of responses to the nuclear dilemma.

Alternative institutions, within which rituals antithetical to the nuclear arms race could flourish, need to be established. A few possibilities include civilian-based defense structures employing Gandhian nonviolent action strategies, institutions for conflict resolution and crisis communication, a nonaligned peace movement, international peacekeeping forces, and institutions to address the causes of war.

Many of the institutional alternatives suggested require a simultaneous cultural reorientation away from the the ritual elements of the arms race, and ways of responding habitually to security threats without an immediate recourse to violence. The process of constructing reality involves creating images of alternatives, much of which occurs at a subliminal symbolic level.[90] The power of ritual behavior can perpetuate the existing networks of reciprocal relations and institutions, or it can be harnessed to assist in a paradigm shift in matters of national policy.

An instructive example is the abolitionist movement of the nineteenth century, which took on a seemingly impossible task and eventually saw the final abolition of slavery as a social institution in the United States. That movement constructed a series of rituals to provide a symbolic underpinning of their efforts. First, there was a ritual public denunciation of the institution of slavery, done in a periodic fashion and employing a rich set of symbolic images. Drawing upon Judeo-Christian images and symbols, the abolitionists developed songs, metaphors, and ritual activities oriented toward the immediate liberation of some slaves (with the "underground railroad") and the eventual elimination of slavery altogether.

These ritual activities of the abolitionists helped to create new shared definitions of the situation and facilitated the construction of an innovative value consensus, so that it became more and more difficult to speak publicly in favor of slavery. The slave trade and its public support was driven underground, while the opposition movement became increasingly public. Eventually, a new consensus emerged within the population and within the dominant political structure. Opposition to slavery became attached to the interests of the Union and served as a rallying cry for the North during the Civil War, regardless of the actual concrete importance of the issue.

The relatively fluid nature of culture, at least when compared to bureaucracies and social networks built on reciprocal relations, makes it possible at times to change cultural definitions in such a way as to undermine the legitimacy of existing institutions. Furthermore, ritual activities can reenforce and fortify alternative institutions, giving them legitimacy and authority to combat dominant power structures.

A first characteristic of rituals that provide alternatives to the nuclear arms race, then, is that they may help to redefine the problem that has created and sustains the nuclear cage. The enemy that is ritually denounced may be framed not in terms of another group of people, or a nation-state, but the nuclear threat itself. The peace movement has utilized a variety of popular rituals, some of which have been borrowed from the repertoires of religions, labor, and civil rights movements, such as public demonstrations and marches, songs, speeches, letter writing, sit-ins, and so forth. It might be fruitful to focus on the creation of such rituals on two levels. First, a series of "stop-gap rituals" could be directed at the denunciation of particular policies, weapons, or actions. A second level of rituals might focus on a deeper layer: those that identify the underlying causes of the arms race—threats to security, dignity, and human rights; injustice and aggression.

Public events might attempt to operate on both levels simultaneously, with an effort to address broader issues as well as more specific questions. One aspect of those rituals would be the construction of new attitudes and strategies for encountering new enemies, on both a cognitive and an emotional level. For example, Gandhi's effort to differentiate between the act and the actor might be reenforced by public declarations, songs, slogans, and symbols that do not vilify individuals or groups of people but instead condemn certain actions and outline ways in which those who commit them might be changed.

Similarly, "new" strategies could be enforced, such as Jesus' suggestion that his followers overcome evil with good. Rituals are often occasions on which people can practice what Sharp calls "political *jiu-jitsu,*"[91] which involves highlighting the sharp distinction between protesters and the violence of the system attempting to repress them, so that even the oppressors may recognize the repugnance of the repressive tactics of the system.

Instead of attacking the core symbols of the opposition head-on, it may be possible to redefine them in a more positive light. One peace activist has suggested, for example, that rather than burning the American flag, as some protesters did in the 1960s, it should have been ritually washed, as a simultaneous expression of respect and criticism that would potentially elicit a much more positive response from the wider public. Other symbols could be "converted" into occasions for transforming the international system, such as cultural, scientific, and economic exchanges as rituals attesting to the common interests of people across national boundaries.[92]

The creation of new rituals and symbols may also create new openings in the nuclear cage. Because rituals are rooted in experience, it may be helpful to investigate systematically the kinds of activities and symbols that in the past have helped to underscore positive international relations, to reduce violence, and so forth. The Live-Aid concert in the summer of 1985, for example, resulted in an audience of millions of people who identified positively with the people of Africa who were trapped in a drought. Whatever the negative implications of such an event (such as a self-righteous feeling of the "do-gooder"), the ritual reenforced the development of empathy for people of other lands and showed participants that it feels good to help others rather than to commit acts of violence against them. Here again, existing institutions and rituals can be drawn upon and amplified to accomplish the desired purposes. One example might be a heightened awareness within Christian churches in the United States and the Soviet Union that as they worship, there are Christians on the "other side" worshipping as well.[93]

Finally, since rituals tend to reify the social structures and institutions in which they occur, the creation by a nonaligned peace movement of ritual occasions that emphasize the international character of the human community could fortify those institutions and give them new legitimacy. Although the structures of bloc politics and global systems of power are obviously not going to change overnight, the ritual celebration of transnational structures in which people begin to take them as real might well undermine the nationalism that provides a major legitimizing force for the structures of war making. One clear indication of the efficacy of the peace movement is the seriousness with which it has been taken by the elites of the two superpowers. Both Bush and Gorbachev have gone to great lengths to coopt the rhetoric of the peace movement in public pronouncements that emphasize their own commitment to peace and arms control.

Though we leave to others a more thoroughgoing analysis of rites that might replace the nuclear arms race ritual, it is clear to us that such alternatives merit further exploration. The functions inherent in rituals, which, in one context, have heretofore served to maintain and accelerate the nuclear threat, could just as well be used to eliminate it.

In the meantime, more questions remain than are answered by the current ritualistic activities carried out by the superpowers in a frantic effort to gain security in the face of potential annihilation. Whether or not the actual use of the new generation of counterforce weapons now being deployed would make it possible to carry out a nuclear war and "restore peace on favorable terms" remains an empirical question best left untested.

Part III

Psychology of Religion

JOHN MCDARGH

Chapter 6

Growing Up in the Nuclear Age: Psychological Challenges and Spiritual Possibilities

In his 1982 presidential address to the American Academy of Religion, theologian Gordon Kaufman argued that religious studies, with its grasp of the dynamics of mythic consciousness, the religious imagination, and the vicissitudes of human hope and despair, has unique resources for understanding and responsibly addressing our life under the nuclear cloud.[1] The essays in Parts I and II of this book illustrate Kaufman's point; they demonstrate that the nuclear threat has an irreducibly religious dimension. But I argue here that finally the "way through" the perils of this nuclear age is necessarily as religious in its structure and substance as is the very danger we face. Benford and Kurtz imply as much in the concluding portion of their chapter (Chapter 5) when they propose looking seriously and appreciatively at the ritualizations that characterize the antinuclear movement.

This chapter picks up where theirs ends by examining the peace movement, especially as it affects and involves young adults, through the twin lenses of ego psychology and the study of religion. It is an inquiry into the kinds of psychological strengths, forms of meaning making, and modes of moral reasoning that motivate and sustain young persons in various levels of commitment to the movement for nuclear disarmament. It is the thesis of this chapter that (1) an extended engagement with the issues of nuclear war makes historically unprecedented demands upon the affective, imaginative, and

91

cognitive resources of all of us, but especially upon late adolescents and young adults, and (2) the greatest psychological challenge of nuclear armament is to the human symbolizing function, precisely the dimension of psychic life that is the locus of religious awareness and self-understanding.

THE PSYCHOLOGICAL IMPACT OF NUCLEAR ARMAMENT

Although American society has been facing the possibility of nuclear war for several decades, remarkably little research has been done until recently to assess the psychological impact of this new threat. Investigations by Sibylle Escalona and by Milton Schwebel at the time of the Berlin crisis in 1961 and the Cuban missile crisis in 1962 were pioneering[2] but not followed up until the mid 1970s, when John Mack and William Beardslee, prominent Boston psychiatrists, were named to an American Psychiatric Association task force studying the psychosocial impacts of nuclear developments.[3] Their area of concentration was on children and adolescents. As part of that study, they obtained questionnaires from 1100 children from various parts of the country.

A qualitative and quantitative analysis of these data shows a profile of anger and depression, a sense of foreshortened time and general unquiet about the future that is a function of the fear of the uncontrollability of nuclear war. The respondents studied were knowledgeable about nuclear issues, their primary source being the media, followed by their teachers. Generally, they did not talk about these matters with their parents and in fact interpreted their parents' silence on nuclear issues as another indication that the adult generation was now unwilling to deal with it.

The findings of the APA task force were corroborated and, if anything, amplified, by a study done of a smaller and more heterogeneous group of elementary students by Eric Chivian and Roberta Snow.[4] The aim of this research was to study the responses in group interviews of school-age children grades 3 through 12 (ages 8-17) in the greater Boston area. The researchers acknowledged that such a study conducted in an area with an unusually high degree of antinuclear political activity may have its own bias. Nevertheless, even that knowledge did not prepare them for the extent and depth of the concerns voiced by the children and adolescents interviewed in classroom groups. Chivian and his colleagues found that the large majority of their young subjects reported that they thought about nuclear war with some frequency. Across the age range these thoughts evoked a marked sense of vulnerability and hopelessness, though the particular expression of such feelings and the modes of handling the accompanying affect varied with age and level of cognitive and emotional development.

Among third- and fourth-grade children (8-9 years), there was a commonly expressed fear of abandonment, the nightmares or the waking fantasies of surviving a nuclear explosion without their families. Their sense of helplessness and hopelessness was articulated as the regret that they might not have the chance to grow up and be astronauts, ballplayers, or parents. By fifth grade (10-11 years) this sense of vulnerability was joined to an increased awareness by some of the political options available to them ("Why can't we march like Martin Luther King did?") and a growing feeling of anger and resentment towards the adult world that is perceived to be responsible for the nuclear impasse ("I want other people to have a chance to grow up—not just adults.")

Children in seventh grade (12-13 years), according to Chivian, displayed considerable cynicism regarding the competence of grown-ups to remedy the situation they had created. Perhaps allied to this cynicism, humor begins to show up as part of the repertoire of defenses used to cope with the prospect of nuclear destruction. Into junior high school and high school (13-18 years) a protested sense of the unfairness of the situation increases. "You've lived your life, but I'm just beginning mine" is a representative angry statement. Coupled with this anger and a heightened politization, however, are more complete defenses against the anxiety provoked by the prospect of war. In many different ways a great many students echoed the sentiments of the young man who asserted, "I try to put it out of my mind. . . . I just don't think about it [because] there's nothing you can do about it."

Might the fears and concerns expressed by the children in these two studies simply reflect the general pattern of uncertainty and apprehension found in young people confronting for the first time and at various ages the reality of death? At one level of analysis they do. The heartfelt outcry one hears in these children's comments is in the first instance a universal and timeless protest against the monstrous unfairness of death, and most particularly that which comes at the hands of one's fellow human being. But the powerful effect mobilized by the prospect of nuclear war differs from that evoked by other natural or human-made disasters in at least one very significant way. In the case of nuclear war, the prospect is one of *total destruction*. Contemplating his or her death under any other circumstances, the child can generally envision being survived, missed, and mourned by family, friends, or at least some enduring community. Here, however, the threatened obliteration is also the terminus of imagination—and not simply for the child.

The qualitatively different order of psychic challenge presented by the prospect of nuclear war has been the subject of probing investigation by psychiatrist Robert Jay Lifton.[5] Lifton's work on this subject has provided the conceptual framework used today by many in the American peace community to think about this problem. Lifton made an extensive psychiatric study of the survivors of the nuclear explosions at Hiroshima and Nagasaki.[6] The response of these survivors to the inundation of massive and mysterious destruction offers a terrible "text," he argues, not only for what will be the psychological reaction of those persons who do manage to survive the initial phases of a thermonuclear war, but for what subtly and insidiously happens to the generations who must contemplate that possibility.

Lifton's work deserves the most careful attention by scholars of religion concerned with the nuclear issue because his theoretical placement of the problem of nuclear armament is squarely within the traditional ambit of religious studies: namely, *the human symbolizing function.* Lifton finds that the work of neopsychoanalytic theorists such as Margaret Mahler and John Bowlby, social psychologists like George Herbert Mead, and philosophers Ernst Cassirer and Susanne Langer converge upon a new psychological paradigm for understanding human motivation and behavior.[7] According to this paradigm, the central motivating issue for human beings is the need to maintain a sense of the continuity of the self and onging life in the face of the annihilating experience of death and separation. Lifton calls his distinctive view of this foundational human problem the "formative-symbolizing perspective." From this perspective it can be seen that the sense of continuity or "symbolic immortality" is in every case achieved by an act of creative personal and communal symbolization. Simply put, we live and allow ourselves to die by the psychic *images* we construct of how the self is related to the vital past, the meaningful present, and the hoped for future.

Historically, human cultural solutions to the need for a sense of symbolic immortality have been of five types. The *biological* mode of symbolic immortality symbolizes the link between one's own existence and future generations through a living legacy in one's own progeny. The *theological* or *religious* mode may be represented by notions of the survival of an immortal soul or continued personal existence on a higher spiritual plane, but more subtle theological modes of symbolic immortality are also historically evident. Where one's life is seen as offered or surrendered for the cause of God, or else identified with the saving activity of a spiritual hero, the human yearning for a meaningful connection with enduring life may also be satisfied.

Symbolic immortality realized in the *creative* mode is found in the enduring contributions to the future through any labor of human hands and minds. *Participation in nature,* a sense that one's own life participates in an eternal cycle of natural life, is the fourth mode of symbolic immortality. Finally, Lifton posits a mode of *experiential transcendence,* a means of symbolic immortality involving sacred or profane experiences of ecstasy in which the threat of death and separation is experientially overcome by a feeling that one has made connection with the "continuous present."

If Lifton is correct about the irreducible necessity of symbolic immortality for human psychic well-being, then we can appreciate why nuclear war presents an historically unprecedented psychospiritual challenge. The "imagery of extinction" that is part and parcel of the total picture of nuclear armament threatens every form of symbolized continuity of life that human communities have hitherto relied upon. The assault upon the biological mode is self-evident. In the "commonwealth of insects and grasses," which Jonathan Schell suggested would be the only viable aftermath of a full nuclear "exchange," there is simply no one to carry on.[8] The dramatic disruption of the natural seasonal cycles that would be precipitated by massive nuclear explosions (e.g., the hypothesis of a "nuclear winter" described in Chapter 5) threatens the natural mode of symbolic immortality as well as the biological.

The desire to tether one's sense of continuity to creative production is equally jeopardized. In the putative aftermath of a nuclear war, little of the creation of our hands would be likely to endure. What of the theological modes of symbolic immortality? Are these, too, touched by the nuclear prospect? According to Lifton, some persons have grasped at certain forms of theological hope—often in perverse and self-defeating ways—as a means of countering the threat of nuclear annihilation.[9] Apart from such instances, however, this mode of symbolic immortality is likewise seriously strained by the prospect of nuclear war. Unless one subscribes to such literalistic apocalyptic scenarios, how God's kingdom and purposes might be realized in the absurdity of a nuclear disaster is not evident and is difficult to make morally or emotionally persuasive.

In view of all this, it is clear that the traditional resources of symbolic imagination are no longer adequate for children (or adults) who must confront not only individual death but the possibility of mass extinction. So the mind erects its defenses. It may grasp at a variety of images, some old and some new, that attempt to give symbolic meaning to the nuclear threat. (Many of these are discussed throughout this book.) Simultaneously, though, the mind may refuse to face the issue at all; it may simply deny its capacity to think or feel or imagine anything about nuclear catastrophe. From his interviews with survivors of the first nuclear blast, Lifton proposed the term *psychic numbing* to describe the constriction of feeling, imagination, and vision that accompanies the sense of living before a doom one is helpless to avoid.[10] The effect of this numbing, Lifton says, is to "inhibit . . . the development and elaboration of culture specific images which make death meaningful by relating it to a vision of continuing life."[11]

THE ANTINUCLEAR MOVEMENT ON THE COLLEGE CAMPUS:
A PROFILE OF STUDENT RESPONSE

The implications of this discussion for the relationship of college students to the disarmament movement may by now be apparent. We would expect that like their younger brothers and sisters they, too, would carry the psychic weight of the nuclear prospect, but that with more age-appropriate defenses this would be more submerged and less in evidence. Certainly on the face of it the students I have the most familiarity with do not give much evidence on a day-to-day basis of being preoccupied with the problems of global conflict. Yet, I have frequently been surprised, and so have they, to discover how close to the surface such fears may lurk and how unexpectedly they may break out. I first became aware of this several years ago in an incident worth retelling for its illustrative value.

As a classroom exercise in a course I was teaching, I asked students to ponder for a moment their own images of the future course of their life and how they would want themselves to be remembered. Then to make that graphic for themselves, I suggested that they try their hand at writing the epitaph they might want to see carved on their own tombstones. The class set busily to work, except for one young man who stared in a kind of stunned silence at his paper. He was an individual who had not to that point struck me as particularly self-reflective or politically aware. When it came time for the students to share with one another what they had written, this young man said in a quaking voice, "I suddenly realized that I did not expect to have a tombstone because I am afraid that there will be nobody left to bury me. . . . I'm talking about the possibility that we are all going to be blown up in a nuclear explosion."

The incident is dramatic, and in this form the eruption of such an unconscious fantasy is, I suspect, rather unusual. But I have found much evidence to suggest that this young man is not alone in his fear; he is perhaps only unusual in being caught by it so unaware and so publicly. Another college student in a journal entry shared an example of the unexpected intrusion of nuclear anxiety in a more private moment: "I was lying in bed one night when I heard a siren. It wasn't a police, ambulance, or fire siren, I know those. It was sustained and high pitched. I know it was probably a car alarm, but when I was hearing it, I broke into a cold sweat and prayed it wasn't an air raid siren. All I could think was, 'My God, they've dropped the bomb on Boston'."

In order to get some sense of how extensively college students would consciously identify a concern with nuclear war as a feature of their perspective on the future, reflection papers were solicited in September, 1982, from eighty-five undergraduates (18-22 years old) at Boston College, none of whom was currently involved with the on-campus disarmament coalition. The students were asked to respond to an open-ended sentence: "When I think about the future, my greatest concerns are..." Over a third of the respondents, in some fashion or another, referred to the possibility that their own hopes for the future could be cut off by events at a global level. A typical response of this sort would be this by a female student:

> When I think about the future, my greatest concern is whether there will be a future which will make these reflections upon it worthwhile and meaningful. I am first concerned about the plausibility of a nuclear war and its shattering consequences. Will anyone survive such devastation and what shape will the earth be in? Could life after a nuclear holocaust be a fate worse than death?

As respondents elaborated upon the character of this threat, one of the central elements that emerged was a sense of *uncontrollability*. Nuclear war was imaged as a potentiality largely outside the power of ordinary citizens—or even the responsible parties—to prevent. The proliferation of nuclear weapons among a number of nations, the accessibility of the technology, and the ever decreasing response time has made the world situation seem less like the 1950s image of a showdown at the OK Corral between the superpowers and more like the landscape of urban terrorism, in which the fatal strike might come at any moment and from an unexpected source. As one respondent expressed this feeling:

> The constant threat of nuclear war is one of my greatest concerns. Suppose some person, state, or country suddenly decides to end all life and launches a nuclear attack. I feel we are all living in a world of fear and uncertainty. In many respects our future depends upon the actions of others. Sometimes we have no control over tomorrow.

If this kind of fear seems chronic among at least some of the students, how is it handled? If it is apparently "missing" or unacknowledged by others, is it repressed? Some responses suggest that one strategy involves a certain fatalism that abandons the possibility of changing the future and narrows attention to the immediate concerns of life. This statement by an 18-year-old male student shows how he attempts to understand this attitude as a form of higher faith:

> When I think about the future, my greatest concerns are getting by today. I have always lived for the present because we never know when we will die. I don't think that worrying about a nuclear war will do me any good because if an important enough person decides to hit the button, it's all over. If we waste our lives away by worrying, we haven't lived. Living in my opinion is loving and being happy with everything (just about). I realize that we don't live in paradise, but we have to make the best of what we have—we can always look forward to life in heaven.

This young man's candid observation is, in my experience, by no means unusual. When fear and a sense of threat break through a prior barrier, one is faced with a sense of helplessness and doubts about personal efficacy. Resignation and a constriction of attention and interest to the immediate and manageable concerns of today provide a safe psychological haven. (One manifestation of this is the "official optimism" described by Chapman in Chapter 8 of this book.) As Lifton comments, "All of these add up to a stance of *waiting for the bomb* and contribute to a self-fulfilling prophecy of universal doom."[12]

The question such responses provoke me to ask is, What would it take to break through the forces of psychic numbing and *not* succumb to a subsequent sense of fatalism? In the terms of this study, how do the responses just discussed differ from the self-descriptions and world views of students who have opted to make some active response to the threat of nuclear war, at least insofar as they have chosen to become involved in various ways in the disarmament activity nearest to hand for them, the antinuclear coalition on their own campus? To assess this, questionnaires were sent in fall, 1982, to twenty members of that group (ten men and ten women).[13] These were compared to similar questionnaires given to a smaller number of the eighty-five students who answered the initial open-ended question. Additionally, in-depth interviews were conducted with six members of the antinuclear group (three men and three women).

One of the distinctive differences between these groups that one might expect to find is a heightened capacity on the part of the activist students to "imagine the real," to hold in consciousness the threat that motivates their involvement in the antinuclear movement. These students were what Chapman calls in Chapter 8 "thinkables," those who are "more willing to experience directly and hold emotionally the reality of the nuclear danger." They are more willing to "listen to images" (as Noel puts it in Chapter 7). At the same time, as already noted, such a consciousness when devoid of an accompanying sense of alternatives can itself be immobilizing and provoke a range of defensive reactions. As Lifton puts the matter: "Awareness, then, involves the full work and play of the imagination. It means imagining danger that is real, but also imagining possibilities beyond that danger, forms of thought and action beyond immediate assumptions."[14] Students who were able to do both were those whose stance was characterized by *hope* and not by *optimism,* to evoke the helpful distinction that Chapman and Noyalis (Chapter 8 and 10) propose.

A comparison of questionnaire responses would seem to bear out this point. On the one hand, students engaged in disarmament activities were more likely to describe themselves as persons who "frequently think and worry about the chances of nuclear war." They were also more likely to believe that there is "a good chance that an all out nuclear war will occur within the next ten years." They harbored few illusions about the "survivability" of a "limited" nuclear war and even questioned whether that kind of language made any sense at all. They were equally strongly skeptical of claims that an effective civil defense is possible against nuclear attack. Several of these involved students spoke frankly about their fears. For example, one young woman interviewed shared a fantasy she said occurs periodically in her life, that when a nuclear attack occurs she will be separated from her family (a fantasy reminiscent of the fears of abandonment Chivian and others found among much younger children).

On the other hand, these students evidenced a much stronger sense that there was something that could be done. They were first of all very much more definite about their own willingness to demonstrate on the nuclear issue, in contrast to only 31 percent of all students in a national study.[15] A majority even expressed an openness to risking arrest in support of a nuclear freeze, versus only 12 percent of the national group. This greater sense of possibility coexisting with a sharp lucidity about the danger of our condition shows itself in their views on the effectiveness of voluntary political action. On the specific matter of the effectiveness of *student* demonstrations swaying government policy, the coalition group was divided, although still more likely to see such activity as at least of some value. However, they were unanimous in their sense that citizen action in general was politically effective.

Not surprisingly, this group also was considerably more knowledgeable about the range of nonstudent peace groups working on the issue at a local and national level. They displayed a clearer sense than noninvolved students of the diversity and creativity of the antinuclear movement in the population at large. Yet, this sense of effectiveness, this capacity to imagine "possibilities beyond danger," would appear to have sources that run deeper than simply their current acquaintance with resources of the peace movement. To get at these sources, we must turn to the material of the in-depth interviews.

In these extended conversations with selected participants in a campus disarmament coalition, a number of patterns emerged that parallel in a remarkable way earlier research by Kenneth Keniston but that, I would argue, have additional significance in the context of the nuclear issue. Keniston found that the serious leadership of the antiwar movement in the 1960s, as opposed to those participants whom he classified as "alienated youth," far from rebelling against the values of their parents were in fact attempting to live out expressed, though perhaps unimplemented, parental values.[16] This was strikingly the case in all six of the subjects interviewed. In three cases, the parents and older siblings (particularly older sisters) actually were already involved in peace activities and were the primary source of the subject's first acquaintance with the movement. This replicates the larger social pattern of adults and professional persons bringing the nuclear issue to the campus community in the form of presentations by groups such as the Union of Concerned Scientists, Educators for Social Responsibility, and other essentially nonstudent organizations. Even in the other cases in which the parents differed in their political analysis from their son or daughter, the students saw their activism as having its source in a value system and world view acquired within the family.

When one examines more closely the nature of the parental influence, another convergence with the Keniston material becomes apparent. Keniston was struck by the enduring influence of mothers upon their activist children, particularly their sons. Among a great many of his subjects he found an "unusual capacity for nurturant identification."[17] Five of the six students interviewed were unequivocal in citing their mothers (and sometimes also older female siblings) as key role models, whose values and outlook were formative for them and inspired their present political loyalties and actions. In their own self-descriptions ("How would you describe yourself to yourself?"), these students repeatedly, if sometimes reluctantly, used terms like *responsible, sensitive, loyal, intense, committed*—words that they would also use for their parents, but especially their mothers.

There is an appropriateness to this maternal identification that becomes apparent when one considers again the unique psychic demands of the nuclear situation. Though the specter of nuclear war clearly engages our fears of personal survival (and even these students were often frank enough to acknowledge this as one motive force), it would be difficult, for reasons that Lifton has elaborated, to sustain an extended involvement with the issue solely out of the anxiety raised by this scenario of personal destruction. The ethical weight of the problem of nuclear war must bear elsewhere, and for these students it does. The nuclear prospect evokes the relationship we have to those who are already the victims of a costly arms race (hence, the link made in argumentation between military spending and world poverty) and the more subtle relationship to those generations yet unborn. It is to this moral relation that Helen Caldicott refers when she says that the question before us is "shall we be good ancestors?"

The profound psychological import of this question has been highlighted by the work of Erik Erikson. In the terms of Erikson's psychosocial developmental schema, the issue addresses that ego strength he calls *generativity*: "the widening concern for what has been generated by love, necessity or accident . . . a concern in establishing and guiding the next generation."[18] The appearance of an incipient sense of generativity on the part of college students is developmentally precocious according to Erikson's schedule of life tasks. In his schema, it is the challenge of consolidating identity and negotiating intimacy that is presumably centerstage for most late adolescents. This may partially explain why the nuclear issue has not seemed to engage the sensibilities of the college-age population in the same way as the Vietnam war, which threatened them very immediately and personally. Nevertheless, the appearance among some students of this capacity for a more inclusive care is worth reflecting on. Perhaps these students, young persons whose commitments are organized around identifications with mothers who themselves were moved by a caring that reached beyond their own families, are precursors of the kind of individual we must take care to nurture and develop.

Don Browning, among other theological commentators on Erikson, has observed that Erikson's increased attention to the problem of human generativity in his later writings reveals an implicitly normative, one might even say religious, agenda that is certainly shaped by the moral exigencies of the nuclear age.[19] Erikson has become concerned to specify what kind of human being, with what kinds of strengths and what sort of vision, will be needed if we as a species are to find our way into a humanly desireable future. His reflections repeatedly return to the model of the generative individual, the person whose sense of mutuality and locus of concern extends beyond the interpersonal, the familial, the tribal, and the national. (See Thistlethwaite's theological development of this theme in Chapter 9).

The concept of generativity, like Lifton's concept of symbolic immortality, stresses the need to symbolize the ties that bind each individual to all of humanity, and to all generations past and future. Lifton has argued, paralleling Erikson, that one of the psychological prerequisites for moving beyond the deadly impasse of an ideology of national security based on nuclear armament is that we must acquire a sense of "shared fate," of the interlocking destinies of all peoples, or more basically, an awareness of our shared humanity.[20] From this perspective, a way through the stalemate of our global showdown would seem to require that we come to see the world as a network of mutual responsibilities rather than as an arena of competing moral claims. But attaining this perspective is in fact a complex developmental accomplishment, at the heart of which is the strenuous strength of that primal virtue that Erikson named *basic trust*.

Significantly, these interviewed students often spoke of their sense of empathy for the situation of the Russian people and showed a consistent effort to appreciate the way in which global power issues might appear to the other side. "You have to understand how many men they lost in the Second World War," one student remarked. "It must be very scary for them," said another, "to know that every nuclear weapon in the world that is not under their control is pointed at them." As opposed to uninvolved students, and even more to students who indicated that they did not favor the idea of a nuclear freeze, these students never cast their analysis of the issue in terms of the right to national self-defense or the obligation to protect "our way of life."[21] By contrast, they tended to discuss the underlying problematic of peace as a matter of *trust*—how to act trustworthily ourselves, and how to solicit that trust from the Soviets.

RESPONSE TO NUCLEAR ARMAMENT:
THE RELIGIOUS DIMENSION

This whole category of trust, I would argue, finally points the discussion to the dimension of the religious. The fragility of our future, the daunting complexity of our circumstances, and hence the enormity of the task of achieving disarmament, profoundly challenges the psychospiritual resources of each person at the most foundational level. It is the individual's sense of basic trust that is at risk in facing the future in a nuclear age, a sense that is laid down in the vicissitudes of earliest development but that historically has been rehearsed, renewed, maintained, and transmitted through religious symbolism.[22] All this is to say that for the students I interviewed, as for all of us, the real question is not, Can we trust the Russians? but rather, In a world of conflicting powers and coercive forces, can we trust that the Ultimate Environment in which we are historical actors wills our well-being, sustains our hopes, and will bring us to fulfillment rather than destruction?[23] At stake then is some formulation of Lifton's posited sense of symbolic immortality, one that can be psychically represented and personally and communally affirmed so that the self is upheld in the face of nuclear reality without sacrifice of either lucidity or action.

However one names and symbolizes the Ultimate Environment, one's interpretation of it and relationship to it is acted out daily in the concreteness of one's political and social life. This was subtly evident in all the conversations of this research. For their part, the activist students, regardless of their relationship to any formal religious tradition, experience themselves as living in what the theologian Paul Tillich called a *kairotic* moment in history, a critical turning point, a moment in which they feel the urgent imperative of the Deuteronomic invitation to "choose life" (Deuteronomy 30:15). Ironically, these students share with the pronuclear Committee for the Present Danger a driving sense of values that are indeed worth ultimate sacrifice and of living in a time when that sacrifice may be required (see Chapter 2). What they have not done is to make the fatal link between the assertion that there are some things worth dying for and the notion that this necessarily involves a willingness to risk nuclear destruction.

Although this sense of historical urgency is empowering, on the one hand, it is a problematic burden, on the other, especially at this age. The discussion of nuclear disarmament has a cruelly coercive character to it. Unlike other claimants for the care and commitment of these students, it presents itself as the subsuming issue, appearing to radically relativize all other concerns. As I have overheard the question put, Why work for the preservation of endangered species, or the release of prisoners of conscience, or gay rights, when the whole planet's survival is at stake? For young men and women such as these, acutely sensitized by their particular development to issues of responsibility, these arguments exert great power. All the more are they persuasive when they appear at a stage in their own development in which a temporary totalism, the need to be as passionately committed and uncompromisingly consistent with one's avowed values as possible, is a component of identity formation.[24] With this all-or-nothing posture, the potentiality for a kind of psychic early "burnout" is high.[25]

For all these reasons, then, for the student activist the passage from college into the next phase of young adulthood and the beginning of family and career is likely to be particularly difficult.[26] Whether a serious degree of commitment to peace work can be maintained and integrated into a pattern of work and relationships will depend on two factors. The first is psychospiritual: Does the individual's sense of an Ultimate Environment, their faith if you will, produce not only the moral demand but also the freedom to rest from that demand? In the words of William James, is he or she able to rely upon a God sufficiently trustworthy to permit an occasional "moral holiday"; that is, to be able to lay down or shift the weight of the burden without disabling guilt. Obviously, this is not simply a matter of private conviction but closely tied to the cultural symbolic resources that may or may not be available.

This factor is also allied to a second, similarly social, concern: Will these student activists be able to locate beyond the university those communities of concern that are sufficiently trustworthy and enduring to persuade them that they will not be alone in their commitments? Will there be cultural paradigms for integrating a peace perspective into a style of life that connects these concerns with the problems of work and family? Here is where the presence of the nonstudent peace organizations and the emergence of creative "peace communities" in some parts of the country offer the greatest hope.[27] As Benford and Kurtz note (Chapter 5), such communities will necessarily be ones that confirm, validate, and ritually celebrate a commitment to peace that in some measure locates the young adult on the margins of a culture where "nuclear superiority" has been an unquestioned article of political orthodoxy.

Here too is where scholars of my own generation should feel the greatest personal challenge. For what is already abundantly evident from this study is that what young people are most in need of from us is finally not our analysis, nor even our collaboration in particular political actions, but rather our modeling of what an ongoing engagement with the issues of peace and justice looks like as a central feature in the fabric of a responsible personal and professional life. They want us not to confirm the uneasy suspicion that many of them carry that the students of the 1960s were unable as adults to "go the distance."

DANIEL C. NOEL

Chapter 7

The Nuclear Horror and the Hounding of Nature: Listening to Images

---

First, a brief word about this chapter. Its style is rather unconventional; but, then, it speaks of unconventional matters in an unconventional time. It is a sort of journal, a story of personal discovery, a journey through images and ideas that the reader is invited to share.

The story should actually begin in the time of Freud and Jung, the great explorers of the psyche. We call their discoveries *depth psychology* because they delved down "beneath" the superficialities of consciousness and culture and found, hidden in those depths, images that hint at processes of which we are habitually unconscious. The psychic image plays a central role in all depth psychologies. Jung went so far as to say that image *is* psyche. Freud showed that the apparently random and innocuous images we use in speaking and writing have meanings we do not consciously suspect. He acknowledged that poets and artists had preceded him in this discovery of the power of unconscious images. Jung spoke of his notion of image as a concept derived from poetic usage, namely, as a figure of fancy or fantasy-image.

If we are to uncover the hidden images that move us, it seems that we must listen more closely to our poets, novelists, and artists—as well as to ourselves. The two may very well be parts of a single process, as I hope to illustrate here. The most recent explorations in this process come from the archetypal psychologists. Growing out of the soil of Jung's thought, archetypal psychology puts great stress on the "poetic basis of mind." It looks for the fundamental images of the psyche in myths as well as individual minds, in poems as well as dreams, in novels as well as neuroses. It moves depth psychology further from the realm of science and closer to the realm of aesthetic appreciation, trying to meet and respond to the image on its own home ground. For the image does have a life of its own. Every image wants to tell us something—indeed many things—that we may not have heard before. If we approach an image as scientists trying to analyze its component parts or as cryptologists trying to decode it objectively, we shall have difficulty hearing its chorus of many voices. Rather we must allow the image its freedom by, as Patricia Berry puts it, "restating" the image over and over again with ears open to its unending echoes.

> By restatement I mean a metaphorical nuance, echoing or reflecting the text beyond its literal statement. . . . Without restatement we tend to get caught in the dream at its face value and draw easy conclusions from it, never truly entering into the psyche or the dream. When we are completely stumped with a dream, there might be nothing better to do than to replay it, let it sound again, listening until it breaks through into a new key.[1]

When confronting the horror of the nuclear threat it is easy to feel as if we are in a dream and even easier to feel stumped. So I find myself on the relatively untrodden path of archetypal psychology, reading and replaying diverse sources (most of them fictional and poetic) that echo with images of the nuclear horror. I have not tried to hunt down any particular images or ideas. I have simply tried to listen patiently with sensitive ears and restate with thoughts and words.

My report on this work, which is still very much in progress, must inevitably be a first-person story. We can study images with objective logical scrutiny of the mind; but to listen to images we must rely on our ears, which are incurably subjective. As archetypal psychology insists, there can be no single meaning for an image. The same image unfolds for each of us in different ways, speaking with different voices. And archetypal psychology suggests that our interpretations of an image may not be as important as the very personal process of listening to it, for in the process of listening and reflecting we discover our own unique responses and find ourselves changed as individuals. So it seems to me that only a personal style of presentation can remain faithful to the method I am exploring. In what follows, I ask the reader to join me in the ongoing process of listening, restating, responding, and changing.

I hope that this will be a helpful demonstration—an antinuclear demonstration, in its way. I hope it will show how images from religion, literature, and depth psychology unendingly intersect and interweave; how all these intersect with my own preoccupations as a student of religion and a target of the current madness; how mere listening can be a mode of research and critical inquiry; and, most importantly, how the very process of listening to the images can forge a new approach to confronting the nuclear horror. If the results seem too tentative and subjective when judged by traditional academic criteria, I ask the reader to remember that it is the personal engagement with images that is the goal here. If my journal—my journey— can stimulate others to listen a bit more carefully to images of the nuclear horror, it will have more than achieved its goal.

I

The aged canon shuffled up the worn stone steps and led me across to the North Wall. Although Canterbury Cathedral's lay tourist guides knew nothing of the wall painting I sought, and the canon himself had to consult a venerable handwritten log before setting out, when I once stood in front of the picture a middle-aged Englishwoman, a stranger, sidled over to me and asked, in a whisper, "Are you here because of *Riddley Walker?*"

I was indeed there because of *Riddley Walker,* Russell Hoban's remarkable 1980 novel, and the sense its readers share of having been initiated into latter-day mysteries, fearsome mysteries, is part of the power of its message. I made my secular pilgrimage to Canterbury in late May 1983, almost a year after beginning my reading of Hoban's novel with his Acknowledgments, where he indicates that the painting in question is 500 years old and the legend of St. Eustace that it depicts is thirteen centuries older than that. But Hoban's story is set some twenty-four centuries into the *future,* 2400 years *after* a nuclear war in the last decade of our own century.

The holocaust we dread has happened, long ago, and the barbarians of a radically devolved forty-fourth century society, hunter-gatherers and primitive agriculturalists in the countryside around Canterbury, have only the caption from the wall painting in the ruins of the cathedral to help them understand how the bombs were developed and why they were used. Indeed, this caption is the only instance of standard twentieth century English in the novel, for along with everything else in the culture of this degenerate future, words have worn down, too. Language has regressed to a sort of Middle-English scatological slang. Much of the somber satisfaction of reading *Riddley Walker,* which its devotees share by conversing in its obscure catch phrases, involves deciphering Hoban's language. Doing so almost forces one to read aloud the strange but usually phonetic spelling. One ends up quite literally *listening to images* of this postnuclear, pretechnological world. And these are images which contribute, as Penelope Mesic has put it in the *Bulletin of the Atomic Scientists,* to restoring "the freshness of delight to language and the freshness of horror to the Earth's ruin."[2]

Foremost among the images of *Riddley Walker,* as already implied, are those regarding the legend of St. Eustace. The salient portion of the caption for the wall painting reads: "At the bottom of the painting St. Eustace is seen on his knees before his quarry, a stag, between whose antlers appears, on a cross of radiant light, the figure of the crucified Saviour. The succeeding episodes lead up to his martyrdom."[3] Out of this caption, Riddley Walker's society has fabricated the people's myth of what happened to humankind "time back way back," when the leaders of "Inland" put the "1 Big 1" into "barms" that "kilt as menne uv thear oan as they kilt enemes."[4]

Like all the "connexion men" or soothsayers for the various settlements, Riddley, the young hero-narrator, has to learn this mythic narrative, *The Eusa Story,* by heart, and in recounting his adventures he transcribes all thirty-three stanzas. It begins with an uncomfortably familiar description, however unfamiliar the spelling may be to the twentieth century reader:

1. Wen Mr Clevver wuz Big Man uv Inland thay had evere thing clevver. Thay had boats in the ayr & picters on the win & evere thing lyk that. Eusa wuz a noing man vere qwik he cud tern his han tu enne thing. He wuz werkin for Mr Clevver wen thayr cum enemes aul roun & maykin Warr. Eusa sed tu Mr Clevver, Now wewl nead masheans uv Warr. Wewl nead boats that go on the water & boats that go in the ayr as wel & wewl nead Berstin Fyr.

2. Mr. Clevver sed tu Eusa, Thayr ar tu menne agenst us this tym we mus du betteren that. We keap fytin aul thees Warrs wy doan we just du 1 Big 1. Eusa sed, Wayr du I fin that No.? Wayr du I fyn that 1 Big 1? Mr Clevver sed, Yu mus fyn the Littl Shynin Man the Addom he runs in the wud.[5]

Eusa protests that there's very little wood around; it's mostly iron and stone. But Mr. Clevver replies that Eusa must "fyn the wud in the hart uv the stoan,"[6] so that one begins to hear the image of a forest—what the English call a wood—in the heart of matter, in the midst of iron and stone.

Here, in this forest, the hunt for the Littl Shynin Man and the 1 Big 1 will take place; Eusa the "noing man," the scientist, is also the hunter with his hounds: "He smaulert his self down tu it he gon in tu particklers uv it. He tuk 2 grayt dogs with him thear nayms wer Folleree & Folleroo."[7] Eventually, the dogs lead a microscopic (or microscope-wielding) Eusa deep down into the dancing particles, into the heart of the wood, which also turns out to be the Hart, the great buck or stag, of this forest in miniature. Here St. Eustace's vision is translated into a mythic version of nuclear physics:

8. In the dark wud Eusa seen a trak uv lyt he follert it. He cum tu the Hart uv the Wud it wuz the Stag uv the Wud it wuz the 12 Poynt Stag stud tu fays

him & stampin its feat. On the stags hed stud the Littl Shynin Man the
Addom in be twean thay horns with arms owt strecht & each han holdin
tu a horn.

9. Eusa sed tu the Littl Man, Yu mus be the Addom then. The Littl Man sed,
I mus be wut I mus be.[8]

For any reader who knows the legend, and even for those who do not (the
twentieth century caption is not transcribed until later in the novel), this is an
astounding image. The tiny Christ, radiant between the stag's horns, has
become both Adam, the archetypal man, and the atom, the basic unit of
matter—at least at the time physicists were helping to develop the first nuclear
bomb. Either of these possibilities retains a Christlike or divine quality,
however, through the Littl Shynin Man's biblical pronouncement: "I mus be
wut I mus be."

As the story continues Eusa turns his anger on the stag:

10. Eusa tuk his weppn in his han he sed tu the stag, Wy doan yu run? Yu no
wut I am goin tu du. The stag sed, Eusa yu ar talkin tu the Hart uv the
Wud. Nuthing wil run frum yu enne mor but tym tu cum & yu wil run
frum evere thing.[9]

This is a curious challenge for a cornered quarry to throw back at a hunter
with the upper hand. But, then, the hunt Eusa and his dogs have been engaged
in is no ordinary hunt. It is the ultimate hunt, and the stag's words in the story
suggest that it cannot succeed, or that the hunter's very success will somehow
be directed against him. And so when Eusa kills the stag and grabs the Littl
Man we sense the worst is yet to come for this hunter who is not only St.
Eustace but, through his name, conceivably also Jesus—or us, in our USA.

For Eusa's part, of course, he is by now hell-bent to find the number, the
recondite formula, of the 1 Big 1 and is pulling the Addom's arms apart until
the latter reveals the secret. Crying in pain, the Littl Man blurts out a series of
archetypal oppositions while Eusa hounds him to "tel mor." Finally he arrives
at the central polarity: "I wan tu aul I wan tu nuthing":

14. Eusa sed, Stop ryt thayre thats the No. I wan. I wan that aul or nuthing
No. The Littl Man the Addom he cudn stop tho. He wuz ded. Pult in 2
lyk he wuz a chikken. Eusa screamt he felt lyk his oan bele ben pult in 2 &
evere thing rushin owt uv him.[10]

So proceeds the splitting of the atom in the mythic memory of the
forty-fourth century. The consequences, in this viewing from the far side of
nuclear disaster, are understandably all negative. After Eusa sees the "Master
Chaynjis uv the 1 Big 1" and writes down the appropriate numbers, the
seventeen remaining stanzas of the story describe his invention of nuclear

bombs, the use of these in a great war, and the horrific aftermath. At the story's end, Eusa confronts the Littl Man, the Addom, once again.

Eusa had let the "Master Chaynjis" escape when he pulled apart the Addom, and now, says the Addom, "yuv got to go on thru them":

> 33. Eusa sed, How menne Chaynjis ar thayr? The Littl Man sed, Yu mus no aul abowt that I seen yu rite thay Nos. down in the hart uv the wud. Eusa sed, That riting is long gon & aul thay Nos. hav gon owt uv my myn I doan remember nuthing uv them. Woan yu pleas tel me how menne Chaynjis thayr ar? The Littl Man sed, As menne as reqwyrd. Eusa sed, Reqwyrd by wut? The Littl Man sed, Reqwyrd by the idear uv yu. Eusa sed, Wut is the idear uv me? The Littl Man sed, That we doan no til yuv gon thru aul yur Chaynjis."[11]

The Eusa Story within *Riddley Walker* turns on the hunt, the cornering and killing of the great stag. This primal act gives Eusa access to the Addom but also carries with it a curse that perhaps only a conclusive self-knowledge can lift. The imagery of hunting, then, is pivotal; and even hunting dogs play their crucial part in abetting humankind's role—possibly a definitive role—of hunter. When an old wise woman tells Riddley a tale called *Why the Dog Wont Show Its Eyes,* he adds, "theres dogs in the *Eusa Story.* Folleree & Folleroo. Theyre more blip dogs nor real 1s tho."[12] The question Riddley leaves to the reader is what *is* the *blip,* the symbolic significance, of these archetypal hounds? We know that at one time St. Eustace was the patron saint of hunting dogs as well as of hunting and that the words *hunt* and *hound* may share a common origin in a root meaning "to seize."

II

But given my background in the psychology of religion, together with my growing apprehension about the confrontative buildup of nuclear weapons by the United States and the Soviet Union, I thought I saw a further significance in Russell Hoban's use of the imagery of the stag hunt, hounds, and the domestication of wild dogs. Returning to the review of his novel in the *Bulletin of the Atomic Scientists,* for instance, we could ponder Penelope Mesic's answer to the question, Why do nuclear arms continue to be made and nuclear power plants continue to be built? Her response is that "the defect in question is not a failure of our moral nature, or there would be no hope, but a failure of our imagination, which is remediable."[13]

Although the academic field of religious studies would not seem to be in the first rank of those enterprises that might remedy the failure of imagination Mesic describes, nevertheless a decent sensitivity within the field toward the primary imaginative language of symbol, rite, and myth could make a valuable contribution. It could at least point us in the direction of those texts that harbor the images capable of illuminating our horror at the nuclear apocalypse we face, images capable, even, of giving us some fresh purchase on its causes and, perhaps, antidotes. It is through such sensitivities, in other words, that those of us engaged in religious studies can help in the much-needed reimagining that must accompany continuing practical efforts to forestall what will come to pass only a few short years from now according to the fictive world history of *Riddley Walker.*

The attempt to participate in the reimagining Penelope Mesic recommends need not focus on Hoban's novel alone. For example, a radio dramatization of Walter Miller, Jr.'s science-fiction classic, *A Canticle for Leibowitz,* allowed me once again to literally listen to a series of images. And once again they were images of a post-nuclear holocaust society struggling to find some meaning in its shattered legacy and regain a measure of scientific prowess. One episode of the story seemed to have special significance.

At this point in the story, Thon Taddeo, the most brilliant secular scientist of his time, visits the abbey where the "Memorabilia" from the time of the "Flame Deluge" have been preserved for nearly 1200 years. Thon Taddeo hopes to recover some of the wisdom of the twentieth century physicist Leibowitz, wisdom that had led to such marvels as the "electrical essence" capable of producing artificial light—and to the "Flame Deluge" as well. When the manuscripts from the Leibowitzian times were brought out of their storage vault, the story tells us, "The thon's assistant assembled several pounds of notes. After the fifth day of it, Thon Taddeo's pace quickened, and his manner reflected the eagerness of a hungry hound catching scent of tasty game."[14] Later discussions between Taddeo and the abbot make it clear that the former has no concern whatsoever for the moral implications of his findings, any more than the hungry hound would care about the tasty game—or "red meat," to remain faithful to the radio version—it was hunting. Here, the image of the hound pursuing its quarry is again used to convey the assault of science upon the secrets of nature, an assault we are obviously meant to see as heading toward a renewal of the holocaust of twelve centuries earlier.

This one brief image in a 278-page book, or rather in a seven-and-a-half-hour radio adaptation, can hardly be put forward as central to Walter Miller's novelistic vision of the nuclear horror. But hearing it after an initial engagement with Hoban's *Riddley Walker* added to the dawning sense that hounds and hunting might have something to teach imaginations locked into the global nuclear stalemate of distrust, deterrence, and deployment. Certainly, I recalled the depiction of Taddeo the amoral scientist as a hungry hound when I stood before the wall painting of St. Eustace at Canterbury.

III

In mid-June 1983, I attended a conference at Newport, Rhode Island, on the theme "Facing Apocalypse." This gathering attempted to look at the nuclear threat through minds attuned to *imagining* what has increasingly seemed worth considering only as a *literal* reality; that is, the end of the world. In facing the nonliteral possibilities of apocalypse from the directions of religious studies, psychology, the history of consciousness, peace activism, and poetry, the conference wanted to give a "face" to apocalypse in our time, an imaginal and therefore flexible identity that could allow us thinkable alternatives to acting out an inevitable physical annihilation.

The series of lectures and discussions at this conference drew me into the effort I am reporting in this chapter: to reimagine the nuclear horror with images I had heard in the novels by Russell Hoban and Walter Miller. The lecturer in Newport whose words were most influential in this regard was Wolfgang Giegerich. His words did not even involve any images of hunting or hounds, but what I heard in his paper provided the context within which those particular images first began to sound in a new key.

Giegerich was a Jungian psychoanalyst from Stuttgart, West Germany, whose talk, "Saving the Nuclear Bomb," began with the admission that the title sounds perverse, that of course *we* are the ones who need saving from the threat of the bomb. But, as he quickly pointed out, he did not mean by "saving the nuclear bomb" that we should safeguard its proliferating production from attempts at "freezes." Rather, he proposed that we protect the bomb from our indifference to its inner symbolic nature, from our failure to heed its imaginal reality.

Our modern frame of mind prevents us from hearing the message of things, Giegerich stated, the streams and trees and animals and objects that once spoke, for instance, in fairy tales. Today, we discard things before ever letting them claim our attention.

> And of all things, it is particularly the nuclear bomb that is speaking to us today. Indeed, it is not merely murmuring like the fairy tale brook or whispering like the wind, it is yelling, shrieking, louder and louder, becoming ever more extreme, so that we need more and more noise, 24-hour TV, disco music, the loudness of high feelings or, on the other hand, perhaps something like the deafening silence of meditation to block out the voice of reality. Because there is no ear to listen to the message the real things have to impart, reality may well have to work itself up to its last resort, to the din of a nuclear explosion—to at least make itself felt, if not heard.[15]

This, then, is what Giegerich had in mind with his perverse title: "Saving the nuclear bomb," he said, "means a third way beyond the entire alternative of pro or con, war or peace. It means listening to its voice, seeing its face, acknowledging its reality, and releasing it into its own essence."[16] And the aim of the lecture, given this perspective, was to move the members of the audience to a point where they might gain a glimpse of the bomb's true countenance, "an inkling of its message."[17]

To approach this point Giegerich chose a roundabout route: a discussion of the history of our attitudes toward nature, from the time when it surrounded us as a menacing wilderness to the time, right now, when we surround it and must protect it as if it were a problem child or senile parent. He traced, with specific historical examples, the process of transition between these two very different situations. Moreover, he commented on science as the continuing extension of this reversal of the relation of nature to human culture:

> In order to establish a truly safe and rational world as the *foundation* of existence, that is, in order to bring salvation to the world and to man, everything irrational had to be shoved one by one from the endless wilderness around us to an interior encircled by us. The labor and process of this moving the irrational from "out there" around us to "in here" is called science, scientific progress.[18]

At the end of the path of scientific progress, according to Giegerich, lies the bomb:

> The utmost result to date of this endeavor to create a world of salvation no longer imbedded in and thus exposed to terror is the nuclear bomb, into the shell and behind the shell of which has been collected and concentrated all the terror that previously had been *spread out* all over the world. . . . It was the counterphobic crusade against the imaginal terror that itself produced the first *literally* existing terror—the very real possibility of an actual and total apocalypse.[19]

IV

The exact connection between Wolfgang Giegerich's startling thesis and my preferred imagery was far from clear to me as I left Newport. I knew by then, however, that it had to do with that fateful reversal upon which he had based his analysis. The domestication of wild dogs and the entire enterprise of hunting, searching out and seizing a quarry with the aid of hounds, came to seem an especially edifying episode in the historical turnabout Giegerich had charted from propitiating the powers of nature to surrounding and dominating them. A few weeks later I received additional support for this surmise from a quite different quarter, reassuring me that my early inferences were not abandoning the images themselves.

The July 1983 issue of *Ms.* magazine contained an article by a woman who was the daughter of a Cherokee mother and a father engaged in secret nuclear research. Marilou Awiakta had in fact grown up during the early 1940s in Knoxville, with her father commuting to the atomic energy facilities at Oak Ridge. For the title of her article she used two questions she frequently asked as a child in those years: "What is the atom, Mother? Will it hurt us?"

By the time she was asking these questions the bomb had already been dropped on Japan, but her mother's reply was not that the atom is inherently evil or that we should cease our inquiries into its nature and uses: "'We have to have reverence for its nature,'" she cautioned her daughter, "'and learn to live in harmony with it'."[20]

Now, some forty years after her childhood experiences, Marilou Awiakta says that "all is not well with the atom," citing the Three Mile Island accident and antinuclear protests. However, she continues to echo her mother's call for a reverence in dealing with it, an attitude that is closer to Giegerich's sense of "saving the nuclear bomb" than to simple opposition. "We must also take time," she observes, "to ponder our affinities with the atom and to consider that our responsibilities for its use are more profound than we may have imagined."[21] In pointing this out, she sounds a familiar note: the need for a more sensitively attuned imagination in the midst of political or strategic preoccupations. Noting with the physicist Neils Bohr that "'when it comes to atoms, the language can be used only as in poetry',"[22] and with Albert Einstein that "'the unleashed power of the atom has changed everything save our modes of thinking',"[23] she closes with an image that heeds the advice of Bohr and Einstein while connecting with the imagery arising from *Riddley Walker* and *A Canticle for Leibowitz*. Awiakta's own preferred image for dealing with the issues she raises is "the sacred white deer of the Cherokee, leaping in the heart of the atom":

> My ancestors believed that if a hunter took the life of a deer without asking its spirit for pardon, the immortal Little Deer would track the hunter to his home and cripple him. The reverent hunter evoked the white deer's blessing and guidance.
>
> For me, Little Deer is a symbol of reverence. Of hope. Of belief that if we humans relent our anger and create a listening space, we may attain harmony with the atom in time.[24]

The sort of "listening space" Marilou Awiakta was hoping for was also, I sensed, the most important contribution that scholarship and teaching in religious studies could offer. Within such a space, the image of hunting reverberated again, now touched with Native American and feminist sensibilities, in Awiakta's vision of the sacred Little Deer leaping in the heart of the atom. It seemed to be almost a composite of Hoban's male, Christian-oriented figures, the Hart uv the Wud and Littl Shynin Man, the Addom. All these figures spoke of a choice placed before us: if human beings must hunt, we can hunt with a spirit of scientific domination, bent only on capturing our prey, or with a spirit of sacred reverence, respecting nature as an independent reality of infinite worth.

Awiakta had more hope than Hoban that we might still choose the way of reverence and thus save ourselves from catastrophe. Yet a lurking pessimism over attaining the harmony that comes from reverence may be concealed in her closing phrase: "we may attain harmony with the atom in time" is a double entendre, intended or otherwise. At some vague future time, "in good time," she says, we may achieve such a relationship. But unless we do so *in time,* she also implies, before it is too late, there may *be* no future, *no* "good time" for a slowly ripening harmony to happen.

Sometime after my encounter with the July 1983 issue of *Ms.,* I reread novelist John Fowles' long essay, *The Tree,* finding there the passage that offered clinching evidence that the images I had begun listening to and listening for were at least significant clues to the meaning of the nuclear horror. It is not just that Fowles refers to a depiction of the legend of St. Eustace. It is rather the point he tries to make with this reference that seems corroborative. He begins by noting "the inability of such artists as Pisanello and Durer to compass the reality of the wild—for all their honesty in other things, such as human portraiture, to look nature entire in the face."[25] Then he focuses on the specific painting that provided the link between his larger discussion and my own preoccupations:

> We all have our favourite pictures, or ikons, and one of mine has long been a painting by Pisanello in the National Gallery in London, *The Vision of St. Eustace;* the saint-to-be sits on his horse in a forested wilderness—he is out hunting—arrested before his vision of a stag bearing Christ crucified between its antlers. Other animals, birds and flowers crowd the background of the small picture. The artifice of the ensemble, above all when compared with Pisanello's own survived work-sketches of individual beast and bird in it, is almost total. . . . I know no picture that demonstrates more convincingly, and touchingly, this strange cultural blindness; and it is fitting that Pisanello should have chosen the patron saint of dogs (and formerly of hunting, before St. Hubert usurped that role) as the central figure, and distorter of the non-human life around him. What is truly being hounded, harried and crucified in this ambiguous little masterpiece is not Christ, but nature itself.[26]

Fowles makes no connections between the moral he draws from the Pisanello painting and the nuclear threat. His notion that nature itself is being hounded in this vision, however, certainly accords with the atom-splitting quest of Eusa in the deep forest of matter—as also with Wolfgang Giegerich's idea about where nature had been hounded *to:* to the last possible hiding place within the bombshell, where it finally must turn and confront us with the very unmanageable wildness we thought we had hunted down and eliminated.

Voltaire had remarked sarcastically on the wickedness of animals in defending themselves when attacked, but Fowles extends the thought: "There is a deeper wickedness still in Voltaire's unregenerate animal. It won't be owned, or more precisely it will not be dis-animated, unsouled, by the manner in which we try to own it. When it is owned, it disappears."[27] Disappears into the shell and becomes the nuclear bomb, Giegerich would doubtless add. And it does so after giving us the warning to which our imagination may be as deaf as Eusa's: "The stag sed, Eusa yu ar talkin tu the Hart uv the Wud. Nuthin wil run frum yu enne mor but tym tu cum & yu wil run frum evere thing."

V

In mid-February of 1984, Russell Hoban replied generously to my inquiry of the previous month. He said he had not read John Fowles' essay but observed that Fowles would have been working on it while he was writing *Riddley Walker* and allowed that Fowles' "comment about nature itself being hounded" was "interesting."

As for the implications of his own novel, Hoban attested that "when I saw the St. Eustace painting the whole world of *Riddley Walker* jumped into my head." Beyond this, he admitted, "it could well be that Walter Miller's *A Canticle for Leibowitz* which I read as a short story years ago was also in my mind." He closed his letter by reminding me that "the possibility of a nuclear war is only one aspect of the work against nature," citing the obstruction of the ozone layer, the "greenhouse effect," acid rain, defoliation, and ocean pollution as examples of "the casual waste of our ecosphere." "None of the dooms impending," he concluded, "can be looked at separately from what we are. *Riddley Walker* addresses itself to various of the mysteries of what we are: to the mystery of our drive to make things happen whatever the cost, to the mystery of the oneness that is always dividing itself into twoness, and to other aspects of the strangeness of our being."

This mystery of what Hoban's Eusa called, for all of us, "the idear uv me," the nature of human nature that the Littl Man told him "we doan no til yuv gon thru aul yur Chaynjis," is inseparable, Hoban believes, from all the "dooms impending." What does the image of humankind the hunter—or perhaps simply *man* the hunter, the predatory masculine in human culture[28]—

teach us about this mystery and therefore these dooms? If the threat of nuclear war is but one aspect of the work against nature, it is surely the most dramatic, the doom impending that more than all other threats to planetary survival should be hardest to deny if only because it can be fulfilled in an instant. Whether humankind as hunter is the cause of this horror; whether the hunter is responsible for that hounding of nature which Giegerich and Fowles and even *A Canticle for Leibowitz* associate with science; whether the hunter, the hounder, is the scientist; and whether this figure, in turn, is the nuclear war maker (however unwittingly): these are questions we may not finally answer until we truly go through all our changes and complete our evolution— assuming we allow ourselves to do so.

But the attentive imagination to which those of us in religious studies can contribute will want to let images such as the hunter with his hounds inform our understanding of how we have come to the point of annihilating ourselves and our planet. The attentive imagination will want to take seriously the images from our deep or recent past that may help us conceive a safer future, one more nearly free from this horror. These could be images like the antlered shaman on the cave wall at Trois Freres; the goddess Artemis turning Actaeon into a stag whose own hounds then turn against him; the head of the Celtic god Cernunnos, again antlered, embossed on the Gundestrup cauldron from Denmark; the Teutonic legend of Wodin's Wild Hunt; the symbolism of the unicorn in the lap of a virgin; the figure of the Questing Beast making its horrific noise of hounds on the chase in Malory's *Morte D'Arthur.* Or perhaps something more contemporary might speak to us: the deer hunter who goes to fight in Vietnam in a popular film, or the deer killed by Karen Silkwood's car in another.[29]

At some point, of course, it would be fair to ask what one *does* with the images one hears. It is difficult, given the threat we are facing—and we may be facing it partly because of our failure to give it an adequately imaginal "face"—it is difficult to be patient with orientations that do not lead directly to effective action. Even the second-order insights of the religious studies scholar, presumably, should enable us to change the situation for the better, make some political difference.

Unfortunately, I cannot at this point say that my own call to listen to the imagery of the hounding of nature or otherwise to reimagine the nuclear horror will lead to the "new forms of collective behavior" cited by Joanna Rogers Macy, the South Asian religion scholar who has become an activist and workshop leader on nuclear issues as well. I admire her efforts and can certainly see, as she describes them, the value of a peace walk or a peace encampment, such as the one at the Greenham Common missile base in England.[30] But although listening to images in the way I have been attempting to do may only represent a complement to the movement into action, or a pause for new forms of collective *reflection* rather than a concrete and immediate step, I would continue to propose it.

VI

I have been instructed in this resolve by a modest synchronicity of which I was only made conscious upon receiving Russell Hoban's letter in early 1984. It happened that he enclosed with it a rambling, almost agonized personal and historical meditation by an English Jungian analyst, David Holt. The essay "Riddley Walker and Greenham Common: Further Thoughts on Alchemy, Christianity and the Work Against Nature," had originally been a lecture delivered in London on the same day, almost a year earlier, that I had stood before the wall painting of St. Eustace's vision in Canterbury Cathedral.

Whether the coincidence at work here should be considered meaningful by anyone besides me is less important than the concluding thoughts Holt has helped me to entertain and prompted me to pass on. His essay contains no discussion of hunting, stags, or hounds. But it moves *between* the novel *Riddley Walker* and the moral imperative of Greenham Common in such a way as to give value to exactly the sort of reimagining I was and am pursuing.

Holt says at the outset that he is trying to let something sound, and be heard, between "two voices":

> On the one hand there is a voice which speaks of the future. It says: there is an act of violence which must not be allowed to happen. We will not let it happen. That is the voice I hear coming from the women camped outside the Cruise missile base at Greenham Common. On the other hand there is a voice which speaks of a future which is already past. It says: there is an act of violence which has already been. Trying to remember it is what keeps us going. That is the voice I hear coming from Russell Hoban's book *Riddley Walker*.[31]

Here, once more, is the image, if you will, of *listening to images*. But beyond that the listening Holt advises is attending to images that come from a chord struck by the blending of both past and future, reflection and activism. Or rather, since he does not actually talk in any detail about Greenham Common, the listening is primarily to the voice of *Riddley Walker* and the "act of violence which has already been," with the voice from the peace encampment kept in mind as counterpoint. In other words, the constant accompaniment of the act of violence that must not be allowed to happen gives a different sound to the voice of Hoban's novel and all that the latter implies about happenings in a half-understood past long ago—such as the hunts and hunters of myth and legend, or the domestication of wild dogs, or the rise of modern science. When we hear the activists' call to preserve the future, these images of the past speak ever louder of the violent hounding of nature, the growing scientific urge to capture and dominate nature by rendering it a collection of mere lifeless objects. They tell us something profoundly important and potentially liberating that we might not otherwise have heard. Perhaps they tell us that only those who hear and reflect on the images of the past can be open to the call of the future.

It is in the spirit of this contrapuntal listening, finally, that I would recommend this process of reimagining to colleagues in religious studies who hope to relate their professional calling to the overriding human issue clamoring for our attention today. I believe, after all, that our sensitivities are in some ways uniquely suited to hearing the messages that images carry. As inhabitants of the modern age, of course, we, too, have had our ears somewhat stopped up by scientific objectivity and the literalizing consciousness that it brings. We, too, must make a special effort to remember the metaphoric mode that is the native tongue of the imagination. But we may be closer than others to the kind of openness that listening requires—the kind of reverence that images, like nature itself, ask of us.

Images are like nature itself. Indeed they are the essence of human nature, harboring a creativity and unpredictability that both enrich and threaten us. As we listen to the hounding of nature we are also listening to the process that has caged up our inner imagining, trying in vain to avoid the threat of the unknown. What we hear may be the footsteps of our own self-understanding—"the idear uv me"—fading into obscurity. Without an openness to our own inner images, how can we know ourselves? If our literalizing objectivity has destroyed what is most essential about us, how can we avoid destroying ourselves? If we are deaf to the violence of the past recorded in human imagination, how can we hear the violence coming in the all-too-pressing future?

But perhaps this self-destructive deafness is actually what we want. David Holt concludes by reminding us of how much is hidden from view inside our own psyches as well as in our nuclear bombs. He urges us to disclose to each other, and thereby defuse, the masochistic wish we may have projected into our future just because it has been hidden in our nature and our history. Holt grants that the possibility that "we should wish for anything so appalling as nuclear war"[32] sounds highly unlikely. But he goes on to say why confronting just such a possibility is crucial and how it will require a remembering, a telling, and a listening, which religious studies is well equipped to teach:

> This unlikeliness of the link between wish and fear is our greatest danger. This is what can make imagination seize up, prevent reflection, and commit

us to totalitarian solutions, whether they be military, political, religious, scientific. To meet it, we need each other's help. There are experiences to be shared which are blind and dumb, still embedded in a matrix of emotion, fear and anguish. To get them into politics, we have to get them into history, into a telling in which we have public as well as private parts.

Such telling requires that we be willing to give of ourselves so that others may have something to get their teeth into. Whatever the wish may be that mushrooms hiddenly in our fear of nuclear holocaust, it is unlikely to objectify itself in discourse if we are shy or embarrassed of appearing absurd, suffering or in anguish.

And the telling requires that we listen, listen as we may never have listened before. A mute witness waits to be heard. . . . To hear its story, our ears should be attentive to something at least as unlikely as the word becoming flesh.[33]

VII

In the summer of 1985, during a trip to England, I was able to meet and talk with David Holt at his home in Oxford. I asked him how his essay had been received. He replied that he had gotten some favorable letters about it but he feared his academic friends disapproved of his going into print with a piece so frankly impressionistic, unsystematically speculative, confessional, and even, in a real sense, unfinished. From my own years of reading and writing academic prose, I could understand that most scholars would have preferred he wait to publish his thoughts until he could couch them in a more conventional mode, one in which he could draw a clear line of argumentation and a definitive conclusion.

However, hearing of this negative reaction I recalled Einstein's oft-quoted words, and wondered if the change in our modes of thinking that he felt was imperative in the nuclear age would ever come about if scholars (among others) were not willing to take some risks in the direction of the sort of heartfelt reimagining Holt and I were attempting. Whatever alteration in thought-style Einstein had hoped for, it was surely long overdue forty years after the explosion in the New Mexico desert that changed everything else.

I left Oxford and pressed on north into Scotland, crossing the border at Gretna near huge nuclear cooling towers, and later passing a nuclear submarine cruising out into the Firth of Clyde from its base at Holy Loch. I eventually ended up at Edinburgh, depressed and perplexed over the juxtaposition of beautiful green glens and misty lochs with these reminders of how we could cancel such beauty in an instant.

I listened to the guide at Holyrood Palace explain that according to legend the abbey that preceded the palace on the site was erected at the behest of David I, King of the Scots, who in 1128 was wounded by a stag while hunting in the forest near where the abbey ruins and palace now sit. When he grabbed the stag's antlers to save himself, he found he was holding a rood (cross) that grew from the stag's forehead. "Seizing this holy weapon," as the guide put it, the king was able to fend off the stag. That night, in a dream, he heard a voice commanding him to make a house for canons devoted to the cross, and thus was founded the abbey, and later the palace, of the Holy Rood. Three different guidebooks on the palace agree that this tale is derivative from the legend of St. Eustace. The history of an image echoed in my ears, along with the history of words: *to hunt, to hound, to seize.*

A few weeks after my return to the United States, at a symposium on the earth as a living organism, I met an accomplished botanist who objected good-naturedly to my religionist jibes about the excesses of science and technology in the nuclear age. He had never heard of *Riddley Walker,* let alone St. Eustace, he said, but in his spare time he had just finished writing a novel himself. It concerned the hunting of the last grizzly bear in California and how this act was somehow related to events at the Diablo Canyon nuclear power plant. I listened as he went on. . . .

Part IV

Reflective Religious Thought

G. CLARKE CHAPMAN

Chapter 8

Approaching Nuclearism as a Heresy

Until recently, few people have noticed that the nuclear arms race is a theological issue.[1] This is curious. As the preceding chapters in this volume have demonstrated, there seem to be multiple layers of religious meaning in our preparations for planetary suicide. We may notice especially two functional criteria of religion: wholeness and ultimacy.

Wholeness, whatever pertains to the totality of our being, has traditionally been labeled sacred. Certainly nuclear weapons affect that totality, for they pose a virtually boundless threat to all of life. *Ultimate concern,* even worship, is our response to whatever affects our deepest weal and woe. And the Bomb may well qualify—both in the objective and subjective dimensions of what we mean by *ultimacy*. It is objectively ultimate, as the cumulative effect of hundreds of explosions could unleash a nuclear winter that would end history. And it also seems subjectively ultimate; each of us could probably confess a secret awe before the atom, a sense of fear yet fascination, helplessness yet exhilaration, as if we stood before divine retribution and omnipotence.

So, like it or not, our supposedly secular world has been tossed by nuclear technology into the midst of theological problems. This has long been intuited by science fiction, popular films, and preachers of Armageddon. It has been used for titillation or entertainment, but now it is time for all of us to take it seriously.

An analysis of this new covert religiousness is offered by Robert Jay Lifton. Naming it *nuclearism*, he describes it as the passionate embrace of nuclear weapons as a solution to death anxiety and a way of restoring a lost sense of immortality. Nuclearism is a secular religion, a total ideology in which "grace" and even "salvation"—the mastery of death and evil—are achieved through the power of a new technological deity. The deity is seen as capable not only of apocalyptic destruction but also of unlimited creation. And the nuclear believer or "nuclearist" allies himself with that power. . . . As with any religion, embrace of nuclearism is likely to be marked by a "conversion experience"—an immersion in death anxiety followed by rebirth into the new world view. At the heart of the conversion experience is an overwhelming sense of awe—a version of Freud's "oceanic feeling" in which one's own insignificance in relationship to the larger universe is so extreme as to feel oneself, in effect, annihilated.[2]

John McDargh's chapter in this book (Chapter 6) ably summarizes Lifton's view of the historical origins of this predicament. Over the years, the traditional ways of symbolizing the continuity of life have been eroded. By now, the modern psyche finds itself terribly exposed to death anxiety. Panicked, we throw ourselves into assorted ideologies that claim to cover total reality. Nuclearism became the culmination of this frenzy. A sacred awe of nuclear weapons is spawned by our amorphous fears, the incomprehensibility of their effects, the sense of grasping the infinite by tapping a primal cosmic force, and an awareness of creaturely vulnerability. In support of his argument Lifton quotes the strikingly religious language used by early eyewitnesses of atomic blasts[3] (see Aho's summary in this book, Chapter 4).

Lifton's analysis is persuasive: we have fallen into the grips of a new and ominous religiousness. But is there no alternative? What can we do? Here I wish to move a couple of steps beyond Lifton, by offering two theses: (1) nuclearism is not only a covert religion but ought to be judged a "heresy"; and (2) the best way to counter this or any false belief system is by eroding the preconceptual models (or paradigms) on which it depends.

JUDGING NUCLEARISM A HERESY

Ought we to go so far as to speak of heresy? Admittedly it is risky because of all the unsavory images and bitter memories it conjures up. Many of these have accrued over the centuries to a word that originally designated a choice of factional or sectarian opinion, hence a one-sided view of a holistic faith perspective. Nowadays bigotry or intolerance is widely recognized as morally wrong, so the word *heresy* may sound outmoded. Every world religion, in fact, tolerates in its midst quite a variety of subgroups and deviations; but toleration may not always be a virtue. From time to time an extreme may be judged so discordant as to threaten the basic identity of a given faith. Every believing community reserves the implicit right to exclude such a mortal threat. It is not a question of good guys versus bad guys, nor of conscientious dissenters versus authority figures, but of an unending contention for wholeness over partiality. That is so, regardless of which opinion is in the majority or the minority. To avoid heresy (or whatever synonym is preferred) is to strive unceasingly to recover the believing community's original vision and to articulate it afresh in our time.

In Protestant history, for instance, the term describing such an occasion is *status confessionis*, a special state of confessing the faith in crisis. Thus, early Lutherans responded to circumstances that, though at first glance innocuous, in actuality put the gospel at risk. Likewise, in our century the Christian churches have been called to a time of special confession of faith in response to Nazism (The Barmen Declaration, 1934) and to South African apartheid (Lutheran World Federation, 1977; Dutch Reformed Mission Church, 1982; the Kairos document of 1985).[4]

Now some voices are calling for a similar confessional stand against the Bomb. For example the Reformed Alliance in Germany proclaimed in 1982 "the issue of peace is a confessional issue. In our opinion the *status confessionis* is given to it because the attitude taken toward mass destruction has to do with the affirmation or denial of the gospel itself."[5] The condemnation here is not of the weapons themselves, but of an idolatrous frame of mind. The issue is less one of munitions than of mindset. Prudential reason might continue arguing forever the circumstances under which the Bomb might or might not be justified. But confessing the faith identifies that idolatry which so befuddles our analyses in the first place.

Using the cases of Nazi Germany and modern South Africa as precedents, we may then venture to hope that nuclearism will likewise prompt the churches and synagogues to recover their own identities in time of crisis. Just as totalitarian racism has been a pseudoreligion threatening the core of Christian or Jewish belief, so is the "totalism" (Lifton's word) of nuclear weapons and their pretentious claims to wholeness and ultimacy. Our hopes for such a reformation must go beyond a few official pronouncements by religious leaders, although they may be helpful. It is far more important that ordinary believers at the grass-roots level struggle to rethink their faith in response to this identified threat, so that from a myriad of such local struggles a new consensus may arise. If Lifton's analysis of nuclearism as an unconscious but functional religion is accurate, then surely the conscious extirpation of this "-ism" is a prerequisite for any modern renewal of Judeo-Christian faith. That truly would be a new reformation.

To avoid self-righteousness, however, the struggle against heresy should be done with humility and a contrite awareness of our own complicity in the very totalism that has gained such popular credence. We do not need witch-hunts or scapegoats. What we do need is prayer, patient self-examination, and an eager hope for new stirrings of God's Spirit in history. Perhaps therefore the latent images of investigator and prosecutor, so customary in ideological contests, should be put aside, and instead the image of the midwife adopted. Midwives historically have served a vital function. They do not force themselves or their preconceptions on the situation or waste time blaming or coercing those around them; instead with patience and skill, they assist a birthing process that they are confident is already underway. And so is born a new life—or a renewed faith—a wholeness that is both new and yet in continuity with the past. With this image in mind, then, people of faith may gently but persistently labor to help their communities of belief come to a new time of confession, a time of spiritual renewal amid the nuclear age.

FACING THE HERESY OF NUCLEARISM AS MIDWIVES

So our discussion has brought us already to the second thesis. Once we grant that nuclearism should be judged a heresy, the question immediately follows of how best to counter it. Little help is found in the history of Western Christianity, with its unhappy succession of schisms and sects, powerplays and persecutions. The time-honored means of repressing error by sword or anathema seem today to have been quite dubious, in terms of both effectiveness and morality. Yet, if we are not to lapse into a swamp of relativism, we dare not despair of truth or jettison the quest for what is truly whole and ultimate. So if a struggle against heresy is to have any value today, it must proceed differently than have past contests. New approaches are required—and not least because nuclearism so easily infects our own unexamined thinking as well!

A driving force behind any belief system is its unnoticed assumptions. Unarticulated preconceptual models of the basic nature of reality are taken for granted, yet quietly regulate the grounding of our ideas. Indeed every world view or ideology, whether claiming to be "religious" or not, has a dimension of faith. That is inevitable, for all our human perceptions are partial constructs; the buzz and blur of all the data around us gain meaning only as they are filtered and shaped by the hunches we supply. Another name for these implicit models is *paradigm*, a term popular since Thomas Kuhn illuminated how even physical science is influenced by such perceptual frameworks. Indeed, revolutions in the history of science often follow a "paradigm shift."[6] The geocentric view of the solar system, for example, was superseded not by new discoveries, but by a new image; afterwards, the evidence fell into place. From these studies in the natural sciences we may infer that the same process pertains to other fields of controversy, such as politics or religion. In short, a change of mind and loyalty is caused not so much by debate and conceptual arguments as by the arrival of a new model of thinking—a shift of paradigms.

This helps explain why the arms race is so intractable, and the peace movement seems to have so few successes. Chapter 2 of this book, by contrast, shows the success of the Committee on the Present Danger in winning public acceptance for its paradigms of danger and security, despite the alternate models advanced by its critics. The lesson to be learned is that the nuclear threat will not diminish until the nations attain what Michael Nagler calls "peace as a paradigm shift."[7] This lesson is not new, but goes back more than forty years to the famous words of Albert Einstein: "The unleashed power of the atom has changed everything except our ways of thinking. Thus we are drifting toward an unparalleled catastrophe. We shall require a substantially new manner of thinking if man is to survive."[8]

Certainly, it is at the preconceptual level that nuclearism must be engaged. This is where theology should have a crucial role to play within the peace movement, for theology analyzes and criticizes the basic symbols humans use to express whatever they perceive to be both total and ultimate. Clear theological thinking is a midwifely duty needed in our time. And, like midwives, we should trust that our human efforts are not alone, but that God is already at work—in this context, by creating a more peaceful world. In the case of Christianity, for instance, our struggle toward a *status confessionis* about nuclearism and the gathering of a new "confessing church" movement could well coincide with and herald a fresh reformation.

FOUR PARADIGMS OF NUCLEARISM

Therefore, let us now sketch how a theological examination of the paradigms behind nuclearism might begin. The following examples are only rudimentary, for obviously a belief system that is so deeply entrenched in the public psyche will need a sustained and team-led critique if it is ever to be dislodged.

We will consider four preconceptual models upon which nuclearism depends: power viewed narrowly as "violence," life together seen in Cold War terms as "zero-sum gaming," future hope deformed into "worst case analysis," and faith misconstrued as "official optimism." So deeply embedded are these assumptions that they are not easily raised to the conscious level. Yet doing so may begin to strip them of the very aura of inviolability that makes them so credible. Our procedure will be in each case to ask three demystifying questions: First, what view of ultimate reality is implied? Second, how does our society show symptoms of this paradigm? Third, what are some of its personal manifestations in daily experience? Finally, to show that alternative and more wholesome views of the four themes do exist within the world's great religions, and selecting Christianity as our normative example, we will suggest briefly how the Christian scriptures offer a peaceable alternate paradigm for the same topic.[9]

Power as Violence

Power, our first topic, is usually defined as the ability to do or act; that is, to actualize what is latent in the very nature of things. Obviously, the notions of power and reality are closely linked! No wonder that a display of power of any kind, whether physical or social, both awes and fascinates the public, and inevitably evokes a "religious" response. The unprecedented energy release of the first atom bombs in 1945 could hardly fail to be regarded religiously, as we have seen in the quotations assembled by Lifton and Aho. Unfortunately, it also reinforced in the public mind the tendency to view power in mainly physical and even violent terms.

Such a view is partly true—but only partly. It is also true that conflict and struggle are universal experiences. But a model of power as violence is a reductionist model, accepting a narrow perception of that tension in coercive, even bloody terms. Nuclearism builds upon that, taking to an extreme Thomas Hobbes' grisly view that the human situation is simply "that condition which is called *war;* and such a war as is of every man against every man."[10] Unfortunately, there are also strands within many world religions that justify such conflictual behavior—from the zealous nationalist tradition begun by Phinehas' blood purge (Numbers 25) to the holy wars of medieval Christendom and the Puritans.[11] Today, we note a resurgence of such militancy in Jewish, Christian, and Islamic fundamentalism, in areas around the globe torn by bloodshed.

First, any thought model rests on a primal notion of what after all is the "really real." The model of power as violence comes down to the assumption that reality is finally mechanistic and materialistic, even though supernaturalist language may be used by some of its pious advocates. What is real is self-existent units of matter in motion, mindless as well as valueless, and crudely determined by patterns of action-reaction. For organisms this means regulation by seeking pleasure and avoiding pain. So on every level, from the microscopic to the global, power is expressed in exertions to impose or ward off domination, usually by violent means. That comes to mold our expectations in life.

Second, our society has many symptoms of this distorted assumption. Consider for instance the unusually high rates of handgun possession, homicide, and crimes of violence. Our everyday English language is filled with violent metaphors: we "fight" for a cause, "target" an audience, and declare "war" on social ills, or "mobilize" for all sorts of "campaigns." The words *vigilante* and *lynch* are distinctively American terms. Another North American invention, the adventure comic strip of the 1930s, usually glorifies a righteous loner driven to violent excess as the only means of restoring justice and thereby stabilizing reality again. In such contrived situations, surely our hero need feel no guilt! A line from the Dick Tracy strip lays bare the satisfying implicit message: "Violence is golden when it's used to put evil down."[12]

Is this message also a veiled invitation to the public to imitate such swashbuckling forms of power? The media and advertising industries are quick to deny this, claiming that these fantasies, now commonplace in film and TV, are harmless, perhaps even cathartic, but social scientists are not so sure. Admittedly the evidence is ambiguous, but some research suggests that our fundamental notions of reality are indeed influenced by our mass entertainments. George Gerbner of the University of Pennsylvania finds a significant correlation between television watching and a preoccupation in real life with violence; heavy viewers of TV tend to have exaggerated estimates of violence and danger in the "real world" and are more likely to expect to become victims of crime themselves.[13] The conventional barrier we draw between fantasy and reality seems fragile—or even porous! A recent interview with a teenage "Pac-Man Junkie" closed with this unwitting self-revelation: "People say these games make kids more violent, but come on, it's just a game. If anything it kind of shows you what it's really like out in the world. You've got to know what's out there. And you *know* it's all out there."[14]

Third, some personal manifestations of this violent paradigm have been suggested already in discussing the social ones. Especially for socially marginalized individuals, bereft of normal, satisfying human relationships, this warped notion of power may suddenly erupt: an airplane hijacking, an assassination, or some urban vigilante act. But even comparatively healthy citizens in our frustrated, high-tech society may well harbor secret fascinations with violence. The signals may be flaunted through gunracks in the rear window or bumperstickers about "God, guns, and guts." Or the evidence may be muted: few neighborhoods realize that in three out of five households spouses or children are abused at least once.[15]

Most individuals, of course, recognize some inconsistency between overt brutality and public morals. So a high premium is placed on mental devices whereby the incongruity can be softened. This no doubt contributed to the popularity of the New Religious Right in the 1980s. A related device is nostalgia. We are awash with TV ads of Grandmother's kitchen, old-fashioned hearthsides, or family reunions. Such sentimental icons of Main Street USA subtly legitimate a patriarchal vision of "normalcy," a turn-of-the-century never-never land when supposedly women and racial minorities knew their place, schoolmarms used the switch freely, and parents "disciplined" their children. Nostalgia can be an effective ally of reactionary politics or repressive force, as the history of Europe also shows. Those who dream of bygone days when law and order was kept by the Colt .45 Peacemaker are often those who dream today of the MX missile as Peacekeeper. Likewise, as Benford and Kurtz demonstrate (Chapter 5), leadership of the Department of Defense in the 1980s yearned for the "war-fighting" strategies of the prenuclear era, before military force had become impotent by its very excess.

Finally, there are, of course, religious alternatives to such a reductionist paradigm of power. For clarifying the contrast we turn to the example of the Christian scriptures. To begin with, the very premise of mechanistic material-ism is incompatible with theism. For Christians, although the material universe is quite real, it is also dependent in origin and in sustenance on a Creator. By definition it is posited as "the Creation." It is not to be viewed as purposeless or atomistic, for it shares in the Creator's goodness. Nor can it be rooted in incessant strife (or as Hobbes put it, "war"), when it is believed that in Christ "all things hold together," for "all things were created through him and for him" (Colossians 1:16,17). Struggle pervades existence, of course, but it is seen as regulative of life's rhythms and anticipating the birth pangs of a New Age. (See Chapter 10, where Noyalis describes how human peacemaking efforts foreshadow the depth and wholeness of final reality.)

Indeed, the New Testament suggests a further claim. Since God has through Christ become bonded to this "real" world, we find that the true nature of power is not violence at all but nonviolence. The resurrection opens the way to newness of life here and now. Many problems were faced by the earliest Christians but, with few exceptions, they renounced military force as well as other coercive short-cuts. In our time Thomas Merton wrote, "nonviolence must be realistic and concrete. . . . But precisely the advantage of nonviolence is that it has a *more Christian and more humane notion of what is possible.*"[16] Instead of a "fetishism of immediate visible results"[17] and the reductionist model of violence, power can be envisioned as a process of nurturing and artistically integrating into higher levels of purposefulness. We may find further midwifely clues to this dynamic process in the writings of Gandhi and Martin Luther King, Jr., for instance, and in current discussions of "civilian based defense."[18]

Life as "Zero-Sum Gaming"

Human life together, our next theme, becomes a pillar of nuclearism when filtered through what is now called *zero-sum gaming*. According to game theory, a field of applied mathematics, some games such as poker are zero-sum because they assume the players' resources are fixed and scarce and distribution is strictly an inverse correlation; that is, any gain by one player requires a corresponding loss for the others. Whatever harms my opponent must benefit me, and vice versa. Participants may enjoy the quick succession of elation and despair as long as it is "only a game," but what if such competitiveness becomes a way of life?

First, the view of ultimate reality implied by this model resembles that of the violence paradigm but also goes further. The world seems not only atomistic and materialist but finite, even diminishing. As the universe winds down, humans are driven to desperation, fighting for survival atop a pile of melting resources. Such a hunch about reality demands that humans become bloody adversaries in the fading twilight of history.

Second, the societal symptoms of this paradigm also overlap those of the false notion of power. Human violence is to be channeled toward our opponents. In our society, care is taken that the young learn this from an early age, albeit in sublimated form. The thousands of hours of TV witnessed by the average child presents a relentless cavalcade of caricatures, "us" versus "them." Pugnacious vigilance thereafter is carried on into adulthood, as we are nurtured by warnings that true romance comes only to those making the right consumer choices or that "the man who wants your job is reading Forbes." Market mechanisms pit each producer against everyone else, and team sports become less an end in themselves and more a partisan means to garner championships and civic pride.

On the international level, our poker games are played for global stakes. The Cold War tally sheet permits only staunch allies or evil empires, with neutrality or local concerns excluded altogether. If an opponent suffers bad crops or social unrest, that is construed as a direct gain for our side; if the same happens to us, it becomes not only a crisis for national security but possibly an enemy plot as well.

Third, our personal lives also are cramped by this adversarial frenzy. Parents compete for their children's affections, convinced that more love for Mommy, say, means less for Daddy. Officemates likewise vie for attention, and often the promotion or praise of one may deepen a sense of personal failure for colleagues. The drive to be "Number One" distorts our leisure hours as well, in the search for winning teams or celebrities with whom to identify or in denigrating gossip about others. This misshapen model of life together is all too familiar. Each of us can recognize lurking within ourselves the appeal of some famous words attributed to coach Vince Lombardi: "Winning is not everything but it is the *only* thing."[19]

Finally, there are alternate ways of imaging our life together. Kenneth Boulding rejects the conventional wisdom of a "static pie of goodies" to be divided somehow. Instead, he says, "Reality is much more complex. There is no single pie, but there is a vast pattern of little tarts, each growing or declining at its own rate."[20] International diplomacy can attain solutions that require neither side to lose but offer gains to all; examples include the nuclear test ban treaty of 1963 and the intermediate nuclear forces treaty of 1987. Such accomplishments rest on what McDargh in Chapter 6, following Eric Erikson, describes as the sense of basic trust and empathy that generative individuals contribute to wider society.

Christians also find in their scriptures a vivid portrayal of human coexistence and fellowship. There contentiousness (Ephesians 4) and self-serving ambition (1 Corinthians 9) are frequently condemned. The genesis of rivalries and hatred is often anxiety about economic scarcities. Scarcity, of course, is no illusory problem, but that does not mean we live in a dying world. The Bible offers instead an encouraging wider vision, a promised fullness of the Holy Spirit that grants, here and now, a foretaste of overwhelming fullness in the Age to Come.[21] Until that fulfillment, the Spirit's chief gift is love. Love spurns the quota mentality and other calibrated responses to human need (1 Corinthians 13:4-7), for its generosity and compassion flow from confidence in the God of reconciliation and hope in the New Creation. When empowered by that vision, life together becomes a reality.

The Future as a "Worst Case Analysis"

Next we examine a curiously inverted form of future hope as a paradigm supporting nuclearism. Chapter 10 by Walter Noyalis explains how war-making extrapolates from the past in a way that makes conflict seem normal, thus blocking openness to a new and better future. In military terms this is called *worst case analysis*. On the battlefield level it may be prudent planning for a commander regularly to overestimate the enemy's forces, while underestimating his own. But on the strategic and diplomatic levels such prudence easily becomes self-serving cynicism. Benford and Kurtz (Chapter 5) show how these scenarios become reified into a part of our social universe. A further example is found in congressional testimony given by the director of defense research and engineering in 1970, explaining why our nation was the first to put multiple warheads on a single missile: "Our current effort to get a MIRV capability on our missiles is not reacting to a Soviet capability so much as it is moving ahead again to make sure that whatever they do of the possible things that we imagine they might do we will be prepared."[22]

But, do not such monumental efforts "to make sure," no matter what "they might do," betray both obsessive behavior and misanthropic hope-lessness? Worst case thinking at this policy-making level perpetuates an unending arms race. In the bluff and posturing required by nuclear deterrence, neither side is likely to be ever satisfied that it has "enough." Indeed, comments Patrick Morgan, "Programs first developed as a hedge against the uncertainties of the future soon come to dictate it."[23] Moreover, this hopelessness guarantees a double standard of judgment. Both superpowers are now deploying new generations of missiles so accurate that they have a capacity of a "disarming first strike" against the adversary. Each superpower, however, denies that such is its intention, while flatly asserting that the other side plans a sneak attack. Clearly such cynicism becomes not only habitual but self-serving.

First the notion of ultimate reality behind hopelessness is an extension of that already surveyed. The cosmos, viewed as an atomistic mechanism and a shrinking storehouse, now becomes outright malicious. Our world is no habitat but an endless boobytrap! The resulting mindset resembles Irving Kristol's definition of a neoconservative: "a liberal who has been mugged by reality."[24] Apparently, one expects such treatment to continue. Humanity is said to live in spite of the cosmos not because of it and with it. The world is reduced to a stage set from some neverending monster movie, with the corollary that the only realism is paranoia.

Second, the social symptoms of this paradigm are seen in the common tendency of human groups to grab for an inequitable share of power, "just in case" of rude surprises from an uncertain future. This happens at all levels, of course, but now it is especially notable on the international scene, in the growing dangers of the arms race. The arsenals of overkill have long since surpassed the minimal demands of Mutually Assured Destruction, for each side is driven to plan according to a "greater-than-expected-threat" from the other. Fear of the future outstrips all other considerations.

There are at least three dangers to this vicious circle of hopelessness. (1) It becomes a self-fulfilling prophecy. Some social science research has found that while "unrealistic trust" of an antagonist is soon corrected by the other's hostile behavior, unfortunately the converse does not happen; in fact *"unrealistic mistrust tends to be self-validating."* (2) Hopelessness forecloses the future by stereotyping the opponent. "The enemy is perceived as evil, but also as operating in monolithic, consistent, rational, sinister, and purposeful ways. Each side minimizes or ignores the existence of conflicting parties and purposes within the opposing group. Also each party attributes to the other a sense of omniscience and rationality that he knows does not exist on his own side."[25] With the aid of a conspiracy theory of evil and a ready heritage of apocalyptic imagery, each superpower feels justified in mobilizing against a satanic foe. (3) Hopelessness is dangerous because it invites an unrestrained arms race, often with tragic results. In a study of 99 "serious disputes" among nations from 1815 to 1965, cited by Bruce Russett, of those that were preceded by an arms race 82 percent ended in war, while of those not so preceded only 4 percent ended in war.[26]

Third, personal forms of worst case thinking betray the future for individuals. We practice two directions of personalized dehumanization. *Object-directed* dehumanization views other persons as either subhuman (e.g., huns, gooks, and such epithets) or superhuman (e.g., the super stud, the yellow peril)—and sometimes both simultaneously! The other category, *self-directed* dehumanization, belittles oneself as a covert way to evade accountability (e.g., "I'm only a cog in the machine; what could I do?"). Either way—or in tandem—the self is seeking protection from the future by an overcompensation in the present. Human interaction is reduced to a primitive level of fear and manipulation by threat. This, by no coincidence, turns out to be a parallel in microcosm of our strategic policy of deterrence.

Finally, there are, of course, alternate visions of the future from the world's religions. Religion, we recall, deals with wholeness and ultimacy. And, it is an anticipation of the wholeness of reality that frees us from the compulsion to force our preconceptions onto the present moment. The U.S. Catholic bishops put it this way, in their 1983 peace pastoral letter: "To believe we are condemned in the future only to what has been the past of U.S.-Soviet relations is to underestimate both our human potential for creative diplomacy and God's action in our midst which can open the way to changes we could barely imagine."[27]

This openness toward the future is sustained for Christians by their Scriptures. The hope of the Kingdom of God is a vision of a shared future, surmounting all worst case fancies and dissolving all enemy phantasms. This mutuality is portrayed in images such as the messianic banquet (Luke 14:15 ff, 22:30; Revelation 19:9), a table fellowship that is explicitly pluralistic (Luke 13:29). Because the future is unitary, it must be shared with all—including those once seen as enemies. Until that glorious future arrives, however, it is most clearly prefigured here and now in a life of mutual forgiveness. For it is through forgiveness that hope attains its most concrete form in the present.

Faith as Official Optimism

Finally, we turn to one of the key supports for the nuclearist heresy, the paradigm of faith seen as official optimism.[28] Will Herberg, a famed sociologist of religion, has described North American religion as founded upon *"faith in faith,"* and he illustrates this by the words of a prominent clergyman: "I begin saying in the morning two words, 'I believe.' These two words *with nothing added* . . . give me a running start for my day"[29] But "to believe" with no object for the verb seems little different from crass self-confidence, even egotism.

This naive tendency rests upon a modern hunger for appearances. For centuries industrialization and modernity have been eroding the traditional bonds and social supports for meaning in human life, leaving individuals exposed to the wintry winds of chaos. Our successive adaptations could never begin to match the accelerations of social change. So a permanent gap widens between substance and appearances in our culture. Meanings have been rendered ephemeral and transitory. In the marketplace packaging sells more than contents, and in elections the candidate's image matters more than qualifications. International relations becomes the artful projection of credibility, national resolve, and "sending the right signal." In short, manipulation of the correct images becomes desperately important in our "officially optimistic society."[30]

Close under the sparkling surface, however, swims a shadowy terror, the dread of vulnerability. Such fear haunts us in the nuclear age, even more than the fear of death. Freud noted that only in its later stages of development could the human mind become aware of death, whereas the experience of helplessness is universal from earliest infancy. Moreover, it seems this dread is even more acute in its social dimensions. Society knits together the canopy of shared meaning that shelters us all, so for a person to glimpse the vulnerability of the group may be more intolerable than glimpsing one's own. In crises such as the battlefield, many individuals choose heroism and readiness to die if only the group can survive. Likewise, a personal "faith in faith" is fed by the wider level of society's "official optimism."

First, the implicit view of ultimate reality behind this model goes beyond materialism, scarcity, and paranoia; indeed, it verges on nihilism. This may surprise those accustomed to the American reputation for invincible confidence in progress. Yet progress is a fairly recent notion in human civilization. No wonder there is a darker intuition of chaos lurking behind the jaunty patter of broadcast news and beaming technocrats. The unspoken and unspeakable suspicion is that perhaps forward motion—like riding a wobbly bicycle—is at best a postponement of collapse.

Second, the social symptoms of this unsteady paradigm are found in the incongruities of our national character. TV ads display life as a beach frolic beckoning us to step over and join in the fun, and smiling entrepreneurs suggest that we be "bullish" and "take stock in [their] America." A favorable climate is needed for investments, expansion, and marketing. So the entire economy bobs and hovers over a steady flow of confidence—much like the old department store demonstrations of vacuum cleaners that kept ping pong balls dancing in mid-air. But the shadow side of such national bravado is never far from the surface. There is little tolerance for frustration when, for instance, Wall Street falters or Iran blusters. Anger, though suppressed, simmers on.

How strange that, in the Land of Opportunity, so much "urban rage" erupts in street crime and freeway shoot-outs.

Likewise in our foreign policy, as we have seen, image comes to outweigh substance. Credibility seems to require a public relations mindset and elaborate rituals to maintain it. The arms race is a consequence, as Richard Barnet points out: "Once the purpose of military spending is to create 'perception,' and weapons are procured primarily as symbols, there is never enough."[31]

Faith as official optimism is a facet of that military nostalgia which longs to return to the prenuclear strategic doctrine of "war-fighting." This "win" mentality might be applauded as a heartening expression of team spirit and idealism, but instead, claims George Kennan, it turns out to be a masquerade. "There is no hope in it—only horror. It can be understood only as some form of subconscious despair on the part of its devotees—some sort of death wish, a readiness to commit suicide for fear of death." It is not faith at all, but its opposite. It becomes in fact an "inability to face the normal hazards and vicissitudes of the human predicament, a lack of faith, or better a lack of the very strength it takes to have faith."[32]

Third, of course, there are personal manifestations of this paradigm in daily life as well. Celebrities must exude self-confidence to retain their fans' adulation, and relentless optimism is mandated for any who aspire to leadership of the home team, the home town, or the ship of state. For North Americans, religion (whether of the conservative or liberal varieties) is popular and even commercially successful to the extent that it helps bolster the uncertain ego amid a high-tech society. Bookstore shelves are heavy with volumes of self-help, reassurance, and human potential nostrums, and box office hits often are those films or musicals that aid us in feeling good about ourselves. Official optimism, it seems, is a commodity in high demand by the average consumer!

Finally, such contrived cheer is foreign to the world's great religions. In them we find not reassurance of human control, but awe of the divine order, not the vaunting of the ego and its labyrinthine mechanisms of protection but the willingness to sacrifice that ego to a higher beatitude. In the case of the Christian scriptures, from Abraham to St. Paul, faith does not avoid but actually requires vulnerability. It accepts the risk of journeying through the unknown and encountering the very shadow side that modern optimism so strenuously averts. Indeed, it may call for a loss of life and self (Mark 8:34 f.) through daring trust in the Lord of life, the Giver of selfhood.

In short, biblical faith finds that it is only through risking one's own security that one finds a deeper identity. As Thomas Merton put it, faith "gives a dimension of simplicity and *depth* . . . to all our experiences," through "the incorporation of the unknown and of the unconscious into our daily life . . . in a living, dynamic and actual manner. The unknown remains unknown. . . . The function of faith is not to reduce mystery to rational clarity, but to integrate the unknown and the known together in a living whole."[33] This depth and wholeness is made possible precisely because faith looks beyond itself. Faith does have an object—something far beyond the apparitions of the human will redoubled to such an intensity that somehow it mistakes itself for divinity. Followers of Jesus would go on to specify that such depth and wholeness must rest upon the God who transcends life and death and who, through death, is able to bring about new life.

CONCLUSION

A case has been presented here for the claim that nuclearism goes beyond ideological opinions or moral arguments concerning the Bomb and is, indeed, a profoundly beguiling covert religion. Its secret effectiveness depends not only on the mixture of awe, horror, and attraction to limitless power that characterize our feelings about nuclear weapons but also on psychic mechanisms of denial and numbing that prevent a clear response to such weapons.

As a belief system, its credibility rests on various root metaphors congenial to our national mindset, and we have considered here four of those paradigms. A constrictive notion of power as violence presumes a fragmented and mechanistic cosmos. The reduction of life together in human communities to zero-sum gaming is linked to fears of scarcity of life's necessities. When the vision of the future is filtered through a worst case analysis, it invites a habitual hopelessness, ever seeking new enemies in a booby trap world. And the trivialization of hope into official optimism betrays its underlying counterpart, nihilism and a dread of vulnerability.

By contrast, quite different perspectives on the ultimacy and wholeness of reality are offered by the world's great religions, and we have selected Christianity as our example. There one can find an alternate vision: paradigms of power as relational and nonviolent, life together as expansive love upheld by the Spirit's fullness, the future as a shared fulfillment already being previewed through acts of forgiveness, and faith as a ready embrace of the unknown, in trust that God is in all and through all.

If this analysis of nuclearism is basically sound, we can gain fresh insight into the seemingly intractable problem of a forty-year arms race. Indeed, until the theological implications of the Bomb are taken seriously and then effectively countered, the world may make little progress toward containing the nuclear threat. But, if a time of genuine reformation is at hand, then we may find the midwifely courage to add our energies to the opening of a new chapter in the human story.

SUSAN B. THISTLETHWAITE

Chapter 9

God and Her Survival in a Nuclear Age

As director of the Los Alamos laboratory that developed the bomb, J. Robert Oppenheimer had the honor of naming its first test. He named that test *Trinity* after one of John Donne's *Holy Sonnets*. Oppenheimer was merely the first, though possibly one of the more erudite, of modern interpreters of the bomb as "the Second Coming in Wrath" (Winston Churchill). Modern fundamentalists such as Hal Lindsey, Pat Robertson, and John Wesley White have specifically identified the bomb with God's judgment and a world-destroying nuclear war with the salvation of the righteous.[1]

To whom can we turn for help in countering the threat of these theologies of salvation by nuclear destruction? The threat itself is very real. Some have argued that nuclear apocalypticism was the viewpoint of Ronald Reagan when he was president.[2] Certainly, in the cultural trend that began in the late 1970s, what used to be regarded as the aberration of the far Right has now become the Center, and what used to be the Center is regarded as the Left. A true Left is currently out in left field. What is true of the general culture is becoming true in theology. Rightist theologies are increasingly portrayed as the moderate option.[3] However, these theologies of salvation by the bomb (which Chapman, in Chapter 8 of this book, describes as "nuclearism") are, in fact, an evisceration of the doctrine of God.[4] What alternatives are there to these rightist theologies?

Protestant liberalism, as represented by the work of Gordon Kaufman and Paul Tillich, offers a critique and specific alternative to nuclearism. Mary Daly, a feminist theologian, provides a different critique and a very different alternative. It is the argument of this essay that the Kaufman-Tillich route is not, in fact, a genuine alternative. Daly's work provides significant gains, but she, and other white feminists such as myself, need to attend to the work of black women writers, who know a lot about survival. The work of these black women particularly challenges the white-dominated West, a location of the nuclear threat, to find a way of talking about God that affirms the goodness and value of the world and also mandates justice in history.

LIBERALS AND THE BOMB

It would seem at first glance that liberals of both a Protestant and Catholic stripe would be the logical ones to provide an alternative, since they are also the targets of fundamentalists. And it is true that a consistent theological statement condemning nuclearism has come from a liberal perspective. Gordon Kaufman's *Theology for a Nuclear Age*[5] addresses nuclearism directly.

Kaufman describes his work as "constructive theology,"[6] by which he means the ongoing work of each generation of Christians to construct a world of meaningful discourse about God. Constructive theology is a recent variant upon the basic themes of liberalism. One definition of *liberalism* in theology is that it is a trend in Protestant theology in the nineteenth and twentieth centuries "which aims to show that Christianity is rational and expedient and reconcilable with the human desire for autonomy."[7] Kaufman's theology is liberal in that he adheres to the notion that theology is rational discourse, is possible discourse, and is necessary to a humanity that finds itself in history and must deal with that fact.

Why is it, asks Kaufman, that only the apocalyptic fundamentalists are asking the meaning of the nuclear threat, this "momentous religious fact right before our eyes?" Kaufman sets it as one of his tasks to pursue the logic of the "fundamentalists on the far religious right who follow out the implications of the biblical apocalyptic imagery of an earthly holocaust as the ultimate expression of God's sovereignty over history," and who "are apparently willing to go so far as to suggest that a nuclear disaster, if it ever comes, could only be an expression of the purposes of god."[8] These fundamentalists further believe that those who work to prevent such a climax to human history are in fact guilty of opposing God's will. Kaufman's conclusion is that the notion of the sovereignty of God itself as "the central traditional claim" of Christian theology is "way 'out of sync'" with the nuclear age.[9]

As constructive theology, rather than a deductive theology (in which God is treated as the only subject and human beings are seen as the passive objects of God's action), Kaufman's proposal is for a project of the human imagination to reconceive the relation of God, the world, and human beings. If one of the constructive tasks of theology is to make a meaningful world, one way to accomplish the task is to excite the human imagination to find a place in that world. The key point, of course, is that, as Kaufman says, a "God conceived in terms of the metaphor of creativity or constructive power . . . will be of a very different sort from a God conceived in terms of violent destructiveness."[10] And, in the logic of Kaufman's argument, each image will either excite human actions to transform creatively the institutions of the world toward construction or find divine justification for destruction or passivity.

Kaufman's enterprise illustrates very well the genius of Protestant liberalism: its embrace of the immanence of God in the world. The immanence of God is most often the point cited as the weakness of liberalism; that is, that its doctrine of God is too subjective, that revelation becomes synonymous with human experience, and hence that there is no judgment on evil.[11] Conservative critics of liberalism always fault its accommodation to modern culture, charging that liberalism makes "man" the measure of all things and dethrones God. They charge that liberalism fails to deal with the sinfulness of human nature and society's innate fallenness.[12]

Liberalism has faults certainly, but not these. Its failure is rather that it has never repudiated the philosophy of Cartesianism or modern philosophical idealism. It holds to a myth of the individual (usually a white male) as the locus of an independently functioning objective reason. From this independent reason liberals generalize to "humanity," with an Anglo-Saxon male face. Liberals look for abstract universals,[13] which undermines their commitment to the immanence of God. The true weakness of liberalism resides not in its embrace of immanence, but in its half-hearted immanence that is colored by romanticism and confined to a particular class and race experience. The embodied character of existence is never embraced, and hence a mind-body dualism remains in its commitment to immanence.

Liberals thus repudiate the flesh of common human experience and extend that repudiation into communal life. As a solitary individual, a liberal is essentially alone, despairing of any genuine sociality. (In Chapter 8 of this book, Chapman links this alienation directly to nuclearism.) This viewpoint has produced a doctrine of God both immanentalist and essentialist. Whereas God is the basis of Existence (the ground of being), God (like the human consciousness) is alienated from the material, physical world. But the physical, material world is the stuff of what it means to be.

The liberal viewpoint has thus produced an alienated rationalism. In 1972 Kaufman wrote with some confidence: "Though the cultural crisis that helped give neo-orthodoxy its hearing is by no means past, we have learned to live with it pretty well and are beginning to hope once again that man [sic] can sufficiently control his destiny to manage both the bomb and the population explosion."[14] Kaufman wrote these words in the second age of the Bomb, the period in which images of nuclear destruction were pushed from the public mind, especially by the Vietnam War. This second period of the Bomb was marked by a naive faith in human rationality—embodied strategically in the concept of deterrence.[15] Even though the acronym MAD (Mutually Assured Destruction) should have revealed easily that this was an unstable situation and anything but rational, it did not. (In Chapter 3 of this book, Chernus shows that the faith in rationality continued to dominate nuclear imagery, at least in the most widely read magazines, in the 1980s.)

Faith in human rationality is a hallmark of liberalism. In 1972 Kaufman's problem with God was the term *God* itself. God is not feeling, not word, not ethics, not ecclesiastical structures, he wrote, but "ultimate loyalty or faith."[16] But as that which transcends any finite reference by definition (i.e., the ultimate), what meaning can the term have "to our modern empirical, secular, and pragmatic temper?"[17] There is no clear empirical evidence for the existence of God, and evidence is the criterion sine qua non of reality in "the way we have come to conceive natural and historical order under the influences of modern scientific, philosophical, and historical studies."[18]

Kaufman's answer to this "problem" is that "God is a symbol for God," in the words of Paul Tillich, whom he quotes.[19] And Kaufman does more than quote Tillich; he constructs a definition of God that depends on Tillich's "God above God" in *The Courage to Be*.[20] Kaufman writes, "God is a symbol—an imaginative construct—that enables men [sic] to view the world and themselves in such a way as to make action and morality ultimately (metaphysically) meaningful."[21]

Kaufman has not varied significantly from this definition of God in 1985. God as symbol is "the ultimate point of reference."[22] That he has not varied significantly in his theological answers may be regarded as surprising,[23] since clearly his assessment of the capacity of human beings to "live with [the bomb] pretty well" has undergone a drastic reassessment. But this reassessment has not included a weakening of the commitment to rationality. Kaufman continues to believe that disembodied reason will enable us to think our way to a concept of God that can "relativize" and "humanize" our situation.[24] "We are attempting to find a contemporary way to think of God, to conceive that reality which grounds our existence, and devotion to which can provide us with significant orientation as we face the frightening pass to which human history today has come."[25]

Yet, Kaufman's God "as point of reference" actually pulls his doctrine of

God away from that which "grounds our being"; namely, our material, embodied life. In this sense the liberal God is wholly unaffected by what happens to us in this frightening nuclear age. Kaufman should be frightened. Kaufman is alone in facing this looming catastrophe. The sense of being alone is the companion anthropology to the liberal doctrine of God. It is well to remember that the "God above God" is Paul Tillich's answer to his assessment of the fundamental existential dilemma of man [sic]—estrangement.[26] Kaufman, in his work of 1981, *The Theological Imagination*, describes the human need for "social interdependence" experienced in childhood and then remarks that "the strong undercurrent of anxiety which most of us experience much of the time appears to be directly correlated with the absence, or potential absence, of such supporting figures."[27]

Kaufman is expressing two of the hallmarks of liberalism: both his own sense of alienation, and his projection of that experience onto the whole of humanity. He writes, "as we mature to adulthood, we become aware that no human being can be absolutely relied on."[28] "In this respect, as Paul Tillich has argued, human anxiety is 'ontological'; it belongs to our human existence as such."[29] From his own experience of existence as alienated and from Tillich's confirmation of this alienation, Kaufman projects this alienation into his definition of the human situation. But this alienation is interpreted wholly in abstract essentialist categories such as "ontological," or our "human existence as such," and never in concrete social and material terms.

The inability of liberals to actually deal with the theological nuclearism of the religious Right is based in the fact that, as Carter Heyward said in addressing the American Academy of Religion, the liberal God "is such a gentleman."[30] That is, the God of liberalism is above the hassle of human history. The liberals' God does not care whether we rule the world or not and hence has nothing at stake. The God of nuclearism has everything at stake. The limited God of liberalism will not harm us—or help us either.

GOD, THE GODDESS, AND THE BOMB

In her work, *Pure Lust: Elemental Feminist Philosophy*, Mary Daly discusses Robert Oppenheimer and the bomb to illustrate the parameters of what she calls the *sadosociety*. The sadosociety depends on the abstractionist, nature- and female-despising works of sadoasceticism. This is the denial of the basis in nature of all life, the reversal of concepts that prepares society to accept as "rational" the notion that destruction is a form of "saving." As American troops once "saved" Vietnamese villages by destroying them, so nuclearists will save the world from "Godless communism" by destroying it.[31]

Oppenheimer was thus an agent of patriarchy's *biocide*: "the degenerative and life violating tendencies" that are becoming more aggressive in the "aging and deterioration of patriarchy itself."[32] When he named the first nuclear test *Trinity* after Donne's poem to the Christian God, he chose this name as the "sadospiritual legitimation of this lust and its technological ejaculations." The opening verse of the poem, "Batter my heart, three person'd God," is well chosen, according to Daly, because it reveals that "the battering of the Earth and of her creatures is the consequence of this disordered sentiment."[33] Daly even quotes the response of Winston Churchill to the report of the successful first test of the new weapon. Churchill, who was relaxing in his zippered siren suit, read the report, then waved his cigar with a flourish. "Stimson," he rumbled, "what was gunpowder? Trivial. What was electricity? Meaningless. This atomic bomb is the Second Coming in Wrath."[34]

For Daly, God is the problem (as Kaufman put it in another context). "The earthy/unearthy males have vaporized and then condensed/reified their self-images into the sublime product, god,"[35] in the process of projecting all that is most holy and sacred onto the cosmos where it cannot undergo natural processes such as death. This theology must be wrathful because it must murder and dismember the Goddess. Unable to do away with nature per se, the underlying reality of which the Goddess is a symbol, Christian theologians have previously been content to ritually murder her and preserve a certain carved remnant in Mary. The advent of nuclear technology, however, makes the complete murder of the Goddess (nature) possible, and it has exposed this fault line at the heart of Christian theology—the ofttimes barely concealed contempt for the earth and its symbol, the Goddess.

"Women," however, "need the Goddess," as Carol Christ explicitly says in her now famous article.[36] In her identification of four reasons why women need the goddess, Christ returns again and again to the symbolism of the female divinity as an affirmation of the bodily, material aspects of human existence. For Daly, the Goddess is the symbol of the reintegration of the radical disconnections between mind and body, spirit and matter, transcendence and immanence whose symptom patriarchy is. Such reconnection or "ontological interacting is participation in Being."[37] It is the way of *biophilia*, or love of life.

Daly's work can be read as corrective to the problem of liberalism, a fact she herself discusses at some length in considering the theology of Paul Tillich. Daly's reading of intellectual history in the West finds that the separation of philosophy and theology in the "Enlightenment" occurred alongside the ritual murder of the Goddess in the European witch-hunts. "For dismemberment of wisdom logically correlates with the dismemberment of the Goddess."[38] The separation of philosophy and theology has had several pernicious effects. One was the decrease in the "personal intensity of concern which motivated the medieval philosopher-theologians."[39] Intimately connected to the emergence of the "disinterested" scholar is the "fact that philosophy was denuded of interest in final causality—a violation compared to lobotomy."[40]

Further, philosophers ceased having any interest in "separate intelligences" or angels. Although Daly acknowledges that today such speculation is the stuff of science fiction, the "philosophy of angels has had power to inspire the philosophical imagination, raising questions about the nature of knowledge, will, change, being in time and space, and intuitive communication."[41] When the spiritual-philosophical imagination is thus bifurcated, genuine creativity, which is rooted in the theological "spirit-force" of life, becomes inaccessible or "deeply buried." We are told it doesn't exist.

The greatness of Paul Tillich, in Daly's view, is that of all recent theologians he did not lose sight of final causality. He "noticed the materialization/fragmentation that prevails in modern philosophy, attributing this to a split between ontological and technical reason."[42] Tillich's analysis of this split between ontological and technical reason is where the problems begin. Tillich always wants ontological reason, or reason in itself, to have control over technical reason, or the process of "reasoning." Since the middle of the nineteenth century, however, "reasoning" has threatened to break away from "reason." Tillich, according to Daly, ends up picturing the process of technical reasoning, as opposed to the abstraction of reason itself, as a "sort of wayward wife who refused to meet the demands of her lord and master and finally not only threatened but actually obtained a divorce—in the middle of the nineteenth century."[43]

It is wholly unsurprising, Daly notes, that this is the period of that separation. It is the first wave of feminism, in which female independence, represented by "technical reason," first emerged. Liberal feminism claimed "technical reason," or the process of reasoning, for its own and opted for the body half of the mind-body split. The tension for liberal feminists has always been that "technical reason" is seen as a threat by liberals themselves, including Tillich, who are always afraid that the "subservient half will break away and become the servant of 'non-rational' forces."[44] The fact that liberal men buy into "this bifurcated vision" is consistent with the other distortions of Western culture.

Science as envisioned by Oppenheimer is the result of this radical disjuncture when nature is seen as the object of scientific inquiry with no ends (final causality) of its own. Tillich's dilemma is even more complex; he can see the problem but subverts the accomplishment of the remedy. Tillich proposes that "ontological reason can be defined as the structure of the mind which enables it to *grasp and to shape reality*."[45] Daly calls this the "'hairy claw' view of ontological reason." Her point is that reality itself is reduced to that which can be grasped. It is rendered thereby a passive recipient of "'reason's' unsolicited attentions."[46] But this actually makes reality into nothing for itself, and in fact, nothing for the would-be philosopher-theologian.

In identifying this flaw of liberal theology, Daly has touched bottom. The God of liberalism is nothing, a vacuum left by the splitting of reality into two halves, one of which presumes to dominate the other, but which in fact is characterized primarily by its own alienation. For liberalism, God is not death, God is nothing.

For Daly, Goddess is definitely not nothing. She is not limited even to the Goddess as Great Mother. "Fixation upon the Great Mother to the exclusion of the myriad other possibilities for Naming transcendence can fix women into foreground categories that block encounters with the inexhaustible Other, stopping the Metamorphic process."[47] That is to say, the divine in Daly's work is not a substitution of female terms for a male transcendent deity nor is the divine reduced to Nature per se. The entire model for divine-human relationship has changed. Limiting the divine to a label instead of understanding the spiraling of metaphoric encounter with shifting images of radical otherness is a symptom, in Daly's view, of "the Standstill Society, the Stagnation."[48] She gives a profound glimpse into what it would mean to actually live in the physical world and in the imagination and not abandon the physical world for an abstractionist human consciousness.

Yet I want to go on to say that Daly also shares some characteristics with Kaufman and Tillich that undermine her commitment to the reintegration of the nature-history split. I get a clue to this in her use of the term *pure* in the title *Pure Lust*. The journey of *Pure Lust* is a movement, a spiral, through "Metamorphospheres" of Wild Weird women who are purified in the real of Fire from the Plastic and Potted Passions and Virtues and are able to break out of these spheres and get in touch with Natural Grace. It is a movement of purification.

It is significant to me that Daly has drawn on Alice Walker's book, *The Color Purple*, to illustrate the movement toward the inexhaustible other.[49] The philosopher (Daly) reads to a student from Walker's book:

> Don't look like nothing, she [Shug] say. It ain't a picture show. It ain't something you can look at apart from anything else, including yourself. I believe God is everything, say Shug. . . . She say, My first step away from the old white man was trees. Then air. Then birds. Then other people. But one day when I was sitting quiet and feeling like a motherless child, which I was, it come to me: that feeling of being part of everything, not separate at all.[50]

Daly continues, "Hearing these words, our Nag-Gnostic philosopher and Novice Nag must feel essentially in accord with Shug and Celie."[51] Daly adds in a note, however, "It is essential to point out that Shug Avery and Celie are in no way responsible for the interpretations of their conversations and behavior presented in this section. I have assumed the Nag-Gnostic prerogative of having Nagging thoughts about them and expressing these. Any Nags— especially Shug and Celie—are, of course, free to disagree."[52]

What I read Daly as saying, however, is that in the realm of purity all differences dissolve. Contrast to her words what Delores Hines has to say about the differences between black and white women's reality.

> We are told that apples and oranges are the same, when we can see that they are not. You cannot easily substitute one for the other in a recipe. Their odors are different. They appeal to people differently. Even a blind person can tell them apart. Yet, a steady stream of rhetoric is aimed at convincing Black women how much alike their lives, experiences, wishes and decisions are to those of our stepsisters.[53]

Kaufman has his own movement of purification. In his volume *An Essay on Theological Method*, Kaufman presents a schema (also operative in *Theology for a Nuclear Age*) of theological analysis that proceeds in three moments. The first moment is "pure phenomenological description," an "attempt to put the varieties of contemporary experience together into a concept of the world as a whole." The second stage is the imposition of the God concept constructed as "the human significance of the ultimate reality." Then comes the third moment, in which "the works of artist and physicists, social workers and philosophers, historians and economists, urban experts and students of the 'third world,' spokespersons for the problems of blacks, women, and other groups, must all be taken into account."[54] After the entire schema is constructed as "pure," then the messy masses are fit in. Granted Kaufman claims that these moments cannot "be taken up in simple, serial order."[55] But in the following paragraph he imagines a theologian embarking on moment 3 who is "grounded" in moments 1 and 2. If these are not serial, their presentation and subsequent function certainly appear that way.

In this sense both Daly and Kaufman regard the concrete, material alienation of women, blacks, "and other groups" to be of import in theological construction, but only in a tertiary sense.

THE SURVIVAL OF THE ANCESTORS, SELF, AND GOD

Audre Lorde commented at a panel on The Personal and the Political at the Second Sex Conference, October 19, 1979, that

> Black panelists' observation about the effects of relative powerlessness and the differences of relationship between black women and men from white

women and men illustrate some of our unique problems as black feminists. If white American feminist theory need not deal with the differences between us, and the resulting differences in aspects of our oppressions, then what do you do with the fact that the women who clean your houses and tend your children while you attend conferences on feminist theory are, for the most part, poor and third world women? What is the theory behind racist feminism?[56]

Simply put, there are women who have no access to any of the spheres Daly describes because of their economic, social, and racial location. There is no reintegration of nature-history without the confrontation of the vast differences in women's historical conditions and a *methodological* shift in light of that difference. We cannot go "Leaping with Wanderlust"[57] over poverty, over racism, over real history.

Our survival and that of God depends on knowing this. "Survival is not an academic skill," as Audre Lord has written.[58] As an academic, and here I speak for myself, I don't know what I need to know about surviving. The irony of writing about this lack of knowledge is not lost on me. But this I do know. Contact with the voices of historical difference and a confrontation with them *as* different is as crucial to our survival and God's as is the reintegration with nature.

In one of her early novels, *Meridian*, writer Alice Walker explores the spiritual truth to her conviction that connection to the heritage of black women is the source of creativity in life and the well-spring of change. Meridian, the chief character, seeks her identity through the legacy left her by other southern black women. Meridian believes in the sacredness and continuity of life, the African spirituality of animism, "the spirit that inhabits all life."[59] Meridian discovers, against impossible odds, the forces in a perverted and distorted racist society that inhibit the natural growth of the living organism toward freedom. She learns that "the respect she owed her life was to continue, against whatever obstacles, to live it, and not to give up any particle of it without a fight to the death, preferably not her own. And that this existence extended beyond herself to those around her because, in fact, the years in America had created them One Life."[60]

The Color Purple can be seen as not only encompassing the themes of Walker's earlier works, but taking them past the tension of longing after resolution to a conclusion. Like her other novels, this is the story of one southern black family and the oppression black women experience in their relationships with black men. She examines subjects of incest and lesbian relationships. In loving Shug, Celie, the main character, who has been sexually abused by her father and physically abused by her husband, comes to value herself and life. Celie has managed not only to survive but to prevail against all odds. The strength she finds is in the solidarity of women who, in choosing freedom for themselves, also permit those around them, both female and male, to find the freedom that is the natural state of human life.

Many have remarked not only on the unusual content of *The Color Purple* but on its unusual style. It is written in the form of letters, to God and from one sister to the other. Letters were one of the few forms of self-expression allowed to a black woman. In adopting this style, Walker herself is claiming allegiance to the generations of women who had no other choice but to express themselves in this form. Walker has also found quilt making to be this same vehicle for the expression of the creativity of the self, for black women were allowed no other artistic outlet.

Black women such as Walker, Zora Neale Hurston, and Toni Morrison, among many others, have used religious imagery, and specifically Christian biblical imagery, to frame their literary works. But the answer to the question of who God is for the black woman writer permits no simple contrast between modes of Christian belief and African spiritualities. What was said of Emily Dickinson can be said of these writers as well: they use the Christian idiom much more than they permit it to use them. It is closer to the major theme of these writers to say that God becomes the black woman protagonist in both suffering and healing. Early in *Meridian* another character says of her, "she thinks *she's* God."[61]

The novel *Meridian* is based not only on the conviction of life itself as sacred, but also on the dilemma of suffering and death giving birth to life. *Meridian*, in its exploration of nonviolent resistance after it has become unfashionable, pursues the notion that unless the struggle is taken on by those who wish to change society, even to the death, they will defeat their own revolution. That which they seek to destroy in society will resurrect itself in their own psyches. And similarly that which they defeat in themselves can become liberating for the community. It may be more accurate to say that it is Life that is divine and that the self-conscious, self-loving black woman who allies herself with life can embody its divinity.

In *The Salt Eaters,* a novel by Toni Cade Bambara, the narrative opens with the question, "Are you sure, sweetheart, that you want to be well?"—the words uttered by Minnie Ransom, the faith healer cum therapist in the Southwest Community Infirmary.[62] The infirmary, one of the unusual features of Claybourne, Georgia, is the facility to which Velma Henry, to whom the question of wellness is addressed, has been taken. Velma, the tireless worker on good causes of the neighborhood, has just attempted suicide.

As Minnie's voice intones its question of wanting to be well, Velma's fractured consciousness allows scenes to drift in and out. Her "soul goes gathering"[63] remembering what it's been like being called in on five-minute notice after all the interesting decisions had been made, called in out of personal loyalty and expected to break her hump pulling off what the men had decided was crucial for community good . . . being snatched at by childish, unmannish hands. . . . Like taking on entirely too much: drugs, prisons, alcohol, the schools, rape, battered women, abused children . . . the nuclear power issue . . . [64]

Velma's healing takes place when she remembers and enters in spirit a place where time fuses the dead, the living, and the unborn, and "Isis lifted the veil"; where the spirits of African religions like Shango preside over the rites of transformation, and Ogun challenges chaos and forges transition; where Obatala shapes creation, Damballah ensures continuity and renewal, and Anancy becomes a medium for the shapes of Brer Rabbit, Brer Bear, Brer Fox, Brer Terrapin, and Signifyin' Monkey; where the griot member of all humankind is reincarnated as the conjure woman, High John, John Henry, the Flying African, Stagolee, the Preacher, the blues singer, the jazz makers; where the sorcerers of African-American literary heritage from the eighteenth century until the present assemble as the Master Minds of global experience. For Bambara, time is a fusion of the ancestors and the future. When the community forgets that, and enters into the linear progression of Western society with its crisis upon crisis: drugs, prisons, alcohol, the schools, rape, battered women, abused children, nuclear war. . . they are broken and can no longer heal either themselves or their world.[65]

For these black women writers, survival depends both on claiming the earth as divine and on claiming a non-Western understanding of history. Mary Daly has pointed out the vacuum at the heart of white, Protestant liberal theology. Yet she and other white feminists who understand the significance of claiming the earth and bodily process in divinity need to hear the difference race makes. From black women writers, I hear that history is to be taken as the location of struggle, of survival, of life and death.

Yes, the survival of God is the survival of nature: the earth and all its splendors, including—but not limited to—human beings. Surely the wanton destruction of the basis of life would be an irreparable rending of the worship relationship that is the content of religion's use of the term God. But survival is not mere persistence in being, nor is it the ideal of progressive material success as defined in the West. God and her survival are threatened both by the other-worldly spirituality of nuclear fundamentalists that makes this earth of penultimate concern *and* by their companion capitalist materiality that measures all life for its monetary values. Survival is the fullness of life, the solidarity between the ancestry of the planet and the race to come. And you can't find that vision in Plato or his heirs.

WALTER J. NOYALIS

Chapter 10

Doing the Truth:
Peacemaking as Hopeful Activity

The preceding chapters have examined the nuclear age in terms of its images, myths, and rituals. If so many in society have "learned to love the bomb," and decisions based on such "love" are being made by political and military leaders on both sides that may, and many think will, lead to nuclear war, the old question remains, For what may we hope? Is the future to be lost to a nuclear winter? Can we any longer assume that the human race will continue on this globe?

These questions about our future as individuals and as a species cannot be ignored. They stem from the foundational human drive to seek meaning. If there is to be no future, then is anything meaningful? Just how central a meaningul future is for us has been explored by psychologists such as Viktor Frankl and Robert J. Lifton. Among theologians, Wolfhart Pannenberg has shown that the future is not only psychologically but even ontologically necessary for meaningful human existence; what we are and how we live have their inner coherence and basis in orientation to the future, to a full outcome— not an end—to existence. Jonathan Schell and Gibson Winter have further dealt with how central for the species is a meaningful future. Lifton and Schell particularly examine the threat of loss of the future through nuclear war.[1]

Current thinking about nuclear war offers at least four ways to react to the nuclear threat of loss of the future: (1) We can lose hope, by a process of psychic numbing. Any sense of a meaningful outcome to life is lost. Since the

152

loss is too great to bear, we encapsulate it by various psychological mechanisms of denial and loss of feeling. (2) We can, in a way that seems curiously "religious," put our trust in nuclear weapons, paradoxically, as a means to prevent their use. We embrace them as saviors from the very destruction they promise to bring, as other chapters in this volume have pointed out. Theories of deterrence seem to carry this weight. (3) We can envision, as some governments do, the possibility of fighting and surviving a limited nuclear war, even a protracted one. Here we trust, again in a quasi-religious way, our technological capabilities to save us from themselves. (4) We can engage in opposition to the possession and use of nuclear weapons, developing attitudes that seem "heretical" to nuclearism.

Each of these options is a stance toward the future; each embodies either a kind of hope or lack of hope. Hope, however, is not optimism. Both pessimism and optimism, as Joseph Powers points out,[2] are mental or emotional states that can inhibit action since they may be based on mistaken readings of unpleasant reality. Thus, they can lead to disengagement from the world and to a kind of action benighted by false premises. Hope, in contrast, is a quality of actions, not of mind. It points to the radical connectedness of our acting with its grounding in the Ultimate. In fact, hopeful actions make real an experience of the Ultimate in concrete living. Thus, the numbing response is pessimistic; deterrence and protracted war-fighting theory involve both pessimism and optimism; but, as a form of peacemaking, active opposition to nuclear weapons involves hope, is hopeful, and as such, is the only option among those named that is truly religious.

This chapter examines how peacemaking can be hopeful activity and as such involve an experience of God. It maintains that in an "experience of God" one discerns the shape of ultimate connections, the ultimate concern at the heart of living. It suggests particularly that such discernment is metaphorical activity since it constructs an image of this ultimate connectedness; peacemaking is precisely an instance of such metaphoric activity. Finally, it suggests that such metaphoric activity has everything to do with concerns about the future.

I

The biblical perspective on peace can serve us as a useful starting point.[3] It sees peace as *shalom*—a structure of universal harmonious connections among all God's creatures, a structure that existed in the beginning, was disrupted by human sin, and will be restored again at the end of time in the "Kingdom of God." But any human action in the present that helps to restore connections with God and His creatures is a step toward the ultimate reconciliation and perfect peace of the Kingdom. In both biblical and contemporary thinking about peace, the idea of "connections" plays a crucial role.

Connections create the structure of life as lived and are grasped directly in their shifting patterns. If the structure of life's connections has been broken, it appears that to restore it, it would be necessary to grasp that structure directly. But how do we grasp a state of affairs as connected? Or how do we know when it needs reconciliation? These insights come through grasping the relation between a concrete moment and its paradigmatic structure.

Structure is simply the way the components of an event fit together, the relationships they have that make the event what it is. Alternate words for *structure* might be *pattern* or *fit*. *Paradigmatic structure* is the way the components fit together in an ultimate way, not only within the event itself but also with all other events. The paradigmatic structure of an event thus is its largest reality, its truth as it has been fully worked out and revealed in the last analysis, which means in an absolute future. Any present structure is only a partial realization of the deepest structure and may even mask the latter, though at any given moment we may glimpse an inkling in a present reality of what it can and ought to become in the future—its ultimate reality.

For example, exactly who I am at any moment of my life is only partially knowable. If I am truly open to the depths of myself, I will also be open to new realizations of my deepest truth. Exactly who I am may not be fully knowable until even beyond my death, if then, until the nexus of all the connections I have with all else, which completes "who" I am, is worked out.

Viewing paradigmatic structure as "horizon" may be helpful for understanding its relational character. *Horizon* primarily means the line where our vision perceives the meeting of sky and earth. What we see on earth as we look to the horizon depends on our position relative to the horizon. The higher we rise, the more we can see—our horizon is broadened. Paradigmatic structure is the broadest horizon we could possibly perceive.

However, in this use of the metaphor, it is not the quantity of objects to be seen that is most important about horizon. More significant is the fact that a horizon is a relation. It is not an object in itself to be seen but a line or pattern described by the relative positions of fields of objects. Everything on the land stands in the distance in relation to the sky because of the curvature of the earth, and what we see of this depends on our position relative to the sky and the earth. Thus, horizon is a function of perception as well as of position.

A horizon, then, is the expression of a figure-ground relationship. The figure-ground relationship is important to any sort of perception. When I see an object, it is against the background of other things. The shape of an object as perceived is a function of its position relative to other objects and to the observer. The truth of this emerges clearly in painting, if we view it as the "configuration" of the figures found there. To see the figures or "objects" in a painting, the eye must perceive them against their background and in relation to the other figures in the painting. It is the spaces between the objects that appear as the background on the surface of the painting. The discerning viewer must be able to see these spaces rather than simply look at the objects. Seen this way, the shape of an object that identifies it to us is really the shape of the edge of the space next to it. Without that space and its shape, the object would disappear, for the figure depends on the ground for its existence. To the eye, the complete lack of form that ensues when figure-ground patterns disappear is the same as nonexistence.

Whereas a completed painting is a present reality, a paradigmatic structure such as the horizon of existence is a future reality since it is still being worked out. Since the future does not yet exist, we imagine it—we develop images that do not represent its content, since it as yet has no content, but point to its structure. The *content* is open, shifting, surprising, as it develops, but the *structure* must be experienced. Thus reconciliation, or peacemaking if you will, depends on our ability to construct an image of a future reality that as yet has no content.

We must use metaphors to construct images of the future, because the strength of metaphors lies in their ability to express the structure of experience even where conceptual clarity cannot be found or is inappropriate, as is the case with the future. By *metaphor* we mean any imaginative construct that is intended to convey the sense of some specific, concrete state of affairs. A metaphor draws bits of data from a storehouse of experiences and memories and organizes them creatively in such a way that they point to something quite different from their original meaning. With a metaphor we can say that case A is understandable in terms of case B even though the literal meaning of case B has nothing to do with case A.

For example, we may speak of a "smiling field." Fields do not literally smile. But to speak of a field as smiling links the associations of smiling with the field as experienced by the user of the metaphor. Although such a metaphor might involve a set of characteristics of a smile (warmth, friendliness, cheer) and apply these to the field, the metaphor cannot be reduced to them. It conveys something unique—the experience of *this* field by *this* person—and asks the reader to summon imaginatively a similar experience. What is more, characteristics may be conceptualized, abstracted, and generalized. Any field may be warm, inviting, cheery. But a metaphor sees something about a specific reality that is matched by no other; it sees the structure, the fit of its parts, and affirms this structure as expressed in the other structure, the fit of the parts to which it is compared. This "fit" can be known only in direct experience and not by abstract conceptualization, for it includes the observer and his or her personal perspectives. We must be engaged and involved to make or appreciate a metaphor.

A metaphor is more than just a personal recognition of connections and correspondences, it is a personal creation of connections. It brings together realities that we had previously experienced as separate. Metaphor thus opens one up to new experience of truth. If perception of what is true is based on experience of the singular, the concrete, and the connected, then metaphor is not only the result of such perception but the path to it as well. Even conceptualizations that are abstracted from multiple experiences of the singular begin in metaphors and need to be constantly refreshed by reference to their original vital encounter with the singular, or they risk not only going stale but even being wrong. The biggest danger with conceptualizations that lose their metaphorical footing is that we may mistake the concept for the reality to which it supposedly points, and this can result in growing divergence between thought and reality. Similarly, to interpret a metaphor simply by laying out the conceptual content of its components (the characteristics of a "smiling" field) is to miss the point that the thrust of metaphor is in the "fit" of its components, in their connections, in the horizon described by their juxtaposition. A metaphor about the future, then, does not yield content about the future but a sense of the paradigmatic structure which is in the future.

Implicit in this analysis is the realization that experiencing a horizon has much in common with making a metaphor. The juxtaposition of objects in metaphor involves the same process of perception as that by which figure-ground relationships are grasped. The tension of the horizon line (or shape) as the *single edge* of two objects makes us aware that the object is concrete, is itself, only because of its relationship to the other object, the background against which it appears. We might say that a metaphor is an imaginative construct that points to and arises from an experience of a horizon. Making a metaphor, then, is creative because it reveals the latent "connections" in our experience of the structure of reality, and this is what makes metaphor appropriate in discourse about the future.

II

This brief examination of structure, paradigmatic structure, horizon, and metaphor equips us to turn to the question, How is God experienced in acts of peacemaking?

"God," or Ultimate Value, is nonobjective.[4] What is meant by *God* is not an object that can be known conceptually in any adequate way. Our concepts identify and delimit contents that we take to be more or less acceptable representations of objects—realities proportionate to our modes of conceptualizing. Ultimate Reality cannot be enveloped or controlled by our minds. This does not mean, however, that we have no experience of Ultimate Reality, but that the sort of experience which is of discrete, "objective" realities and which gives rise to concepts is inappropriate. Our experience of God is much more like the experience that leads to metaphors, and our speech about God must therefore be metaphorical.

The experience of God, to use a much-favored metaphor, involves experience of the "horizon of being." Experience of God as horizon involves an experience of the paradigmatic structure of meaning and existence, the background against which all concepts must be seen. Without this horizon, our knowing could not take place. As the Ultimate Horizon, God is not an object among others, but is necessary and given in the act of knowing objects, the prerequisite for every existent and the ultimate expression of the connectedness of all things. So we speak of a "preconceptual" or a "nonconceptual" awareness of God, as God is not directly an object of conceptual experience but the necessary basis for any experience.

Since the ultimate or paradigmatic structure is a future reality, experience of God must point us toward the absolute future. As indicated earlier, a sense of the future, of paradigmatic structure, is integral to our search for meaning. Wolfhart Pannenberg has analyzed how present human existence is determined by the future. For the purpose at hand, his suggestion of how we grasp the future is interesting.[5] We find meaning through an anticipatory or proleptic grasp of the structure of the future. What is proleptically grasped is not the content of the future but its real structure. His use of the German word *Vorgriff* (literally, "grasp before") is fruitfully ambivalent; it carries the weight of "preconception" (that is, the "preconceptual" awareness of God as in horizon analysis), and it suggests a reaching out to the future in a temporal sense, as if to speak of grasping the future before its time. Since the future as content-laden does not exist, one is limited to a sense of the horizon, the background structure of that future. It is as though that structure is grasped as the deeper structure of any reality, not reducible to the way things are now fitted together, but open to working itself out in the actual future. In any moment when we sense the deepest ground of our life, he claims, we grasp proleptically its future. We are open to an experience of God.

This experience must also be an experience of the absolute future, the Kingdom of God. Indeed, as Pannenberg points out, the term *Kingdom of God* is used in the New Testament as a roundabout way of speaking about God himself.[6] God involves the ultimate pattern of all reality, the ultimate restoration of all broken connections—in the future, yes, but already at work now. Whenever action is taken to restore connections, God is experienced as present and peace is experienced, too. In the moment of peace God is fully revealed to us.

Thus, the disciples of Jesus saw, in their experience of the risen Jesus alive after the crucifixion, the breaking through of the absolute future where the full reality of God is to be found. *What* they saw could not be conceptualized because it had no content that could fit into any conceptual framework available to them. Yet the experience, Pannenberg thinks, was of something real, not simply wish fulfillment or merely an intramental construct.[7] So they used a metaphor, "resurrection from the dead," to speak of what they had seen. The metaphor conveys no description of the otherworldly state of Jesus but points to the relation, the grounding of the present in its deepest structure, that of the future. What was true for Jesus is true in some sense for us all—our most specific, concrete reality, what we indeed are, is tied to its outcome in the future (God is our "horizon"). To the extent that what we are and think now (present content) is not adequate to that structure, we are abstract, not yet real. Yet, by grasping proleptically that future as the horizon of present, we open up the present. Its content is not the last word; we are not slaves to how we conceptualize it. Though we never grasp the future thematically, we can touch it in the experience of awareness, in specific engaged encounter with what is real.

This encounter is precisely a metaphorical act. If we use concepts from past experience to express it, we do so metaphorically—they cannot be limited to what they used to mean; their content is opened up. They are now images pointing not to a clearly defined set of facts but to the pattern of an experience, to the Ultimate Reality as known only in such encounter. Metaphor anchors us to concrete experience. So the process of imagination that creates a vision of a reconciled, peaceful future according to its experienced structure must be a process of metaphorical understanding.

Though the analysis thus far seems to point to knowing as a response to subjective experience, it also applies to doing, to creative activity, for in creative activity, knowing and doing are one. The experience of working creatively is itself an experience of the truth of that which one is doing. Thus, creative activity can also involve an experience of the Ultimate.

To illustrate this point, consider the process of creating a nonrepresentational work of art. There is no identifiable subject in a nonrepresentational painting—it is not a painting of something so that it mimics the appearance of the subject. An artist may indeed contemplate a subject, but the effect is to render creatively its specific reality, its deep structure, in a nonrepresentational way. The artist sees a subject—a landscape, a stone wall—and discerns the connections, the interfaces between its myriad dimensions. A utilitarian eye may see a field to be excavated or a wall to be fixed or removed. The artist sees shape and shadow, tone and texture, figure and ground. Never is the figure separated from the ground, but the ground comes to expression in the arrangement of figures. The figure itself is layer upon layer of figure-ground relationships. The dynamics of the interaction of these elements is the structure, and in contemplating the whole one can almost see forming, as a crystal forms, the connection with, and grounding of the subject against, the background of all other reality.

To paint it, the artist uses as elements the surface of the canvas, composition, medium, tones, and values. One's attention is focused on the work; the possibilities inherent in the canvas are the range of possibilities for the painting. The work takes shape, its own shape, carried along by the development of its own inherent structure. What may have begun as contemplation of an "object" is now "abstract." But it is a rendering of truth, as perceived by the artist responding to the demands of the subject and the materials. It is not arbitrary—a finished painting would not "work" as well if done differently. If done differently, it would simply be a different painting, a different perception, a different truth.

Only in the act of painting does the artist come to experience the truth of the painting. The experience of working it out reveals its true dimensions. If we happen to start out with an idea, it will be modified, shaped, changed as we see the painting grow. The work demands that the artist be true to it, adapt to it.[8] The result is not an identifiable subject. A third party will be hard-pressed to say what it is a painting of, but will be challenged to respond, not to its subject but to its *subjectivity*—to its patterns, connections, modulations—and to see these against the background of his or her own subjectivity, thus opening up possibilities perhaps only latent for the artist. "What" a painting is, then, is a function of all its connections. Only some of these become explicit in the work, though all are implied. The outcome may be surprising, even disturbing, but it cannot be exactly predicted, since it depends on the truth as revealed in the act of painting.

This analogy suggests that creative action, dynamic interaction of person and person or person and situation, can involve a discovery of the ultimate grounding of the concrete. This is so dependent on the action that the action is itself the awareness. But it is not an awareness that can be precisely forecast as to its content, for it has no content that can be abstracted from the experience and dealt with independently. The action is metaphoric, and each making of a metaphor is different; it reveals further surprising dimensions of ultimate grounding.

III

Now, how is making peace metaphorical? Does not action—making— spring from knowing and awareness, and is it not the act of knowing that is metaphorical? The Western religious and philosophical tradition has tended to answer in the affirmative. Christian thought in the Middle Ages usually asserted that the deepest nature of humankind "participated" in that of God, who was infinite intellect. The fulfillment of human nature and the highest human operation was, therefore, the intellectual contemplation of God, the Absolute Truth. The primacy of the mental-spiritual life over the life of action was generally upheld.

At the beginning of the modern era, Descartes emphasized this primacy of the mental to the point of proclaiming a total dichotomy between the knowing subject and the material object. Because this Cartesian dualism isolated the subject completely from the objective environment, it undercut the possibility that any objective truth in the environment could become a basis for action. Consequently, action became idiosyncratic, something deduced from personal existence and responsible to personal existence alone. This Cartesian legacy, not surprisingly, sees little in human action that could be an experience of God. It holds the experience of God to be purely within the subject, and action proceeds from that interior experience more than from any claim that an external state of affairs expressing the Ultimate may have on the subject.

But is it not possible that, contrary to the prevailing Western view, an action itself—and peacemaking in particular—can generate awareness of concepts and constitute awareness of the ultimate, of the future horizon of being? Is it not possible, in fact, that in making peace, as in abstract painting, the action is the awareness, the experience of deepest Truth? If we have a prior idea of peace and simply try to put it into effect, we may be disappointed if it does not turn out the way we envisioned it. We need to be open to have our vision corrected by the encounter with the situation. The experience of peacemaking, then, must be an experience of a structure from which can emerge a vision and a metaphor. These must retain their roots in the experience to have any claim to validity. (In Chapter 7 Daniel Noel also concludes that metaphor is the key to overcoming Cartesian dualism and reuniting thought and action, concept and concrete experience.)

Let us examine some examples of peacemaking, of reconciling activity, to see how it works. Making love is such an example. We can make love genitally, or with a look or a touch, or in conversation, in giving a gift, even in an argument—whenever there is sensitive congeniality in action. Congeniality discerns the patterns of concrete existence in the beloved, in the self, and in the relationship. It discerns them as they shift with the moment and helps to create them. Love is not so much an emotion or an idea as a commitment to respond in action to the value of the beloved. But the outcomes of making love are not always conceptually predictable. The depths of the person and the contours of the relationship become real only as they are lived in concrete acts, as they depend on concrete acts for their shape. Yet the actions respond to the dynamics of the relationship. The structure does not exist without the actions, yet it is not reducible to them. By loving we know the love; our sense of it is shaped, sometimes in new and surprising ways. To proceed from too rigid an idea of how love should look may lead us to act inappropriately. But appropriate action is a dialectic; it is shaped by the awareness we have of the grounding of the relationship in its ultimate future and so expresses that grounding, points to it.

Similarly, in nonviolent resolution of conflicts, we feel our way, we sense the appropriate thing to do while responding to the dynamics of the freedom and the divergent interests of the parties. Violence forces the issue into a preconceived outcome regardless of the dynamics of the situation. There may be procedures to follow and psychological principles to understand in resolving conflict, but in meeting the situation we must have a feel for its dynamics, which we can have only by being involved, *through the experience of working it out*. Here, we sense the truth behind the conflict, the existential bases deeper than the conflict and masked by it. We sense these as they are true for the parties involved. This puts us in touch with the broadest grounding of the parties in the Ultimate.

The way the Ultimate is concretely realized in a conflict depends on its not being forced. It may be surprising to all. It will involve some change. But any solution that *imposes* a preconceived outcome is automatically distant from, not involved with, the grounded life of the parties. This is violence, for it controls and manipulates, and its outcomes do not embody the deep structure of the existence of the parties. Nonviolence, however, finds solutions that point to the deepest interests of the parties, to the structure of their lives. Only by building such outcomes do we know these connections, not by conceiving them in abstraction beforehand. Thus, the resolution is a metaphor for the wholeness of being, and working it out is an anticipation of that wholeness.[9]

The way of Mohandas Gandhi offers a case in point of such a perspective on peacemaking. [10] Gandhi saw God as Truth (Satya). However, God as truth is not an abstraction or mental construct but a concrete value to be realized and experienced concretely in *Satyagraha* (truth force, seizing and holding to truth). *Satyagraha* is thus the experience of God, the force of consciousness that, as Truth, pervades and binds the universe.

For Gandhi, this truth is never realized absolutely but only relatively. We do not grasp it completely due to our limited and egocentric minds. But we can become relatively more open to it through love, which diminishes egocentrism as it respects the truth and value of the other. Such respect can never do violence against the other in order to force an outcome; such force is egocentric in that it forgets the limits of our ability to see truth.

For Gandhi, a situation of conflict is violent in that it springs from a similar failure to perceive ultimate truth due in some fashion to egocentrism. Such a situation must be resolved for it stands in the way of our deepest need to experience the truth. But its resolution must be nonviolent or the truth is once again obscured. Thus, conflict resolution is itself an experience of God, since it brings to light the truth, whether the conflict is resolved through reasoning and persuasion, personal symbolic suffering (such as the fasts Gandhi undertook), or civil disobedience (such as the famous Salt March). These are experiences of God since they are geared to converting and reconciling opposing parties to the truth, however it may appear. Coming to experience Truth is one and the same with the process of reconciliation of conflicting parties through the action of loving resistance. So the action is a metaphor of Ultimate Being.

IV

We now return to the theme of hope and hopelessness to examine how this sheds light on making peace and making war. As one of the theological virtues, hope proceeds from our rootedness in God. It is nevertheless far from an optimistic attitude to the future. Such an attitude might say "I am optimistic that there will be no nuclear war. Who would be so crazy? Besides, God would not allow it." Or, "Deterrence has worked so far; it will continue to work." The optimists have been wrong about every war we have had until now. The trouble with such optimism is that it envisions the content of the future; it attempts to predict and so does not take into account the freedom of history to move beyond our conceptualizations.

War-making, including preparing for war, and especially for a protracted nuclear war, involves a similar optimism—that our technological capacity and penchant for control can account for every future contingency. It, too, tries to predict the future (as Clarke Chapman clearly demonstrates in Chapter 8 of this book). But war-making also proceeds from hopelessness. It envisions the future simply by extrapolating from a content currently known, from an understanding of the past and the present that is taken as the ultimate potential for the future. It assumes that the unreconciled, unpeaceful world that relies on nuclear weapons is the norm—that conflict is the norm and can be avoided finally only by the threat of greater conflict. It does not see any deeper grounding for human existence than self-interest defined as current or expected benefits. To the extent that we see this extrapolation as definitive, there can be no possibility, newness, or surprise, because the ground of imagination has become closed to ongoing future experience.

The maxim "If you want peace, prepare for war" is thus the maxim of hopelessness, of the failure to imagine an open future due to conceptual identification of the structure of the future with the events of the past.[11] What *we* think becomes the future; our sense of its content precludes experiential awareness of the specific, concrete horizon of our being. The nuclear vision of the future is thus closed, constricted, profoundly antimetaphorical. (The examples of nuclear fatalism offered by John McDargh in Chapter 6 of this book testify to this.) If there is any saving grace in nuclear weapons, it lies in the Bomb's power to expose this dimension of the war-making mythos. The prospect of the destruction of the species through war has compelled many people to see war in an entirely new attitude.[12] This now means to see the hopelessness behind *all* war, to see how removed war is from the true horizon of our life.

This is not to say that it is wrong to expect benefits from the future. The problem arises when the *content* of what is expected is separated from awareness of human grounding in a nonmanipulable way in the absolute future, the free future. To oppose nuclear war, on the other hand, is to become aware of this deepest grounding. It is hopeful activity, even if we sense little basis for optimism in current history. To write on the subject, to speak, to demonstrate, to engage in civil disobedience are concrete actions geared to change the situation. As such, they themselves point to that deeper horizon, the grounding in the future. They do not assign the future a specific content but they say that its reality, its structure as presently experienced, is incompatible with nuclear conceptualization. They are metaphors of an open future that is known only in exploring its surprising manifestations, in committing ourselves to a practical value. Working for peace, building a peaceful world, is not mere opposition to nuclear weapons, it is a positive expression of a specific truth—in Christian terms, the Kingdom of God that is the working out of the deepest truth of creation. And in experiencing the structure of true peace while attempting to help it blossom, we encounter in the veiled metaphorical manner of our actions the Ultimate Truth itself. As metaphors, these actions are experiences of the concrete reality of the Ultimate and express its shape, its structure.

Peacemaking, then, reminds us of what war-making forgets, that our constructs of reality are profoundly metaphorical. The truth of our life is not conceptually known. It is *done*, lived out. We live out the nonviolent alternative to war, discerning its shape as we go along. Peacemaking is thus creative, able to compose, to texture and tone, a peaceful reality because of openness and commitment to the deepest structures of living, of our ultimate future. War-making, which in its nuclear expression may be the ultimate form of Cartesian dualism, is closed to these structures, denies the possibility of such vision, and lives in a conceptualized future of its own making, alienated from the concrete structures of life. Thus, it threatens the future of us all.

Part V

Conclusion

IRA CHERNUS and EDWARD TABOR LINENTHAL

Chapter 11

The Religious Dimensions of the Nuclear Age

The nuclear age is an immense enigma. How in the world did we get to this point? Where in the world are we headed? Where should we be headed? How can we get there from here? These are the puzzling problems that continue to call out for solutions. The chapters in this book offer a wide variety of pieces that may help us solve the nuclear puzzle. These pieces can be put together in an even wider variety of ways. In this concluding chapter, we want to suggest some ways that we see to put them together, and we want to urge readers to think about alternative solutions of their own. We shall first look at each of the four subdisciplines of religious studies represented here, focusing on the question, Why have weapons of mass annihilation not yet been eliminated? Then, we shall put together those four sections to sketch one interpretation of the nuclear puzzle as a whole.

Some parts of this concluding chapter review the main themes of the preceding chapters, drawing out their implications and interweaving their common threads. Other parts are more speculative, suggesting hypotheses that deserve further exploration. We believe that there is a lot more to the nuclear age than meets the eye. If the paradoxes of this age are ever to be resolved, it will demand some deep digging into the hidden patterns of our personal, cultural, and social lives. Americans, like all people, are immersed in national and cultural traditions, as well as universal human realities, that shape our every experience. Like fish looking for water, we cannot see our human environment simply because it is everywhere. Academic study gives us an opportunity to step back and look more self-consciously at ourselves and our world. It calls upon us to examine the evidence carefully and draw reasonable conclusions. It also calls upon us to make educated guesses about the hidden pieces of the puzzle that must be brought to light. In this chapter we invite the reader to join us in both steps of the academic process.

THE FOUR SUBDISCIPLINES

History of Religions

The religious dimension of the nuclear age appears most clearly in the symbolic images that we use to think and talk about nuclear weapons. Historians of religion trace these images as they change in response to changing historical circumstances. Beneath the change, however, they find enduring patterns that remind them of familiar motifs from the world's religions. Even in this most secular age, it seems, people continue to seek a world steeped in sacrality. As the nuclear age has unfolded, an everwidening symbolic canopy has been woven around our central symbol of religious meaning and numinous power—the Bomb. But if the Bomb does play this role, once reserved for God alone, it differs from all previous deities in that we are its creators, not its creatures.

Wielding this new deity, we can claim omnipotence and cosmic significance for ourselves. Understandably, then, as a nation we grasp the Bomb with religious zeal. Individuals identify with their nation, the nation identifies with its nuclear arsenal, and all seem to merge in a single reality that transcends all limits. As we consecrate the Bomb it consecrates our lives in a spiral that is as terrifying as it is exhilarating, for we are no longer sure whether we wield the Bomb or it wields us. So we repeat the ritual incantation: we need nuclear weapons to protect our national security and our freedom. Perhaps we actually seek the security of religious structures to protect us as we aspire to freedom from human finitude, the freedom of omnipotence.

Endowing the Bomb with traditional religious symbolism, we reassure ourselves that the divine power we now embody in our national life is the same power our forebears served in war and peace. As we join ourselves with divinity in accustomed ways, the past and the present seem to merge. The reality of fundamental change is denied. Though we pay lip service to the radical changes wrought by modernity and nuclear weapons, we let religious symbolism affirm that the passage of time actually has no enduring effects. Needing to believe that nothing has changed and able to believe that nothing need change, we may easily come to believe that nothing should or even could change.

Sociology of Religion

Sociologists of religion have long noted that whenever the familiar order of life is threatened by some potentially uncontrollable force, the response is likely to have decidedly religious dimensions. The invention of nuclear weapons introduced a potentially uncontrollable force into our lives, and our response as a society recalls familiar patterns of religious life. The Bomb has been received as a numinous power—dreadful in its capacity to destroy but irresistibly appealing in its capacity to save. While we depend on it for security and stability, we feel that it makes our lives more precarious. Thus, we see it both as a friend deterring threatening foes and as itself a foe. The resulting ambivalence and confusion only heighten our sense of insecurity.

Religions typically respond to such confusion by giving the source of the threat a meaningful place in their world view. For example, both scientists and religious believers have adapted familiar religious language to speak about nuclear weapons. In effect, they make divinity a metaphor for the Bomb, allowing us to see the Bomb as a savior protecting us against the chaos it can itself create. Clinging to this new vision of order, we also cling to the social institutions that support it. Political and military structures become, in our day, what religious structures once were—the link between individuals and the cosmic order.

At the heart of this social process is the need to feel in control. Through religious and social interpretation, the Bomb's inherent threat of uncontrollable power is denied. But, although the irrationalities of the nuclear age may be covered over, they can never be swept away. This subtle interweaving of the controlled and the uncontrollable confronts us at every turn as we explore the nuclear dilemma. Perhaps we can no longer distinguish order from disorder; perhaps our sociological crisis now threatens to reach its breaking point. If so, we must feel an ever stronger need for control. So we focus on the order and rationalize the confusions by making the unfamiliar seem familiar. We turn to our traditional world view, which generated the problem, for our solution and our salvation. Alternative possibilities seem more threatening than attempts to rationally manage the current crisis.

Psychology of Religion

The symbolism of the Bomb offers an all-encompassing religious structure that should make us feel secure, confident, and saved from anxiety. Yet beneath the surface calm of our everyday lives there is a growing anxiety that must be constantly repressed. Psychologists of religion attempt to ferret out these psychodynamics and interpret their causes and implications. From a psychological viewpoint, religion should provide a basic trust in the sum total of reality—the Ultimate Environment—as a life-enhancing unity that fosters an unending process of personal growth. Today, however, the threat of nuclear annihilation raises grave doubts about any future prospects for the individual and for the Ultimate Environment itself. Reality seems no longer to open out into endless possibility but rather to hem us in with its fragmented pieces, leaving us wondering whether there is any unified Ultimate Environment at all. Behind our pervasive fragmentation lies what Robert Lifton has called the "broken connection," not only of death to life but of mind to bodily sensation and reason to imagination.

The Bomb, the epitome of the Western technological mind, also epitomizes the triumph of rational thought over metaphoric imagining. Our abstract, empirical, literal thinking has no meaningful place for sensory or symbolic images, nor for the terrors of the psyche's shadow side. All these instinctual realities can only become enemies to be caged, repressed, or even destroyed. Perhaps this is why the West, in counterpoint to its ideal of pure rationality, has periodically "lost its senses" in furious outbursts of senseless slaughter. These irrational rages may reflect the irrepressible demands of instinct, matter, and unconscious imaginings. They return us to the natural foundation that links us to past and future, a foundation that can be hunted and hounded but never destroyed. Yet this war against our own nature has broken so many essential connections that we are bereft of a unified trustworthy Ultimate Environment. The Bomb has turned this sense of "broken connection" into a gaping fissure, but it may be more the most virulent symptom than the cause of our crisis.

Now, we are called upon to come to our senses and make sense out of the most senseless threat imaginable. But we may be stymied because we insist on trying to imagine nuclear holocaust purely literally. If the connection between thought and sensory imagination were restored, we might be able to hear the foreboding mythic images arising from the unconscious wellsprings of truly human thought. These images make the future present in a concrete bodily way, speaking to us of a catastrophe that has already occurred: the open-ended nature of both our world and ourselves has been largely destroyed. The Bomb, the epitome of modernity, wreaks its violence on us simply by existing.

However, we are so insensible to nature and human nature that we cannot hear the voice of a future that is already here. We accept the spiralling arms race because we can not imagine any alternatives or feel genuinely responsive to the future we are preparing to destroy. We can only try to control the problem by turning to the same literalizing technology that created the problem in the first place. Thus, although the nuclear age is replete with imaginative religious symbols, they can not serve their traditional role of fostering trust in, and concern for, the Ultimate Environment. Our deafness prevents our symbols from making sense, and so we confirm our insensibility to the threat of extinction.

Reflective Religious Thought

The foundations of the nuclear age are built out of preconceptual paradigms—those presuppositions about reality that pass unnoticed because they are so deeply embedded in our culture. Reflective religious thought examines those paradigms in light of the religious paradigms of the past and present. The most basic preconceptual paradigm of modernity (shaped largely by white males in the West) is the irreducible separation between self and world. Seeking scientific truth as the only valid truth, we see ourselves as rational observers, totally detached from the world. And we see the world as mere fragments of matter with purely mechanistic relationships marked more by tension than reconciliation. Our goal is to predict, and thereby control, those relationships. So competition, control, and coercion are the bases of modern Western values. Since the world seems devoid of harmony, purpose, or connection with humanity, there is no moral check on technology's destructive capacities.

We seem confident that our literal technical calculations can extrapolate from the present to predict and control the future. Beneath this optimism, though, lurks a nagging dread. Reality appears to be random, and the meanings we give to its intrinsic absurdity appear equally arbitrary. Clinging for security to our conceptual abstractions, we only detach ourselves even further from the concreteness of our biological and historical reality. For many people, God Himself (with an appropriately male pronoun) is increasingly abstract and detached from the complex historical particularities of the material world.

Despite our superficial optimism, then, we actually feel compelled to believe that things will get worse, not better. In a world of permanent fragmentation and conflict, we will always have to be on our guard, prepared for the worst-case scenario. Inevitably, the prophecy fulfills itself; when everyone is creating visions of the future that assume the worst, the future is bound to get worse. We could imagine a genuinely new and better future only through open-ended metaphorical thinking that roots the mind in material and historical reality. But that is precisely the kind of thinking now proscribed and stigmatized by the leaders of our society as "mere subjectivity."

So we remain optimistic yet hopeless. This is no contradiction. The optimists' frantic attempts to control history betray their detachment from, and mistrust of, history's concrete connections of past, present, and future. Behind that mistrust lies their dread of an everthreatening nihilism, which their rationalized disembodied God cannot overcome. This may be the true face of the nuclear age—an age with no place for subjective involvement and meaning, no place for openness to the unpredictable, no means to reconcile mind and body or known and unknowable. Regardless of what the future might actually bring, the nuclear age, it seems, must create a present without hope. If we are indeed hopeless—detached from the concrete reality that threatens us and the biological heritage that is threatened—we would understandably have little incentive to work for change.

PUTTING THE PIECES TOGETHER

We divided this book, and this concluding chapter, into four subdisciplines of religious studies—a convenient but artificial and somewhat arbitrary structure. The reader will find diverse issues and approaches treated within each subdiscipline. The reader will also find virtually all the important themes crossing these artificial lines: Aho and Chernus both focus on the numinous quality of the Bomb and its "experts"; Linenthal and Benford and Kurtz show us how elites try to redefine reality; Noel, Thistlethwaite, and Noyalis share a concern for the tensions between rational thinking and metaphorical imagining; both Chapman and McDargh explore optimism in relation to nuclearism and numbing. Many other examples could be cited. Indeed, our concluding survey has already suggested that only all the subdisciplines in concert can provide a comprehensive understanding of the nuclear age. A brief recapitulation of the major shared themes will make this apparent.

The recurring references to goals of order, stability, and control show that the nuclear age flows directly from the main currents of modern Western culture. Other recurring themes show the price of modernity: a fragmented world of broken connections between life and death, order and disorder, clarity and mystery, consciousness and inner depths. In such a world, life becomes steeped in contradiction and self-contradiction. Confusion breeds anxiety, helplessness, hopelessness, and mistrust of reality. Our efforts to gain control of our world in customary ways only potentiate these feelings and mire us deeper in the nuclear dilemma. In sum, the preconceptual paradigms of the modern age foster a psychological disorder that is only exacerbated by societal efforts to maintain order, and all this is acted out on history's stage of symbolic meanings.

At the same time, though, the nuclear age also reflects a paradoxical attempt to escape the pains of modernity by undoing the work of modernity.

Through the Bomb we hope to turn back the clock and recover a life centered on an infinite saving power that offers meaning through transcendence. We fill our public life with ancient images, although we remain largely deaf to their religious meaning. Of course, the ancient religious and modern secular cultures of the West are not totally antithetical. A pervasive tone of dualism, with all responsibility for evil projected onto the "other," is one strong link binding them together. A desire to escape time by denying the reality of change is another. On the whole, though, there is a deep contradiction between our affirmation and rejection of the modern world. Whereas we seek escape from an unfulfilling past into an ever better future, we also hold fast to the past and try to return to it. And we pursue both goals by building paradox upon paradox: we hope to forge a peaceful future by preparing for a war that may destroy every future—a war viewed as both saving transformation (a traditional perception of war) and total annihilation (an old fantasy become real possibility through the new technology of nuclear weapons).

Because nuclear castastrophe is unimaginable on the literal level, we can apprehend it only through the symbols of the creative imagination. If we willingly fall back into numbed passivity, hoping to escape the issue, we allow the prevailing contradictory images to rule over us. Yet, if we try to break through our psychic numbing and imagine the impending future, we immediately encounter a maze of seductively appealing images, drawn from a religious past and a nuclear present, that fascinate and mesmerize us. And we try to appropriate these images in the mode of modern literal rationality, thereby intensifying our numbed denial. So it matters little whether we choose to think about the Bomb or not to think about it. Under the present conditions, both options reinforce each other in deepening our acquiescence in the status quo. Trapped in our ambivalence toward the past and present, we face the future helplessly because we can not imagine a meaningful future at all.

We embrace the Bomb in part because it enshrines all these contradictions in a paradoxical unity. It opens up that vanishing sense of religious meaning we long for and gives us a rich panoply of powerful images. We also embrace it because it denies the reality of contradiction with its abstract, rationalized, objective image of the world. It protects us from the sense of numinous mystery that we fear. So the religious dimension of the nuclear age reflects a desperate but false hope of ultimate transcendence. Modernity has evoked this hope in a uniquely desperate and deadly form just because modernity has denied in advance the possibility of its fulfillment.

It is not surprising that we speak so readily of "nuclear madness." The maze of contradictory double-binds that ensnares us is precisely the kind of world that makes for madness, creating deep schisms in both individual and societal life. When bewilderment runs so deep, it may be inevitable that we stop trying to understand, stop trying to respond, and thus stop trying to escape. We may even find relief in this paralyzing madness, for madness is a form of numbed death in life. If we are already dead, what can the Bomb do to us? Perhaps it can release us and transform our lives; most suicides believe in the transcendent power of their act. If it cannot change things for the better, at least the Bomb can explode the trap that binds us and release us from our fear and pain. One last eruption of transcendence may finally take us beyond every human limit.

WHAT SHOULD WE DO?

When issues of great import are at stake, there is something frustrating about academic analysis. One naturally asks, "What should I do, concretely, right now?" The traditional answer of the academy—study, ponder, understand— seems especially unsatisfying in the face of a life-and-death threat of unprecedented magnitude. Yet the interpretations offered in these chapters suggest that a new thoughtfulness is needed now more than ever. Understanding is crucial, not only as a prelude to action but as a form of action in itself. For as Ninian Smart points out in his foreword, the crux of the nuclear dilemma is not in our behavior but in our attitudes and ways of experiencing reality. The critical arena is not the field of political or social or technological action, but the field of symbols, images, and paradigms within which action occurs. If we are to imagine new possibilities for the future, we must begin with new ways of experiencing the past and present. We must make our known reality a metaphor for an unknown future. We must grow into that future by finding new ways to understand and apprehend the past and present.

Can we say what this means in practical terms? Our authors offer various suggestions. Chapman urges a return to the biblical paradigm of reconciliation and trusting embrace of the unknown. McDargh offers a psychological analogue to this paradigm: a basic trust in the Ultimate Environment and a generativity that nourishes the future. Benford and Kurtz suggest ritual actions that can help lead from danger to safety. Noyalis reminds us that thought and contemplation are themselves creative actions when they explore the realm of metaphor. Noel offers an example of this exploration in his journey of listening to the images. Thistlethwaite urges a return to the bodily roots of thought and points to a specific community where this rootedness is discovered in the roots of a people's past.

All our authors agree that we must learn to imagine a new kind of world today if we are to have any kind of world at all tomorrow; some call us into a future that may be radically different from the past and the present. They call for acceptance of the incalculable, the uncontrollable, the irreducibly mysterious. And they seek concrete images that can lead the way to a future in which known and unknown are embraced together. Such images must themselves be unpredictable, open ended, and metaphorical. They must image the world they seek to open up: a world imbued with the unpredictable power of imagination.

Yet, these essays also suggest that we need not abandon altogether the reality that we know today. If the new departures we need are essentially religious in nature, then the religious dimensions of the nuclear age may themselves offer a point of departure for our new explorations. The Bomb grips us so powerfully because its symbols are complex and open ended, capable of taking on ever new meanings. If our present need is for a new mode of experience more than a new content of experience, may we not be able to build on the content that already exists by evoking its inherent capacity to grow? If our need is to recapture the consciousness of the symbolic and metaphorical dimensions of life, may we not—indeed must we not—learn to see the nuclear age in a symbolic mode?

Once we understand the nuclear age as a unique constellation of symbolic images, we recognize that those images can be adapted to move us toward a radical transformation. Whatever the content of our transformation, it will call for strong will, clear purpose, and meaningful sacrifice. It will call for new myths, rituals, and social organizations. It will call for some measure of continued balanced rationality, tempered with revitalized imagination. And it will call for renewed consciousness of the numinous and its promise of redemptive transcendence. All of these, which now serve policies that assume a continuing need for nuclear weapons, can play a vital role in the search for alternative security stances.

Above all, the transformation we can envision will call for honesty in facing the true dimensions of our terror. Here, too, the images of the nuclear age can serve us simply by existing as cultural mirrors of the terror we all share. If we can learn to see and hear these images as reflections of our own creative imaginations, we may begin to build a world of wholeness where life and death, order and chaos, and joy and terror can live together in proper balance. If we can learn to see a connected world of abundant symbolic meanings, we may find ourselves moving into a radically new situation whose contents reflect our new vision of the world. Uncovering the religious dimension hidden beneath our nuclear arsenal—recognizing the deepest sources of the Bomb's grasp upon us—we may discover ourselves naturally releasing our grasp on the Bomb. As we are able to think more creatively about the "other" and about real security, nuclear arsenals may no longer have a place in our conceptions of proper world order. This in turn would release public policy decisions regarding nuclear weapons from the prison of political fear to their rightful place as a part of the process, slow as it might be, toward political and social transformation.

The nuclear age offers us a rich history for inspection. This inspection, this understanding, is the key. If we can understand the nuclear age in all its complex reality—symbolic and metaphoric as well as literal—we can understand the need for a new order and in that very act begin to create the humane order that all the world's religions envision. It is the process that matters most. As a step in the process, this book offers no single answer, no single concrete action that can save us. Rather it offers a way into a new orientation, a new point of view, a new vocabulary and way of thinking. It invites the reader to join in the process, to explore new attitudes and approaches, to put ideas together in new ways. The interpretations we have offered in this conclusion are only a few of the many possibilities that these chapters can open up for all students of the nuclear age.

Notes

1. *Nuclear Images in the Popular Press: The Age of Apocalypse*

1. *Life* (August 20, 1945), p. 32.
2. *Reader's Digest* (February 1946), pp. 121–26.
3. *Life* (November 19, 1945), pp. 27–35.
4. Cf. Chapter 2, pp. 44–47.
5. *Life* (February 27, 1950), p. 30.
6. Ibid., pp. 19–40.
7. *Reader's Digest* (March 1951), pp. 59–60. Armageddon is the place where the final apocalyptic battle will take place, according to some biblical traditions.
8. *Reader's Digest* (April 1951), pp. 29–30.
9. *Life* (August 28, 1950), pp. 26–27.
10. *Life* (March 30, 1953), p. 24.
11. *Life,* (March 29, 1954), pp. 17–23.
12. On the role of the nuclear priesthood, see Chapter 4, in this book.
13. *Life* (April 12, 1954), pp. 32–33.
14. *Reader's Digest* (August 1954), pp. 1–8.
15. *Life* (June 10, 1957), pp. 24–29.
16. *Reader's Digest* (April 1958), pp. 41–46.
17. For the centrality of "will" in nuclear imagery, see Chapter 2.
18. *Life* (September 15, 1961), pp. 95–108.
19. *Life* (January 12, 1962), pp. 2, 4, 34–43.
20. This is a good example of the "official optimism" described by Chapman in Chapter 8.

21. *Reader's Digest* (June 1962), pp. 106–108.

22. *Life* (May 4, 1962), pp. 44–45.

23. *Reader's Digest* (April 1962), pp. 106–110.

24. *Life* (July 20, 1962), pp. 26–35.

25. *Life* (November 9, 1962), pp. 38–39.

26. This nonlogical aspect of religious symbolism is discussed more fully in Chapter 10.

2. War and Sacrifice in the Nuclear Age: The Committee on the Present Danger and the Renewal of Martial Enthusiasm

1. Guest's stanza found in Michael Yavenditti, "The American People and the Use of Atomic Bombs on Japan: The 1940s," *Historian* 36 (February 1974): 229; Manuel is quoted in Fred Halliday, *The Making of the Second Cold War* (London: Verso, 1983), p. 5.

2. Columbia Broadcasting System, *From Pearl Harbor into Tokyo: The Story as Told by War Correspondents on the Air* (New York: Columbia Broadcasting System, 1945), p. 296.

3. See Les K. Adler and Thomas G. Paterson, "Red Fascism: The Merger of Nazi Germany and Soviet Russia in the American Image of Totalitarianism," *American Historical Review* 75 (1970): 1046–64.

4. Carl Solberg, *Riding High: America in the Cold War* (New York: Mason and Lipscomb, 1973), p. 40.

5. Quoted in Richard J. Barnet, *Roots of War* (Baltimore: Penguin Books, 1973), p. 19.

6. William G. McLoughlin, *Revivals, Awakenings, and Reform,* Chicago History of American Religion Series (Chicago: University of Chicago Press, 1978), p. xiii.

7. Jerry W. Saunders, *Peddlers of Crisis: The Committee on the Present Danger and the Politics of Containment* (Boston: South End Press, 1983), p. 43.

8. Lawrence Freedman, *The Evolution of Nuclear Strategy* (New York: St. Martin's Press, 1981), p. 94.

9. Saunders, *Peddlers of Crisis,* p. 198.

10. Norman Podhoretz, "The Present Danger," *Commentary* 69 (March 1980), p. 31; and Podhoretz, *Breaking Ranks* (New York: Harper and Row, 1979), p. 363.

11. Norman Podhoretz, "The Culture of Appeasement," *Harper's* (October 1977), p. 29; Richard Polenberg, ed., *America at War: The Home Front, 1941–1945* (Englewood Cliffs, N.J.: Prentice-Hall, 1969), p. 3.

12. Norman Podhoretz, "The Future Danger," *Commentary* 71 (April 1981), p. 38.

13. "Peace With Freedom: A Discussion by the Committee on the Present Danger before the Foreign Policy Association, 14 March 1978," in Charles Tyroler, II, ed., *Alerting America: The Papers of the Committee on the Present Danger* (Washington, D.C.: Pergamon-Brassey's, 1984), p. 29.

14. Peter Berger, "Indochina and the American Conscience," *Commentary* 69 (February 1980), p. 39.

15. Tyroler, *Alerting America,* p. 3; "The 1980 Crisis and What We Should Do about It," in Tyroler, ibid., p. 176; "Peace with Freedom," in Tyroler, ibid., p. 31.

16. "Has America become Number 2?" in Tyroler, ibid., p. 235; Richard Pipes, *Survival Is Not Enough: Soviet Realities and America's Future* (New York: Simon and Schuster, 1984), p. 102; Richard Pipes, "Why the Soviet Union Thinks It Could Fight and Win a Nuclear War," *Commentary* 64 (July 1977), p. 26.

17. Norman Podhoretz, "Making the World Safe for Communism," *Commentary* 62 (April 1976), p. 37.

18. Saunders, *Peddlers of Crisis,* p. 195; Podhoretz, "Making the World Safe for Communism," p. 40; Podhoretz, "The Present Danger," p. 37.

19. Podhoretz, "The Present Danger," pp. 37, 29, 40.

20. Podhoretz, "The Future Danger," p. 36; Robert Conquest and John Manchip White, *What to Do When the Russians Come: A Survivor's Guide* (New York: Stein and Day, 1984), p. 177; Jeane Kirkpatrick, *The Reagan Phenomenon and Other Speeches on Foreign Policy* (Washington, D.C.: American Institute for Public Policy Research, 1983), p. 12.

21. Podhoretz, "The Future Danger," pp. 29–47.

22. Norman Podhoretz, *The Present Danger* (New York: Simon and Schuster, 1980), p. 61.

23. Gray is quoted in Robert Scheer, *With Enough Shovels: Reagan and Bush on Nuclear War* (New York: Random House, 1982), p. 12.

24. Richard J. Barnet, *Roots of War* (Baltimore: Penguin Books, 1971), p. 255.

25. Charles Tyroler, "Peace with Freedom," in *Alerting America,* p. 34; Pipes, *Survival Is Not Enough,* p. 66.

26. Sidney Hook, H. Stuart Hughes, Hans Morgenthau, and C. P. Snow, "Western Values and Total War," in Peter G. Filene, *American Views of Soviet Russia, 1917–1965* (Homewood, Ill.: Dorsey Press, 1968), p. 364; Ronald Reagan, "Remarks to the National Association of Evangelicals, March 8, 1983," in Strobe Talbott, *The Russians and Reagan* (New York: Vintage Books, 1984), pp. 115–16.

27. For a good introduction to controversies surrounding nuclear winter see, Lester Grinspoon, ed., *The Long Darkness: Psychological and Moral Perspectives on Nuclear Winter* (New Haven: Yale University Press, 1986); and Russell Seitz, "'Nuclear Winter' Melts Down," *The National Interest* (Fall 1986), pp. 3–17.

28. For a detailed discussion of the ideology of strategic defense, see Edward Tabor Linenthal, *Symbolic Defense: The Cultural Significance of the Strategic Defense Initiative* (Urbana: University of Illinois Press, 1989).

3. Nuclear Images in the Popular Press: From Apocalypse to Static Balance

1. *Time* (March 29, 1982), p. 19.

2. *Readers Digest* (October 1982), p. 66.

3. *Time* (April 12, 1982), p. 14.

4. *Time* (March 29, 1982), p. 25.

5. *Time* (January 2, 1984), p. 45.

6. *Time* (December 5, 1983), p. 100.

7. *Time* (March 29, 1982), p. 26.

8. *Time* (April 19, 1982), p. 21.

9. *Reader's Digest* (February 1984), p. 168.

10. *Reader's Digest* (December 1980), p. 107.

11. *Time* (January 2, 1984), p. 35.

12. Ibid., p. 26; cf. *Reader's Digest* (March 1985), p. 90.

13. *Time* (April 19, 1982), p. 21.

14. *Time* (November 30, 1981), p. 60.

15. *Reader's Digest* (December 1980), p. 107.

16. *Time* (April 12, 1982), pp. 12, 14.

17. *Time* (November 30, 1981), p. 60; cf. *Reader's Digest* (November 1984), p. 137.

18. *Reader's Digest* (June 1981), pp. 66, 70; cf. (March 1985), p. 89.

19. *Time* (November 2, 1981), pp. 34, 36.

20. *Time* (January 2, 1984), p. 31.

21. *Time* (March 21, 1983), p. 16.

22. *Time* (January 2, 1984), p. 26.

23. *Reader's Digest* (December 1980), p. 106.

24. *Time* (June 14, 1982), p. 22.

25. *Time* (December 5, 1983), p. 39.

26. *Reader's Digest* (August 1981), pp. 107, 110.

27. *Time* (December 5, 1983), pp. 44, 40.

28. *Time* (March 29, 1982), p. 25.

29. Ibid.

30. Ibid.

31. The importance of "stability" as a motive for the arms race is discussed from another perspective in Chapter 5.

32. *Time* (February 27, 1984), p. 34.

33. *Time* (December 5, 1983), p. 39.

34. *Time* (March 21, 1983), p. 26; cf. *Reader's Digest* (March 1985), pp. 90–91.

35. *Time* (March 21, 1983), p. 17.

36. *Reader's Digest* (June 1981), p. 70; cf. (March 1985), p. 91.

37. *Time* (October 10, 1983), p. 12.

38. *Time* (December 5, 1983), p. 16.

39. *Time* (March 29, 1982), p. 22; cf. *Reader's Digest* (March 1985), p. 90.

40. *Reader's Digest* (January 1979), pp. 65, 67.

41. Cf. Chapter 6.

42. See Chapter 2 for the central role of this theme in nuclear imagery.

43. *Reader's Digest* (June 1981), p. 70.

44. *Reader's Digest* (December 1980), p. 107.

45. *Time* (September 26, 1983), p. 18.

46. *Time* (March 29, 1982), p. 23.

47. *Time* (November 2, 1981), p. 34.

48. *Time* (November 28, 1982), p. 30.

49. *Time* (October 24, 1983), p. 41.

50. *Time* (December 5, 1983), p. 16.

51. *Reader's Digest* (January 1983), pp. 97, 98, 100.

52. *Time* (April 4, 1983), p. 8; cf. *Reader's Digest* (November 1984), pp. 136–40.

53. *Time* (April 4, 1983), p. 9.

54. Ibid., pp. 22, 19.

55. *Time* (March 29, 1982), p. 23.

56. *Time* (June 14, 1982), p. 22.

57. *Reader's Digest* (August 1981), p. 107.

58. *Reader's Digest* (December 1980), p. 104.

59. *Time* (March 29, 1982), p. 25.

60. Ibid., p. 24.

61. *Time* (June 14, 1982), p. 22.

62. *Time* (March 29, 1982), p. 24.

63. *Time* (December 5, 1983), p. 44.

64. *Time* (November 30, 1981), p. 60.

65. *Time* (December 5, 1983), p. 16.

66. *Reader's Digest* (November 1982), p. 143.

67. *Time* (December 5, 1983), p. 39.

68. Ibid.

69. *Time* (May 30, 1983), p. 16.

70. *Time* (April 12, 1982), p. 14.

71. *Time* (December 5, 1983), pp. 100, 40.

72. Ibid., p. 44.

73. *Time* (March 29, 1982), p. 26.

74. The relationships between this view of the world and the nuclear arms race are developed at greater length by Chapman in Chapter 8.

4. "I Am Death . . . Who Shatters Worlds": The Emerging Nuclear Death Cult

1. Robert Coles, "The Psychology of Armageddon," *Psychology Today* (May 1982), pp. 13–14, 88; Ken Briggs, "Graham Warns of Arms and Dangers in TV Evangelism," *New York Times* (January 1981), p. 7; William Martin, "Waiting for the End," *Atlantic Monthly* 249 (1982), pp. 31–37.

2. Rudolf Otto, *The Idea of the Holy,* trans. John W. Harvey (New York: Oxford University Press, 1973 [1923]).

3. William Laurence, *Men and Atoms* (New York: Simon and Schuster, 1959), p. 120; cf. pp. 121–22.

4. In 1942 Edward Teller correctly calculated that the heat production of a fission bomb is sufficient to ignite first deuterium and then nitrogen. This nitrogen reaction could lead to an uncontrolled nuclear explosion enveloping the entire earth. Later calculations by Oppenheimer and Arthur Compton indicated that, although this scenario is empirically possible, it is probable only three times in 1 million. But doubts persisted until after the Alamogordo test (Nuel Pharr Davis, *Lawrence and Oppenheimer* [New York: Simon and Schuster, 1968], p. 132). See also Pearl Buck, "The End of the World? One Noble Prize Winner Interviews Another," *The American Weekly* (March 8, 1959), p. 11.

5. Otto Frisch, *What Little I Remember* (London: Cambridge University Press, 1979), p. 164.

6. Laurence, *Men and Atoms*, p. 129.

7. Weisskopf, "The World According to Weisskopf," NOVA, no. 1108, April 8, 1984, WGBH Transcripts, Boston, MA: WGBH Educational Foundation.

8. Quoted in Henry De Wolf Smyth, *Atomic Energy for Military Purposes: The Development of the Atomic Bomb under the Auspices of the United States Government, 1940–1945* (Princeton: Princeton University Press, 1945), pp. 253–54.

9. Quoted in Davis, *Lawrence and Oppenheimer*, p. 233.

10. Laurence, *Men and Atoms*, p. 118.

11. A. H. Compton, *Atomic Quest: A Personal Narrative* (New York: Oxford University Press, 1956), pp. 215–16.

12. Robert Jungk, *Brighter than a Thousand Suns*, trans. James C. Cleugh (New York: Harcourt, Brace and World, 1958), p. 200.

13. Davis, *Lawrence and Oppenheimer*, p. 242.

14. Ibid., p. 239.

15. Quoted in Laurence, *Men and Atoms*, p. 118.

16. Ibid., pp. 116–20. For similar experiences of the captive German physicist Otto Hahn and the Japanese physicist Yoshio Nishina upon hearing of the bomb, see Jungk, *Brighter than a Thousand Suns*, pp. 210–14.

17. Kenneth Bainbridge, "A Foul and Awesome Display," *Bulletin of the Atomic Scientists* 31 (1975): 46.

18. Quoted in Stanley Blumberg, *Energy and Conflict: The Life and Times of Edward Teller* (New York: G. P. Putnam's Sons, 1976), p. 141.

19. Edward Teller, *The Legacy of Hiroshima* (Garden City, N.Y.: Doubleday, 1962), p. 17.

20. Leslie R. Groves, *Now It Can Be Told: The Story of the Manhattan Project* (New York: Harper and Row, 1962), p. 296.

21. Ibid., p. 303.

22. Jungk, *Brighter than a Thousand Suns,* p. 202.

23. The case of Teller is complicated. Lifton considers him the most extreme exemplar of religiously based "nuclearism" (Lifton and Falk, *Indefensible Weapons: The Political and Psychological Case Against Nuclearism* [New York: Basic Books, 1982], p. 91.) But he fails to cite examples from Teller's experience of the Bomb to support this contention. Indeed, Lifton admits that Teller rebuked those of his colleagues who saw in the Bomb "improbable and fantastic calamities." On the contrary, he exhorted them to be "rational" and "not seek refuge in a make believe world" of nuclear annihilation. Nevertheless, Teller frequently and unashamedly invokes religious rhetoric in his own discussions of the bomb. "First of all," he once soberly confessed to Leo Szilard, "I have no hope of clearing my conscience." "The things we are working on are so terrible that no amount of protesting or fiddling with politics will save our souls." (Quoted in Leo Szilard, *Leo Szilard, His Version of the Facts: Selected Recollections and Correspondence,* ed. Spencer R. Weart and Gertrud Weiss Szilard [Cambridge: MIT Press, 1978], p. 207–9.) See also Blumberg, *Energy and Conflict,* pp. 156–57.

24. Laurence, *Men and Atoms,* p. 130.

25. "At twilight on the sixth day of Creation, so say the Hebrew commentators to the Old Testament, God made for man a number of tools that give him also the gift of creation." So begins Bronowski, who then audaciously adds: "If they were alive today, they would write, 'God made the neutron.'" "Here it is at Oak Ridge in Tennessee," he continues, "the blue glow that is the trace of neutrons: the visible finger of God touching Adam in Michelangelo's painting, not with breath but with power" (Jacob Bronowski, *The Ascent of Man* [Boston: Little, Brown and Co., 1973], p. 341).

    William Laurence speaks of "suffering from some kind of hallucination" when ushered into the same sacred precincts: "One stands before them as though beholding the realization of a vision such as Michelangelo might have had of a world yet to be, as *indescribable* as the Grand Canyon of Arizona, Beethoven's Ninth Symphony, or the presence 'whose dwelling is the light of setting suns.' . . . Here, for the first time in history, man stands in the presence of the very act of elemental creation of matter. Here in the great silences . . . new elements are being born, a phenomenon that, as far as man knows, has not happened since Genesis" (Laurence, *Men and Atoms,* pp. 97–98).

26. For further insights, see Chapters 1–3 and 8 of this book.

27. Davis, *Lawrence and Oppenheimer,* p. 224.

28. Stewart Alsop and Ralph E. Lapp, "The Strange Death of Louis Slotin," *Man against Nature,* ed. C. Neider (New York: Harper and Bros., 1954).

29. "Batter My Heart" in John Donne, *The Complete Poetry of John Donne,* ed. John T. Shawcross (Garden City, N.Y.: Doubleday-Anchor Books, 1967), p. 344; and "A Litany," pp. 355–56, sec. iv, verses 28–36.

30. Davis, *Lawrence and Oppenheimer,* p. 225.

31. Donald R. Roberts, "The Death Wish of John Donne," *PMLA* 62 (1947): 965–68.

32. For example, "Metempsychosis" (Donne, *Complete Poetry,* pp. 307–29), "A Funeral Elegie" (pp. 286–89), and "Of the Progress of the Soule" (pp. 289–306).

33. *Bhagavadgita,* 11: 26–30.

34. Donne, "Batter My Heart," *Complete Poetry,* p. 344, lines 1–6, 12–14.

35. Heimar Kipphardt, *In the Matter of J. Robert Oppenheimer,* trans. Ruth Speirs (New York: Hill and Wang, 1964), pp. 91–92; Davis, *Lawrence and Oppenheimer,* p. 240; Laurence, *Men and Atoms,* p. 118.

36. *Bhagavadgita,* 11: 12, and 10: 34, 11: 32.

37. Laurence, *Men and Atoms,* p. 117. "We felt," said Oppenheimer, "the world would never be the same again" (Davis, *Lawrence and Oppenheimer,* p. 240).

38. For more on ritual elements of the nuclear death cult, see other chapters in this book, particularly Chapter 5.

39. Chevalier, *The Man Who Would Be God* (New York: G. P. Putnam's Sons, 1959), pp. 272–73.

40. Davis, *Lawrence and Oppenheimer,* p. 160.

41. Ibid., p. 163.

42. Frisch, *What Little I Remember,* pp. 159–62.

43. Alsop and Lapp, "The Strange Death of Louis Slotin," pp. 10–11.

44. Davis, *Lawrence and Oppenheimer,* pp. 225–26.

45. Philip M. Stern, *The Oppenheimer Case: Security on Trial* (New York: Harper and Row, 1969), especially pp. 434–40. Cf. Chapter 5, p. 81.

46. Alvin Weinberg, "Social Institutions and Nuclear Energy," *Science* 177 (1972), p. 34.

47. Quoted in J. Gustave Speth, Arthur R. Tamplin, and Thomas B. Cochran, "Plutonium Recycle: The Fateful Step," *Bulletin of the Atomic Scientists* 30 (1974): 20.

48. Thomas Sebeok, *Communication Measures to Bridge Ten Millennia* (Washington, D.C.: U.S. Govt. Dept. of Commerce, National Technical Information Service, 1984).

49. See the numerous letters to this effect in Szilard, *Leo Szilard.*

50. Jungk, *Brighter than a Thousand Suns,* pp. 107–8.

51. Ibid., pp. 91–99. For the background and substance of the Franck report (1945) that sought to keep nuclear research out of military hands in America and place it under international control, see pp. 183–86 and 348–60.

52. Ibid., p. 81.

53. See Chapter 1, for examples of the conflicting popular images of the Bomb.

54. Norman Cohn, *The Pursuit of the Millennium* (New York: Oxford University Press, 1970).

55. Quoted in Otto, *The Idea of the Holy,* p. 99.

56. Hal Lindsey, *The Late Great Planet Earth* (Grand Rapids, Mich.: Zondervan, 1970).

57. John Wesley White, *Arming for Armageddon* (Milford, Mich.: Mott Media, 1983), pp. 39–40. White cites two conversions, one by a physicist, the other by a commander of a Minuteman base in Wyoming, to support his contention that nuclear priests themselves are convinced that the world is about to end in nuclear holocaust. "In trying to save millions from nuclear war, might it happen despite his [the colonel's] best efforts? . . . So that night . . . [he] came forward and confessed Jesus as his Lord and Savior. Thereafter come peace or war," we are assured, "he was Christ's" (ibid.).

58. Lindsey, *The Late Great Planet Earth,* p. 163.

59. Ibid., p. 164.

60. Ibid., p. 168.

61. White, *Arming for Armageddon,* p. 19.

62. Ibid., p. 171. Cf. 142–44.

63. Ibid., p. 179.

64. Ibid., p. 201.

65. Cf. I Corinthians 15:51–54 or I Thessalonians 4:15–18.

66. Hal Lindsey, *The Rapture* (New York: Bantam Books, 1983), p. 24.

67. Herman Kahn, *On Escalation* (Baltimore: Penguin Books, 1968), p. 194.

68. "Pretribulationists" believe that Rapture precedes Tribulation and include in their number both Lindsey and White. "Posttribulationists," who hold the opposite, are represented by Robert Gundry, *The Church and the Tribulation* (Grand Rapids, Mich.: Zondervan, 1973).

69. Hal Lindsey, *There's a New World Coming* (Eugene, Ore.: Harvest House, 1973), pp. 307–308.

70. Georges Bataille, *Death and Sensuality: A Study of Eroticism and the Taboo* (New York: Walker and Co., 1962), pp. 221–51.

71. Max Weber, *Essays in Sociology,* trans. and ed. Hans Gerth and C. Wright Mills (New York: Oxford University Press, 1958), pp. 77–78.

72. Michael Blain, "The Role of Death in Political Conflict," *Psychoanalytic Review* 63 (Summer 1976): 249–65.

73. O. K. Johnson, "INEL Tightens Its Security Measures," *Idaho State Journal*

(November 30, 1984), p. B–1; Joel Connelly, "The Militarization of Hanford," *Seattle P-I Focus* (January 20, 1985).

74. Robert Bellah, *The Broken Covenant* (New York: Seabury Press, 1975), p. 142.

75. Otto, *The Idea of the Holy,* p. 132.

76. Quoted in Studs Terkel, *The Good War* (New York: Ballantine Books, 1984), p. 437.

5. Performing the Nuclear Ceremony: The Arms Race as a Ritual

1. Clifford Geertz, *The Interpretation of Cultures: Selected Essays* (New York: Basic Books, 1973), p. 112.

2. Kurt Finsterbusch, "The Sociological Literature on Nuclear Issues." *Society* 22 (January–February 1985): 2–3. In *Social Problems,* where one might expect such discussions, Finsterbusch found seventeen articles; however, ten appeared in a special 1963 issue, immediately following the Cuban missile crisis.

3. Lester R. Kurtz, with the assistance of Robert Benford and Jennifer Turpin, *The Nuclear Cage* (Englewood Cliffs, N.J.: Prentice-Hall, 1988).

4. Thomas Ford Hoult, *Dictionary of Modern Sociology,* (Totowa, N.J.: Littlefield, Adams & Co., 1974), p. 275.

5. A. R. Radcliffe-Brown, "Religion and Society," in *The Social Anthropology of Radcliffe-Brown,* ed. Adam Kuper (London: Routledge & Kegan Paul, 1977), p. 105.

6. William Graham Sumner, *Folkways: A Study of the Sociological Importance of Usages, Manners, Customs, Mores, and Morals* (New York: Mentor Books, [1906] 1940). Sumner suggested that "ritual is the perfect form of drill and of the regulated habit which comes from drill" (p. 67).

7. See Robert L. Herrick, "Review of *Secular Ritual,* edited by S. F. Moore and B. G. Myerhoff, and *Rituals of the Kadyan State* by H. L. Seneviratne," *American Journal of Sociology* 86 (September 1980): 396–99; and Sally Falk Moore and Barbara G. Myerhoff, eds., *Secular Ritual* (Amsterdam: Van Gorcum & Co., 1977).

8. Erving Goffman, *Interaction Ritual: Essays in Face-to-Face Behavior* (Chicago: Aldine, 1967).

9. Moore and Myerhoff, *Secular Ritual.*

10. Goffman, *Interaction Ritual,* p. 57.

11. See e.g., Robert Jay Lifton, "Imagining the Real" in Robert Jay Lifton and Richard Falk, *Indefensible Weapons: The Political and Psychological Case against Nuclearism,* pp. 3–125 (New York: Basic Books, 1982).

12. Arnold van Gennep, *Les rites de passage.* Published in English as *The Rites of Passage,* trans. Monika B. Vizedom and Gabrielle L. Caffee (Chicago: University of Chicago Press, [1909] 1960); Victor Turner, *The Ritual Process: Structure and Anti-Structure* (Ithaca: Cornell University Press, 1969); cf. Lester R. Kurtz, "The Politics of Heresy," *American Journal of Sociology* 83 (May 1983): 1085–1115.

13. John Dillard, "Nuclear Potlatch," unpublished paper (University of Texas, Austin, 1983). Dillard noted parallels between the arms race and the potlatch among the Kwakiutl, in an effort to channel competition into nonwarfare activities. He suggested, however, that the potlatch item (in this case, nuclear weapons) should be replaced with a more benign alternative. Hence, the implication is not that the ritual form be abandoned but that the content of the ritual be changed.

14. Goffman, *Interaction Ritual,* p. 42.

15. There is consensus across the political spectrum that there is enormous uncertainty in dealing with the issue. The Office of Technology Assessment of the Congress of the United States study on *The Effects of Nuclear War* (Totowa, N.J.: Allanhead, Osmun & Co., 1980) concluded that "The effects of a nuclear war that cannot be calculated are at least as important as those for which calculations are attempted" (p. 3). Cf. Lifton, "Imagining the Real"; A. S. Collins, "How a Nuclear War Would Be Fought on Land," *Bulletin of the Atomic Scientists* 35 (May 1979): 28–30; Harold Brown, *Thinking about National Security: Defense and Foreign Policy in a Dangerous World* (Boulder, Colo.: Westview Press, 1983), p. 79; James Fallows, *National Defense* (New York: Vintage Books, 1982), p. 140; Donald M. Snow, "Strategic Uncertainty and Nuclear Deterrence," *Naval War College Review* 34 (1981): 27–41; Solly Zuckerman, *Nuclear Illusion and Reality* (New York: Vintage Books, 1983), p. ix.

16. Roger Molander, "How I Learned to Start Worrying and Hate the Bomb," *Washington Post* (March 21, 1982): pp. D1, D5. This kind of narrowly focused thinking often reflects a purely intellectualized grasp of reality, detached from concrete reality. See Susan Thistlethwaite's discussion of this central feature of the nuclear age in Chapter 9.

17. Executive Office of the President, *Major Themes and Additional Budget Details: Fiscal Year 1984* (Washington, D.C.: U.S. Government Printing Office, 1983), p. 201. For further examples, see Chapter 4.

18. Geertz, *Interpretation,* p. 113. Geertz defined a people's *ethos* as "the tone, character, and quality of their life, its moral and aesthetic style and mood; it is the underlying attitude toward themselves and their world that life reflects." The "world view is their picture of the way things in sheer actuality are, their concept of nature, of self, of society" (p. 127).

19. *Ibid.,* p. 114.

20. Andrew Cockburn and Alexander Cockburn, "The Myth of Missile Accuracy," *New York Review of Books* 28 (November 20, 1980), p. 40; Stephen Hilgartner, Richard C.. Bell, and Rory O'Connor, *Nukespeak: The Selling of Nuclear Technology in America* (New York: Penguin Books, 1983).

21. See Walter R. Fisher, "Narration as a Human Communication Paradigm: The Case of Public Moral Argument," *Communication Monographs* 51, no. 1 (1984): 1–23.

22. Goffman, *Interaction Ritual,* p. 43.

23. Lifton, "Imagining the Real," pp. 1–22, outlined several "nuclear illusions" shared by those who appear to believe that a nuclear war is "survivable" or "winnable," including the illusions of limit and control, foreknowledge, preparation, stoic behavior under nuclear attack, recovery, and rationality. For similar and additional examples, see Ira Chernus, "Mythologies of Nuclear War," *Journal of the American Academy of Religion* 50 (June 1982): 255–73; G. F. Kennan, *The Nuclear Delusion: Soviet-American Relations in the Atomic Age* (New York: Pantheon, 1982); Robert Scheer, *With Enough Shovels: Reagan, Bush and Nuclear War* (New York: Random House, 1982); George W. Ball, "The Cosmic Bluff," *New York Review of Books* 30 (July 21, 1983): 37–41; Bernard J. O'Keefe, *Nuclear Hostages* (Boston: Houghton Mifflin, 1983); Emma Rothschild, "The Delusions of Deterrence," *New York Review of Books* 30 (April 14, 1983): 40–50; Bruce Russett, *The Prisoners of Insecurity: Nuclear Deterrence, the Arms Race, and Arms Control* (San Francisco: W. H. Freeman, 1983); Zuckerman, *Illusion and Reality;* Fallows, *National Defense.*

24. See, for example, Paul H. Nitze, "Atoms, Strategy and Policy," *Foreign Affairs* 34. no. 2 (1956), pp. 187–98, and Herman Kahn, *On Thermonuclear War* (Princeton: Princeton University Press, 1960).

25. For examples, see P. H. Nitze, "Assuring Strategic Stability in an Era of Detente," *Foreign Affairs* 54 (January 1976), pp. 223–26; Richard Pipes, "Why the Soviet Union Thinks It Could Fight and Win a Nuclear War," *Commentary* 64 (July 1977), pp. 21–34; Colin Gray, "Nuclear Strategy: The Case for a Theory of Victory," *International Security* 3 (Summer 1979), pp. 54–87; Harold Brown, *Department of Defense Annual Report to the Congress, Fiscal Year 1981* (Washington, D.C.: U.S. Government Printing Office, 1980); Colin S. Gray and Keith Payne, "Victory Is Possible," *Foreign Policy* (Summer 1980), pp. 14–27; Robert Jastrow, "Why Strategic Superiority Matters," *Commentary* 75, no. 3 (1983), pp. 27–32; C. W. Weinberger, *Department of Defense Annual Report to the Congress, Fiscal Year 1984* (Washington, D.C.: U.S. Government Printing Office, 1983). Secretary Weinberger, in his 1984 *Annual Report to Congress,* denied that he shares such beliefs. He argued that rather than trying to *win* a nuclear war, our objective would be *"to restore peace on favorable terms"* (p. 32, emphasis in the original).

26. Collateral damage usually refers to the destruction of population centers, and so on, that are in close proximity to intended military targets. A number of "experts," including two former secretaries of defense, Robert McNamara and Melvin Laird, have insisted that a nuclear war could not be kept limited. R. E. McNamara, "The Military Role of Nuclear Weapons: Perceptions and Misperceptions," *Foreign Affairs* 62 (Fall 1983), p. 71; Melvin R. Laird, "What Our Defense Really Needs," *Washington Post* (November 4, 1982), p. A15.

27. Office of Technology Assessment, *Effects.*

28. Joint Committee on Defense Production, Congress of the United States, *Economic and Social Consequences of Nuclear Attacks on the United States* (Washington, D.C.: U.S. Government Printing Office, 1979).

29. These congressional studies examined only the expected damage to the United States and the Soviet Union. Current U.S. strategic doctrine, called the *countervailing strategy,* is based not only on the theory that "escalation" could be "controlled" but that a nuclear confrontation could be "contained" to the "theatre" (region) in which the war begins. Implicit in this doctrine is the hope that should a nation violate the taboo against the use of nuclear weapons, their use would be limited to other than American soil. For elaborations of the "countervailing strategy," see Harold Brown, *Department of Defense Annual Report to the Congress, Fiscal Year 1980* (Washington, D.C.: U.S. Government Printing Office, 1979), pp. 74–81; idem., *Annual Report 1981,* pp. 65–68; Walter Slocombe, "The Countervailing Strategy," *International Security* 5 (Spring 1981), 18–48.

30. Carl Sagan, "Nuclear War and Climatic Catastrophe: Some Policy Implications," *Foreign Affairs* 62 (Winter 1983–84), p. 259. See R. P. Turco, O. B. Toon, T. P. Ackerman, J. P. Pollock, and Carl Sagan, "Nuclear Winter: Global Atmospheric Consequences of Multiple Nuclear Explosions," *Science* 222 (December 23, 1983), pp. 1283–92; Paul R. Ehrlich, Mark A. Harwell, Peter H. Raven, Carl Sagan, George M. Woodwell, et al., "Long-Term Biological Consequences of Nuclear War," *Science* 222 (December 23, 1983), pp. 1293–1300; Philip Shabecoff, "Scientists See No Hope in Atom War," *New York Times* (December 9, 1983). For a more comprehensive treatment of the nuclear winter phenomenon by the scientific community, see Committee of the Atmospheric Effects of Nuclear Explosions, Commission on Physical Sciences, Mathematics, and Resources, National Research Council (National Academy of Sciences), *The Effects of a Major Nuclear Exchange* (Washington, D.C.: National Academy Press, 1985); Paul R. Ehrlich, Carl Sagan, Donald Kennedy, and Walter Orr Roberts, *The Cold and The Dark: The World after Nuclear War* (New York: W. W. Norton, 1984); Mark A. Harwell, *Nuclear Winter: The Human and Environmental Consequences of Nuclear War* (New York: Springer-Verlag, 1984).

31. Wayne Biddle, "Pentagon Agrees Nuclear Warfare Could Block Sun, Freeze Earth," *New York Times* (March 2, 1985). The conclusions about a Nuclear Winter have not been interpreted by the defense establishment as calling into question the efficacy of "limited" nuclear war strategies. Instead, the adherents to

the nuclear ritual have followed their traditional path, pointing to this research as bolstering their argument for rapid development of the Strategic Defense Initiative or "Star Wars" technology; U.S. Department of Defense, *The Potential Effects of Nuclear War on the Climate.* Report to Congress (March 1, 1985).

32. G. F. Kennan, "Zero Options," *New York Review of Books* 30 (May 12, 1983), p. 3.

33. For other approaches to this problem, see Chapters 1–3 and 8.

34. Max Weber, *Economy and Society,* vol. 1 (New York: Bedminster Press, 1968), p. 24. Prayer, for example, according to Weber, "has a purely business-like, rationalized form that sets forth the achievements of the supplicant in behalf of the god and then claims adequate recompense therefore" vol. 2 (p. 423).

35. Moreover, the military is structured in such a way as to fight previous battles; for example, Luttwak contends that the current U.S. military structure is "geared to restage the D-Day landings": Edward N. Luttwak, *The Pentagon and the Art of War: The Question of Military Reform* (New York: Simon and Schuster, 1984), p. 21.

36. Fallows, *National Defense,* p. 35.

37. MIRVs refer to Multiple Independently Targeted Reentry Vehicles or the placement of several warheads on a single ballistic missile, each of which can be programmed to strike a separate target.

38. Herbert Frank York, *Race to Oblivion: A Participant's View of the Arms Race* (New York: Simon and Schuster, 1970).

39. McGeorge Bundy, "A Matter of Survival," *New York Review of Books* 30 (March 17, 1983), pp. 3–6; James R. Killian, Jr., *Sputnik, Scientists, and Eisenhower* (Cambridge: MIT Press, 1977); Luttwak, *The Pentagon;* York, *Race to Oblivion.*

40. York, *Race to Oblivion;* Zuckerman, *Illusion and Reality.*

41. Max Weber, *The Protestant Ethic and the Spirit of Capitalism,* trans. Talcott Parsons (New York: Scribner's Sons, [1904–1905] 1958).

42. It has been estimated that the U.S. arsenal consists of approximately 29,000 nuclear weapons, whereas the Soviet Union possesses some 17,400; Ruth Leger Sivard, *World Military and Expenditures 1983* (Washington, D.C.: World Priorities, 1983), p. 15.

43. See, for example, John Foster Dulles, "The Evolution of Foreign Policy," *Department of State Bulletin* 30, no. 761 (1954): 108; Robert S. McNamara, *Defense Program and 1964 Defense Budget* (Washington, D.C.: U.S. Government Printing Office, 1963); James Schlesinger, *1975 Defense Budget and FY 1975–79 Defense Program* (Washington, D.C.: U.S. Government Printing Office, 1974); Executive Office of the President, Office of Management and Budget, *Budget of the United States Government, Fiscal Year 1984* (Washington, D.C.: U.S. Government Printing Office, 1983); Brown, *Annual Report 1980;* Weinberger, *Annual Report 1984.*

44. Weinberger, ibid.

45. Zuckerman, *Illusion and Reality,* p. 128.

46. George F. Kennan, "A Modest Proposal," *New York Review of Books* 28 (July 16, 1981), p. 14.

47. See Jonathan Schell, *The Fate of the Earth* (New York: Alfred A. Knopf, 1982), regarding the potential effects of a nuclear war. Schell asserted that we are now threatened with a "second death"—"the death of the species."

48. See Chapters 1–3 and 8, for examples of this.

49. Bernard Brodie, *The Absolute Weapon* (New York: Harcourt Brace, 1946), p. 76.

50. See Herman Kahn, *Thermonuclear War;* and idem., *Thinking about the Unthinkable* (New York: Horizon Press, 1962) for comprehensive statements representing this perspective. Brodie's work has been hotly debated over the years and has had little favor in political or military circles for at least a decade. Porro, however, asserts that his argument dominated published works by *civilian* strategic thinkers until the early 1960s; Jeffrey D. Porro, "The Policy War: Brodie vs. Kahn," *Bulletin of the Atomic Scientists* 38 (June 1982): 17.

51. Rothschild, "Delusions of Deterrence." Moreover, Rothschild contended that due to the "uncertain judgments about changing technology and political psychology on which the interpretation of the deterrent threat depends," military expansion "turns out to be inherent in deterrence policies" (p. 50).

52. The concept employed here has its inspiration in Berger and Luckman's notion of the "social construction of reality"; Peter L. Berger and Thomas Luckmann, *The Social Construction of Reality: A Treatise in the Sociology of Knowledge* (Garden City, N.Y.: Doubleday-Anchor Books, 1967). It has been used elsewhere, notably by David G. Bromley, Anson D. Shupe, Jr., and J. C. Ventimiglia, "Atrocity Tales, the Unification Church, and the Social Construction of Evil," *Journal of Communication* 29 (Summer 1979): 42–53; and Richard Stivers, *Evil in Modern Myth and Ritual* (Athens: University of Georgia Press, 1982).

53. Emile Durkheim, *The Division of Labor in Society* (New York: Free Press, [1893] 1933).

54. Georg Simmel, *On Individuality and Social Forms: Selected Writings,* ed. Donald N. Levine, (Chicago: University of Chicago Press, 1971).

55. Kai Erikson, *Wayward Puritans* (New York: John Wiley and Sons, 1966); Mary Douglas, *Purity and Danger: An Analysis of Concepts of Pollution and Taboo* (London: Routledge & Kegan Paul, 1966).

56. Simmel, *On Individuality,* p. 48.

57. See Kurtz, "Politics of Heresy."

58. Durkheim, *Division of Labor;* Erikson, *Wayward Puritans.*

59. See Nachman Ben-Yehuda, "The European Witch Craze of the 14th to 17th Centuries: A Sociologist's Perspective," *American Journal of Sociology* 86 (July

1980): 1–31; Albert James Bergesen, "Political Witch Hunts: The Sacred and the Subversive in Cross-National Perspective," *American Sociological Review* 42 (April 1977): 220–32. Mary Douglas, *Natural Symbols: Explorations in Cosmology* (New York: Pantheon Books, 1982), suggests that the tendency to value social boundaries and "guard the orifices" is particularly strong in social groups in which there is a strong emphasis on the group and a weak "grid"; that is, a system of internal control. It could be argued that the United States is in exactly such a situation. Soviet leaders similarly perceive themselves as besieged by a hostile environment and incapable of sufficient internal control, despite their efforts to suppress dissidence.

60. Victor Turner, *The Forest of Symbols* (Ithaca: Cornell University Press, 1967) and *Ritual Process.*

61. See, for example, Lippman and Merz's analysis of American news reports on early Soviet developments; Walter Lippman and Charles Merz, "A Test of the News" [a special supplement], *New Republic* (August 4, 1920), pp. 1–42. For a broader analysis of the image of the Soviet Union in the American news media, we are indebted to William A. Dorman, "The Image of the Soviet Union in the American News Media: Coverage of Brezhnev, Andropov and MX," unpublished paper (War, Peace and News Media Conference, New York University, March 18–19, 1983).

62. Francis X. Clines, "Reagan Denounces Ideology of Soviet as 'Focus of Evil,'" *New York Times* 132 (March 9, 1983), p. A1.

63. See Kurtz, "Politics of Heresy."

64. Simmel, *On Individuality.*

65. Douglas, *Natural Symbols,* p. ix.

66. John Barron, "The KGB's Magical War for 'Peace,'" *Reader's Digest* (October 1982), p. 207.

67. Produced in 1983 by the American Security Council Foundation for the Coalition for Peace through Strength. The quotations that follow are from a transcript of the film obtained from the American Security Council Foundation, Boston, Virginia.

68. See Jerry W. Sanders, *Peddlers of Crisis: The Committee on the Present Danger and the Politics of Containment* (Boston: South End Press, 1983). For a related analysis of the CPD, see Chapter 2.

69. Emile Durkheim, *The Elementary Forms of the Religious Life,* trans. Joseph Ward Swain (New York: The Free Press, [1897] 1915); Radcliffe-Brown, "Religion and Society," p. 107. Students of ritual have long noted that "from the viewpoint of the actor, rites can alter the state of the world because they invoke power." Edmund Leach, "Ritual," in *International Encyclopedia of the Social Sciences,* ed. David Sills (New York: Macmillan and The Free Press, 1968), p. 524. Cf. William Robertson Smith, *The Religion of the Semites* (New York: Meridian, [1889] 1956).

70. See James Aho's discussion in Chapter 4 of the organizational attributes of the "nuclear death cult."

71. Goffman, *Interaction Ritual,* p. 43.

72. The authority of the clergy, for example, and religious institutions is increased substantially by their successful direction of key rituals like marriages and burials, during which time other ritual participants are dependent upon the clergy for instructions concerning their role in the ceremony. That authority lingers long after the ritual itself is completed, especially if the clergyperson has fostered a convincing performance in his or her role.

73. Turner, *Forest of Symbols.*

74. Defense Secretary Weinberger's *Annual Report 1984* includes an eleven-page appendix (Appendix E) with a glossary of 500–600 acronyms. Zuckerman asserted that "it is a linguistic process that may simplify communication but it all too often ends by confounding reality." *(Illusion and Reality,* p. 41).

75. "A Complex of Tricky Issues," *Newsweek* (April 26, 1982), p. 29.

76. Russett, *Prisoners of Insecurity,* p. ix.

77. Richard Falk, "Nuclear Weapons and the End of Democracy," *International Foundation for Development Alternatives Dossier* 28 (March–April 1982): 56–64. Cf. idem., "Political Anatomy of Nuclearism," in Lifton and Falk, *Indefensible Weapons,* p. 131; Kosta Tsipis, *Arsenal: Understanding Weapons in the Nuclear Age* (New York: Simon and Schuster, 1983), p. 3; Lifton, "Imagining the Real," p. 26. Falk went so far as to argue that the advent of nuclear weapons has precipitated long-term adverse consequences for democratic forms of government: "democracy, as a political framework, seems to be a permanent casualty of the nuclear age" ("End of Democracy," p. 63).

78. Despite norms against "breaking rank," "every role has its defrocked priests to tell us what goes on in the monastery": Erving Goffman, *The Presentation of Self in Everyday Life* (Garden City, N.Y.: Doubleday-Anchor Books, 1959), p. 164. Falk commented that "it is notable that what dissent from nuclear orthodoxy we have observed . . . has all been the work of ex-officials with little hope of return to government." ("Political Anatomy," p. 135). See, e.g., Admiral Rickover's testimony before Congress after his forced retirement; Hyman Rickover, "Advice from Admiral Rickover," *New York Review of Books* (March 18, 1982).

79. For a complete transcript of the Oppenheimer security hearings, see United States Atomic Energy Commission, *In the Matter of J. Robert Oppenheimer: Transcripts before Personnel Security Board and Texts of Principal Documents and Letters* (Cambridge: MIT Press, 1971).

80. Falk, "Political Anatomy," p. 130.

81. See Peter Berger's discussion of the process as *alienation,* in which "the dialectical relationship between the individual and his world is lost to consciousness": Peter L. Berger, *The Sacred Canopy: Elements of a Sociological Theory of Religion* (Garden City, N.Y.: Doubleday-Anchor Books, 1969), p. 85.

82. See John Lofland, *Doomsday Cult: A Study of Conversion, Proselytization and Maintenance of Faith* (Englewood Cliffs, N.J.: Prentice-Hall, 1966); Leon Festinger, Henry W. Riecken, and Stanley Schachter, *When Prophecy Fails* (Minneapolis: University of Minnesota Press, 1956); and Chapter 4.

83. An analogy inspired by Max Weber's concept *(Protestant Ethic)* of bureaucracy as an "iron cage" that acts back upon its creators, ironically producing irrational consequences as a result of rationalizing human activity through bureaucratic organization. See Kurtz et al., *Nuclear Cage,* and Daniel Noel's comments on the "cage" image in Chapter 7.

84. The most fundamental critiques of the ritual are invariably formulated by former insiders who stand at the margins of the ritual, such as many participants in the peace movement, by those who have denounced their roles, or by other "outsiders" such as the U.S. Catholic bishops: see their critique of the ritual in U.S. Catholic Bishops, "The Challenge of Peace: God's Promise and Our Response," *Origins: NC Documentary Service* 12 (October 1982): 307–27.

85. Ground Zero, *Nuclear War: What's in It For You?* (New York: Pocket Books, 1982), p. 65.

86. Ball, "Cosmic Bluff," p. 38.

87. A case in point is the recent increase in public rhetoric concerning "counterforce weapons" (or, in its most recent version, "countersilo" weapons); that is, highly accurate weapons allegedly capable of destroying military targets. The most publicized counterforce weapons are the Ground Launched Cruise Missiles (GLCMs) and Pershing II missiles deployed in Western Europe; the "MX," dubbed the "Peacekeeper" by the Pentagon; and the Trident submarine armed with D-5 warheads.

88. Lawrence Freedman, *The Evolution of Nuclear Strategy* (New York: St. Martin's Press, 1982), p. xv.

89. Cf. Simmel, *On Individuality,* p. 370.

90. See Chapters 7 and 10.

91. Gene Sharp, *National Security through Civilian-Based Defense* (Omaha, Neb.: Association for Transarmament Studies, 1985), p. 22.

92. Witness, for example, the recent change in the way Americans view the People's Republic of China since the reestablishment of trade relations between the two countries.

93. Bruce Rigdon, an expert on the Russian Orthodox Church who teaches at McCormick Theological Seminary in Chicago, claims that on any given Sunday morning there are more people worshipping in churches in the Soviet Union than in the United States (personal communication). Such a recognition by church-goers in the United States might help to undermine the legitimacy of perceptions of the Soviets as evil.

6. *Growing Up in the Nuclear Age: Psychological Challenges and Spiritual Possibilities*

1. Gordon Kaufman, "Nuclear Eschatology and the Study of Religion," *Journal of the American Academy of Religion* 52, no. 1 (March 1983): 3–14.

2. Sibylle Escalona, "Children and the Threat of Nuclear War," in *Behavioral Science and Human Survival,* ed. M. Schwebel (Palo Alto, Calif.: Behavioral Science Press, 1965); Milton Schwebel, "Nuclear Cold War: Student Opinion and Professional Responsibility," in Schwebel, ibid. For more recent studies by the same authors, see M. Schwebel and B. Schwebel, "Children's Reactions to the Threat of Nuclear Plant Accidents," *American Journal of Orthopsychiatry* 51, no. 2 (1981): 260–70; S. Escalona, "Growing up with the Threat of Nuclear War: Some Indirect Effects on Personality Development," *American Journal of Ortho-psychiatry* 52, no. 4 (1982): 600–607; Milton Schwebel, "Effects of the Nuclear War Threat on Children and Teenagers: Implications for Professionals," *American Journal of Orthopsychiatry* 52, no. 4 (1982): 608–18. See also Michael Carey, "Psychological Fallout," *Bulletin of the Atomic Scientists* 38 (1982): 20–24; and Melanie Morrison, "'How Old Will You Be in the Year 2000?' Adolescents Reflect on Nuclear War," *Sojourners* (July–August 1982). At the end of Chapter 1, Ira Chernus notes that concern for the nuclear issue in the popular press was similarly diminished between the Cuban missile crisis and the late 1970s.

3. William Beardslee and John Mack, "The Impact on Children and Adolescents of Nuclear Development," in *Psychosocial Aspects of Nuclear Development,* Task Force Report #20, American Psychiatric Association, Washington, D.C.

4. The study by Chivian and colleagues was reported in a presentation at the conference on "Families and the Nuclear Crisis," Wheelock College Center for Parenting Studies, October 23, 1982.

5. Robert Jay Lifton, *The Broken Connection: On Death and the Continuity of Life* (New York: Simon and Schuster, 1979).

6. Robert Jay Lifton, *Death in Life: Survivors of Hiroshima* (New York: Touchstone Books, 1976). Lifton's observations have not been without criticism. Rachelle Linner in her essay "City of Myth and Reality: Listening to Hiroshima's Survivors" *(Commonweal* 113, no. 14 [August 9, 1985], pp. 425–28) contends that Lifton has not adequately attended to the ways in which a great many survivors of Hiroshima, the *hibakusha* as they are called in Japan, have found great meaning and purpose in leading the nonviolent struggle in Japan and the world for the end to nuclear armament. But cf. Lifton, *Death in Life,* index, s.v. Peace Movements.

7. Robert Jay Lifton, *The Life of the Self: Toward a New Psychology* (New York: Simon and Schuster, 1976).

8. In accounting for the rise of "nuclear consciousness" in the United States, it is important to note the considerable impact on at least some segments of the

population of Jonathan Schell's book *The Fate of the Earth* (New York: Alfred A. Knopf, 1982), which originally ran in three segments in the February 1982 *New Yorker Magazine.*

9. See James Aho's discussion of the "fundamentalist Bomb" in Chapter 4 and G. Clarke Chapman's observations on theological dimensions of "nuclearism" in Chapter 8 for some specific examples.

10. Lifton, *Broken Connection,* pp. 7–8.

11. Robert Jay Lifton and Richard Falk, *Indefensible Weapons: The Political and Psychological Case Against Nuclearism* (New York: Harper and Row, 1982), pp. 100–10.

12. Lifton and Falk, *Indefensible Weapons,* p. 42. For an extended discussion of the religious significance of this fatalism, see Chapters 8 and 10, by G. Clarke Chapman and Walter Noyalis.

13. This particular group was located on a Catholic university campus. It styled itself a coalition although there were no identifiable subgroups that formed it. There was, however, considerable diversity in its membership. It was begun under the sponsorship of a lay woman on the university chaplaincy who remained, at the time of this study, a very important mover of the group.

14. Lifton and Falk, *Indefensible Weapons,* p. 112. Cf. the interpretations of this notion of imagination in this book by Noel and Noyalis, Chapters 7 and 10.

15. A *Newsweek* poll conducted by the Gallup Organization, 507 personal interviews with full-time students on 96 campuses in the United States. Reported in *Newsweek Magazine* On Campus issue (November 1982).

16. Kenneth Keniston, *Young Radicals: Notes on Committed Youth* (New York: Harcourt, Brace and Jovanovich, 1968), pp. 60–66. "The most impressive feature of the radical commitment in these young men and women is the sense of continuity most of them feel with their pasts" (p. 35). For further resources on this period, see Kenneth Keniston, ed., *Radicals and Militants: An Annotated Bibliography of Empirical Research on Campus Unrest* (Boston: Lexington Books, 1974).

17. Keniston, *Radicals,* pp. 51–55.

18. Erik Erikson, *Childhood and Society* (New York: W. W. Norton, 1963), p. 267, and *Insight and Responsibility* (New York: W. W. Norton, 1964), p. 130.

19. Don Browning, *Generative Man: Psychoanalytic Perspectives* (New York: Delta, 1973).

20. Lifton and Falk, *Indefensible Weapons,* p. 114.

21. The correlation between maternal identification and the mode of moral reasoning that characterizes these student reflections upon nuclear war may be more than coincidental. The critical work of Harvard professor Carol Gilligan on the moral developmental schema of Lawrence Kohlberg proposes the thesis that women

characteristically, though not exclusively, tend to see moral dilemmas in terms of mutual responsibilities and interrelationships of the involved parties. This as opposed to the more "male" tendency at Kohlberg's higher levels of moral reasoning to think in terms of competing claims for justice and adjudicating principles. See Carol Gilligan, *In a Different Voice: Psychological Theory and Women's Development* (Cambridge: Harvard University Press, 1982) and the related ideas of Thistlethwaite in Chapter 9.

A perspective on the problem of how to accurately and empathetically perceive our relationship to "the enemy" that discusses the matter in psycho-dynamic terms as the problem of the withdrawal of projections is developed in two essays by John Mack, "The Perception of U.S.-Soviet Intentions and Other Psychological Dimensions of the Nuclear Arms Race," *American Journal of Orthopsychiatry* 52, no. 4 (1982): 590–99, and "But What About the Russians?" *Harvard Magazine* (March–April 1982), pp. 21–24, 53–54.

22. Erikson, *Childhood and Society,* p. 250.

23. For a theological discussion of this understanding of faith, see H. Richard Niebuhr, *Radical Monotheism and Western Culture* (New York: Harper and Row, 1960); and James Fowler, *Stages of Faith: The Psychology of Human Development and the Quest for Meaning* (New York: Harper and Row, 1981).

24. Erik Erikson, *Identity: Youth and Crisis,* (New York: W. W. Norton, 1968), pp. 133–34.

25. The awareness that a sustained commitment to peace work involves a confrontation with the limits of our capacities and with the potentiality of our own personal and collective destruction has stimulated the creation of retreats and workshops for persons involved in this work that draw on Eastern and Western spiritual traditions for resources of renewal. See Johanna Rogers Macy, *Despair and Personal Power in the Nuclear Age* (Philadelphia: New Society Publishers, 1983).

26. For a study of the psychological and social factors involved in the maintenance of a sense of global responsibility into the adult years, see Cheryl Hollman Keen, "Sources and Support for a Sense of Global Responsibility in College Students and Adults" (unpublished dissertation, Harvard Graduate School of Education, 1981).

27. Robert D. Holsworth, "A World Worth Living In: The Making of a Counter-culture in the New Peace Movement," paper delivered to the Annual Meeting of the Society for the Scientific Study of Religion, Providence, Rhode Island, Fall 1982.

7. *The Nuclear Horror and the Hounding of Nature: Listening to Images*

1. Patricia Berry, *Echo's Subtle Body: Contributions to an Archetypal Psychology* (Dallas: Spring Publications, 1982), p. 72.

2. Penelope Mesic, *"Riddley Walker* by Russell Hoban" (review), *Bulletin of the Atomic Scientists* (June–July 1982), p. 50.

3. Russell Hoban, *Riddley Walker* (New York: Washington Square Press, 1982), p. 123.

4. Ibid., p. 33.

5. Ibid., p. 30.

6. Ibid.

7. Ibid.

8. Ibid., p. 31.

9. Ibid.

10. Ibid., p. 32. This passage takes on additional meaning if we recall that the Hebrew name *Adam* is related to *dam* ("blood") and *adamah* ("earth").

11. Ibid., p. 36.

12. Ibid., p. 21.

13. Mesic, *"Riddley Walker,"* p. 49.

14. Walter Miller, Jr., *A Canticle for Leibowitz* (New York: Bantam Books, 1959), p. 160.

15. Wolfgang Giegerich, "Saving the Nuclear Bomb" (manuscript), pp. 2–3, since published in *Facing Apocalypse,* eds. V. Andrews, R. Bosnak, and K. Goodwin (Dallas: Spring Publications, 1987).

16. Ibid., p. 3.

17. Ibid., p. 4.

18. Ibid., p. 12.

19. Ibid., p. 13.

20. Marilou Awiakta, "What Is the Atom, Mother? Will It Hurt Us?" *Ms.* (July 1983), p. 47.

21. Ibid.

22. Ibid.

23. Ibid., p. 48.

24. Ibid.

25. John Fowles, *The Tree* (New York: Ecco Press, 1983), unpaginated.

26. Ibid.

27. Ibid.

28. This judgment would be implied by the eloquently voiced and persuasively supported discussions of patriarchal misogyny in Susan Griffin, *Woman and Nature: The Roaring inside Her* (New York: Harper and Row, 1980) and Carolyn Merchant, *The Death of Nature: Women, Ecology and the Scientific Revolution* (New York: Harper and Row, 1983). Compare Susan B. Thistlethwaite's views in Chapter 9.

29. In his spirited defense of hunting, the philosopher Ortega y Gasset suggests that it is the interjection of the element of reason—represented by, among other things, the use of domesticated dogs—that makes hunting supersede itself and become what it is not in essence: pure killing and destruction. See Jose Ortega y Gasset, *Meditations on Hunting,* trans. Howard B. Wescott (New York: Charles Scribner's Sons, 1972); and also Paul Shepard, *The Tender Carnivore and the Sacred Game* (New York: Charles Scribner's Sons, 1973).

30. Joanna Rogers Macy, *Despair and Personal Power in the Nuclear Age* (Philadelphia: New Society Publishers, 1983). Two other notable efforts at using workshops on "imaging" to empower peace activism are those led by Elise Boulding, a sociologist who concentrates on having her hearers imagine a weaponless future, and Mary Watkins, a psychotherapist (and speaker at the 1983 "Facing Apocalypse" conference) who evokes imaginal dialogues between apathetic and activist voices within each member of her audience. Cf. Walter Noyalis' argument in Chapter 10 of this book, that metaphoric imagination—what I would call "listening to images"—is itself a form of action that can create a more peaceful future.

31. David Holt, "Riddley Walker and Greenham Common: Further Thoughts on Alchemy, Christianity and the Work against Nature," *Harvest* 29, p. 30.

32. Ibid., p. 53.

33. Ibid.

8. *Approaching Nuclearism as a Heresy*

1. For an extended discussion of the following, see G. Clarke Chapman, *Facing the Nuclear Heresy: A Call to Reformation* (Elgin, Ill.: Brethren Press, 1986). An abbreviated form of this essay appeared in *Union Seminary Quarterly Review* 39, no. 4 (1985): 255–68.

2. Robert Jay Lifton, *The Broken Connection: On Death and the Continuity of Life* (New York: Basic Books, 1983), p. 369; see also pp. 376, 385. He has written widely on this subject, but perhaps most useful for the beginning reader is Robert Jay Lifton and Richard Falk, *Indefensible Weapons: The Political and Psychological Case Against Nuclearism* (New York: Basic Books, 1982), especially Chapter 2.

3. Lifton, *Broken Connection,* pp. 369–76.

4. See Chapman, *Facing the Nuclear Heresy,* Chapter 2; John W. de Gruchy and Charles Villa-Vicenio, eds., *Apartheid Is a Heresy* (Grand Rapids, Mich.: Eerdmans, 1983); *The Kairos Document: Challenge to the Church,* foreword by John W. de Gruchy (Grand Rapids, Mich.: Eerdmans, 1986).

5. Quoted by Jürgen Moltmann, "Discipleship of Christ in an Age of Nuclear War," *On Human Dignity: Political Theology and Ethics* (Philadelphia: Fortress, 1984), p. 129.

6. Thomas Kuhn, *The Structure of Scientific Revolutions* (Chicago: University of Chicago Press, 1970).

7. Michael Nagler, "Peace as a Paradigm Shift," *Bulletin of the Atomic Scientists* 37, no. 12 (December 1981): 49–52. See also Edward LeRoy Long, *Peace Thinking in a Warring World* (Philadelphia: Westminster, 1983); and Chapman, *Facing the Nuclear Heresy,* Chapter 5.

8. Quoted, for example, as the epigraph in *Psychiatric Aspects of the Prevention of Nuclear War* (New York: Group for the Advancement of Psychiatry, 1964), p. 223. See also (on p. 313) the preamble to UNESCO's constitution: "Wars begin in the minds of men."

9. For a fuller discussion of these four topics, their analysis, and some biblical alternatives, see Chapman, *Facing the Nuclear Heresy,* Chapters 6 through 9.

10. Thomas Hobbes, *Leviathan,* Part I, Chap. 13.

11. See Robert Jewett, *The Captain America Complex,* 2d ed. (Sante Fe, N.M.: Bear and Co., 1984); and Michael Walzer, *The Revolution of the Saints: A Study in the Origins of Radical Politics* (New York: Atheneum, 1976), especially Chapter 8.

12. Quoted by Jewett, ibid., p. 142. The implications of this vigilante mentality for pop culture and mass entertainment are well described in Robert Jewett and John S. Lawrence, *The American Monomyth,* 2d ed. (Lanham, Md.: University Press of America, 1988).

13. George Gerbner and Larry Gross, *Trends in Network Drama and Viewer Concept of Social Reality, 1967–73* (Violence Profile, No. 6, Annenberg School of Communications, University of Pennsylvania, December 1974).

14. "True Confessons of a Pac-Man Junkie," by Steve, as told to Marion Long, *Family Weekly* (January 2, 1983), pp. 6 f.

15. Long, *Peace Thinking,* p. 112.

16. Thomas Merton, "Blessed Are the Meek: The Christian Roots of Nonviolence," *The Nonviolent Alternative,* ed. Gordon C. Zahn (New York: Farrar, Straus and Giroux, 1980), p. 213. See also the further discussion of the theological meaning of nonviolence by Walter Noyalis in Chapter 10 of this book.

17. Ibid.

18. See Gene Sharp, *The Politics of Nonviolent Action* (Boston: Porter Sargent, 1973); and *Making the Abolition of War a Realistic Goal* (New York: Institute for World Order, 1981). On a simpler level, see Ron Sider and Richard Taylor, *Nuclear Holocaust and Christian Hope* (Downers Grove, Ill.: InterVarsity, 1982), Chapters 13–15.

19. Quoted by Lifton, *Broken Connection,* p. 159 n.

20. Kenneth Boulding, *Stable Peace* (Austin: University of Texas Press, 1978), p. 76.

21. See the writings of M. Douglas Meeks, for example, "Toward a Trinitarian View of Economics: The Holy Spirit and Human Needs," *Christianity and Crisis* 40, no. 18 (November 10, 1980), pp. 307–16.

22. Quoted in Alan Geyer, *The Idea of Disarmament! Rethinking the Unthinkable* (Elgin, Ill.: Brethren Press, 1982), p. 92.

23. Patrick Morgan, *Deterrence: A Conceptual Analysis* (Beverly Hills, Calif.: Sage Publications, 1977), p. 209.

24. Quoted by George Hunsinger, "Karl Barth and Liberation Theology," *Journal of Religion* 63, no. 3 (July 1983): 247.

25. *Psychiatric Aspects of the Prevention of Nuclear War,* p. 261. See also the chapters in this book by Benford and Kurtz (Chapter 5) and Chernus (Chapter 1) for numerous examples of such stereotypic and mythic images.

26. Bruce Russett, "The Contribution of Political Science," *Proceedings of the Symposium: The Role of the Academy in Addressing the Issues of Nuclear War* (Geneva, N.Y.: Hobart and William Smith Colleges, 1982), pp. 91 f.

27. National Conference of Catholic Bishops, *The Challenge of Peace: God's Promise and Our Response* (Washington, D.C.: United States Catholic Conference, 1983), par. 258.

28. See G. Clarke Chapman, "Faith as Official Optimism: A Nuclearist Heresy," *Christianity and Crisis* 44, no. 12 (July 9, 1984), pp. 271–73.

29. Will Herberg, *Protestant-Catholic-Jew: An Essay in American Religious Sociology* (New York: Anchor Press–Doubleday, 1960), p. 89.

30. See Douglas John Hall, *Lighten Our Darkness: Toward an Indigenous Theology of the Cross* (Philadelphia: Westminster, 1976), Chapters 1–3.

31. Richard Barnet, *Real Security: Restoring American Power in a Dangerous Decade* (New York: Simon and Schuster, 1981), p. 39. Compare his wry comment (p. 27): "The entire purpose of the nuclear arsenal is to influence the behavior of six

or seven Soviet leaders. As an education system, it has the highest per-pupil cost of any in the world."

32. George Kennan, "On Nuclear War," *The Nuclear Delusion: Soviet-American Relations in the Atomic Age* (New York: Pantheon Books, 1982), p. 199.

33. Thomas Merton, *New Seeds of Contemplation* (New York: New Directions, 1962), p. 135.

9. God and Her Survival in a Nuclear Age

1. See, for example, Hal Lindsey, *The Late Great Planet Earth* (Grand Rapids, Mich.: Zondervan, 1970), and Lindsey's other widely selling books. For numerous other examples, see James Aho's discussion of the "fundamentalist bomb" in Chapter 4 of this book.

2. See the issue, "Doomsday Religion," in *Sojourner's* (June–July 1984), especially Yehezkel Landau, "The Present and the Prophets," pp. 24–25.

3. A particularly instructive way of tracking this development is to observe which views dominate current mergers of Lutherans or Presbyterians. Data on the direction of the Lutheran discussions is helpfully available in the "Merger Watch" section of *Dialog,* a Lutheran journal. See particularly, *Dialog* 25 (Winter 1986), pp. 58 ff.; and 25 (Summer 1986), pp. 214 ff.

4. Susan B. Thistlethwaite, "I Am Become Death: God in the Nuclear Age," Johnson Foundation Lectures, 1987.

5. Gordon Kaufman, *Theology for a Nuclear Age* (Philadelphia: Westminster Press, 1985).

6. Gordon Kaufman, *An Essay on Theological Method* (Missoula, Mont.: Scholars Press, 1978), p. 41.

7. Karl Rahner and Herbert Vorgrimler, *Dictionary of Theology* (New York: Crossroad, 1985), pp. 275–76; the complexity entailed in defining *liberalism* precludes anything more than a definition in process. Although Kaufman's theological perspective takes issue with the classic starting point of liberalism (e.g., in Schleiermacher) that experience (God-consciousness) is the primary theological datum as a *given,* his views are consistent with the later development of liberal theology. Compare, for example, Kaufman, *God the Problem* (Cambridge: Harvard University Press, 1972), pp. 68 ff., with Friederich Schleiermacher, *The Christian Faith* (Edinburgh: T. and T. Clark, 1976), pp. 142 ff.

8. Kaufman, *Nuclear Age,* pp. 5, 8.

9. Ibid., pp. 5–8.

10. Ibid., pp. 25–26. Cf. Walter Noyalis' discussion of the theological role of imagination, metaphor, and creativity in Chapter 10 of this book.

11. See Karl Barth, "The Word of God and Experience," in *Church Dogmatics,* vol. I, part 1 (Edinburgh: T. and T. Clark, 1936), pp. 226–60.

12. Karl Barth, *Church Dogmatics,* vol. III, part 3, pp. 312–49.

13. See Susan B. Thistlethwaite, *Metaphors for the Contemporary Church* (New York: Pilgrim, 1984), for a review of this aspect of modern liberalism.

14. Kaufman, *God the Problem,* p. 5.

15. Ira Chernus, "War and Myth: 'The Show Must Go On'," *Journal of the American Academy of Religion* 53 (September 1985): 456–57.

16. Kaufman, *God the Problem,* p. 5.

17. Ibid., p. 7.

18. Ibid., p. 10.

19. Ibid., p. 82, quoting Paul Tillich, *Dynamics of Faith* (New York: Harper and Row, 1957), p. 46.

20. Paul Tillich, *The Courage to Be* (New Haven: Yale University Press, 1952), pp. 15, 182, 186–90.

21. Kaufman, *God the Problem,* p. 109.

22. Kaufman, *Nuclear Age,* p. 33.

23. Kaufman now speaks of God as "web of all existence" and identifies nature with the evolutionary process as well as the human pursuit of progress. See *Nuclear Age,* Chapter 3.

24. Ibid., p. 34.

25. Ibid., p. 41.

26. Tillich, *Courage to Be,* pp. 48, 52, 54, 75–77, 87, 90, 125–27, 132, 138, 169.

27. Kaufman, *The Theological Imagination* (Philadelphia: Westminster Press, 1981), p. 59.

28. Ibid., p. 60.

29. Ibid., p. 52, citing Paul Tillich, *The Courage to Be.*

30. Carter Heyward, "Feminist Studies in Religion," 1985 Address to the American Academy of Religion.

31. Mary Daly, *Pure Lust: Elemental Feminist Philosophy* (Boston: Beacon Press, 1984), pp. 47 ff.

32. Ibid., p. 102.

33. Ibid., p. 48. See Aho's discussion of the poem, and of the eroticism in theological nuclearism, in Chapter 4 of this book.

34. Ibid., p. 49, quoting Lansing Lamont, *Day of Trinity* (New York: Atheneum Press, 1965), p. 261.

35. Daly, *Pure Lust,* p. 73.

36. Carol P. Christ, "Why Women Need the Goddess: Phenomenological, Psychological and Political Reflections," *Womanspirit Rising: A Feminist Reader in Religions,* ed. Carol P. Christ and Judith Plaskow (San Francisco: Harper and Row, 1979), pp. 273–87.

37. Daly, *Pure Lust,* p. 73 Cf. the remarks of John McDargh in Chapter 6, n. 21, and Daniel Noel in Chapter 7, n. 28, in this book.

38. Ibid., p. 54.

39. Ibid.

40. Ibid., p. 154.

41. Ibid., p. 155.

42. Ibid., pp. 155–56.

43. Ibid., p. 156.

44. Ibid., p. 157.

45. Ibid., p. 158 (emphasis Daly's). One way that reason tries to grasp and shape reality, in both religion and nuclearism, is through ritual. Cf. Chapter 5 of this book by Benford and Kurtz.

46. Ibid., pp. 158–59.

47. Ibid., p. 403.

48. Ibid., p. 405. Again, see Noyalis' views on the theological role of metaphoric imagination in Chapter 10 of this book.

49. Ibid., pp. 399–404.

50. Ibid., p. 400, quoting Alice Walker, *The Color Purple* (New York: Harcourt Brace Jovanovich, 1982), p. 167.

51. Ibid., p. 400.

52. Ibid., p. 400 n.

53. Dolores Hines, "Racism Breeds Stereotypes," *The Witness* 65 (February 1982), p. 7.

54. Kaufman, *Essay on Theological Method,* pp. 59–61.

55. Ibid., p. 61.

56. Audre Lorde, "The Master's Tools Will Never Dismantle the Master's House," in *This Bridge Called My Back: Writings by Radical Women of Color,* ed. Cherrie Moraga and Gloria Anzaldua (Watertown, Mass.: Persephone Press, 1981), p. 100.

57. Daly, *Pure Lust,* p. 411.

58. Lorde, "The Master's Tools," p. 99.

59. Alice Walker, *Meridian,* p. 5.

60. Ibid., p. 204.

61. Ibid., p. 22.

62. Toni Cade Bambara, *The Salt Eaters* (New York: Vintage Books, 1981), p. 3.

63. Ibid., p. 152.

64. Ibid., pp. 25 ff.

65. *Black Women Writers (1950–1980), a Critical Evaluation,* ed. Mari Evans (Garden City, N.Y.: Doubleday, 1984), pp. 64–65. This paragraph is a paraphrase from the Evans volume. From their psychological perspectives, McDargh in Chapter 6 and Noel in Chapter 7 of this book also stress the need for images linking past and future generations in the nuclear age.

10. Doing the Truth:
Peacemaking as Hopeful Activity

1. Viktor E. Frankl, *Man's Search for Meaning* (New York: Washington Square Press, 1963); Robert Jay Lifton, "Imagining the Real," in Robert Jay Lifton and Richard Falk, *Indefensible Weapons: The Political and Psychological Case against Nuclearism* (New York: Basic Books, 1982); Wolfhart Pannenberg, *What Is Man?* (Philadelphia: Westminster Press, 1970); Jonathan Schell, *The Fate of the Earth* (New York: Alfred A. Knopf, 1982); Gibson Winter, *Liberating Creation* (New York: Crossroad, 1981).

2. Joseph Powers, *Spirit and Sacrament* (New York: Seabury Press, 1973), pp. 41–44.

3. Ronald J. Sider and Richard K. Taylor, *Nuclear Holocaust and Christian Hope* (New York: Paulist Press, 1982); J. Carter Swain, *War, Peace, and the Bible* (Maryknoll, N.Y.: Orbis Books, 1982).

4. Powers, *Spirit and Sacrament,* pp. 1–61.

5. Wolfhart Pannenberg, *Basic Questions in Theology,* 2 vols. (Philadelphia: Fortress Press, 1970–1971); idem., *Revelation as History* (Toronto: Macmillan, 1968); idem., *Theology and the Kingdom of God* (Philadelphia: Westminster Press, 1969).

6. Pannenberg, *Kingdom,* pp. 55–56.

7. See Wolfhart Pannenberg, *Jesus—God and Man,* 2d ed. (Philadelphia: Westminster Press, 1977), pp. 53–114.

8. Some artists do not work this way, but begin with a complete visualization of the painting in their minds. Theorists of aesthetics thus debate whether the process takes place on the canvas or in the mind.

9. In Chapter 8 of this book, G. Clarke Chapman discusses the biblical and theological roots of nonviolent conflict resolution. He also shows the links between nonviolence and a biblically based view of the world as open-ended and eternally growing toward its ultimate horizon. Cf. John McDargh's stress on the need for faith in an Ultimate Environment in Chapter 6.

10. For this discussion of Gandhi, I rely on Ignatius Jesudasan, *A Gandhian Theology of Liberation* (Maryknoll, N.Y.: Orbis Books, 1984). James W. Douglass has offered an analysis of the convergence of Gandhi with the Christian ideal of nonviolence in *The Non-violent Cross* (New York: Macmillan, 1968). For another approach to Ghandhi's relevance, see Chapter 5, pp. 85–7.

11. Other essays in this book amply document this central feature of the nuclear arms race. See, in particular, the discussions of "worst case scenarios" in Chapter 2, pp. 25–7, Chapter 5, pp. 82–3, and Chapter 8, pp. 134–6.

12. Within Roman Catholicism, the Second Vatican Council called for an "entirely new attitude" toward war (section 80), a call that the American bishops attempted to answer in their seminal pastoral letter on nuclear war, *The Challenge of Peace: God's Promise and Our Response.*

Notes on Contributors

James A. Aho is Professor of Sociology at Idaho State University. His numerous publications on religion and violence include *Religious Mythology and the Art of War* (1981) and *The Politics of Righteousness* (1989), a study of the radical Christian patriot movement in the American inter-mountain West.

Robert D. Benford is Assistant Professor of Sociology at the University of Nebraska-Lincoln. He has published articles on the nuclear threat, conflict resolution, and social movements, and he is currently working on a book analyzing the ebb and flow of antinuclear activism in the United States.

G. Clarke Chapman is Professor of Religion at Moravian College. He is the author of *Facing the Nuclear Heresy: A Call to Reformation* (1986) as well as articles on theology and peace and on theologians Dietrich Bonhoeffer and Jürgen Moltmann.

Ira Chernus is Associate Professor of Religious Studies at the University of Colorado at Boulder. His previous publications include *Mysticism in Rabbinic Judaism* (1982), *Dr. Strangegod: On the Symbolic Meaning of Nuclear Weapons* (1986), and articles on both Jewish mysticism and the religious dimension of the nuclear age. He has been co-chairperson of the Religion, Peace, and War Group of the American Academy of Religion.

Lester R. Kurtz is Associate Professor of Sociology and director of the Religious Studies program at the University of Texas at Austin. He has written *The Politics of Heresy* (1986) and *The Nuclear Cage: A Sociology of the Arms Race* (1988). He has served as chair of United Campuses to Prevent Nuclear War (UCAM).

Edward Tabor Linenthal is Professor of Religion and American Culture at the University of Wisconsin, Oshkosh. He is the author of

Changing Images of the Warrior Hero in America (1982) and *Symbolic Defense: The Cultural Significance of the Strategic Defense Initiative* (1989), and he is currently writing a study of the cultural functions of American battlefields.

John McDargh is Associate Professor of Theology at Boston College. Author of *Psychoanalytic Object Relations Theory and the Study of Religion* (1983), he is continuing his research on the relationship of psychotherapy to religious development and traditional spiritual disciplines.

Daniel C. Noel is Professor of Alternative Education at Vermont College of Norwich University, focusing on interdisciplinary religious studies. He has written *Approaching Earth: A Search for the Mythic Significance of the Space Age* (1987) as well as numerous articles, and he has edited *Echoes of the Wordless Word* (1974) and *Seeing Castaneda* (1976). He is currently studying the archetypal psychohistory of the Strategic Defense Initiative.

Walter J. Noyalis is Associate Professor and Chairman of Religious Studies at Anna Maria College. His research focuses on hermeneutics and peacemaking as well as action/reflection models of education for peace and justice.

Susan B. Thistlethwaite is Associate Professor of Theology and Culture at Chicago Theological Seminary. She has published *Metaphors for the Contemporary Church* (1983), *A Just Peace Church* (1985), and most recently co-authored with Mary Potter Engel *Constructing Christian Theology from the Underside* (1989).